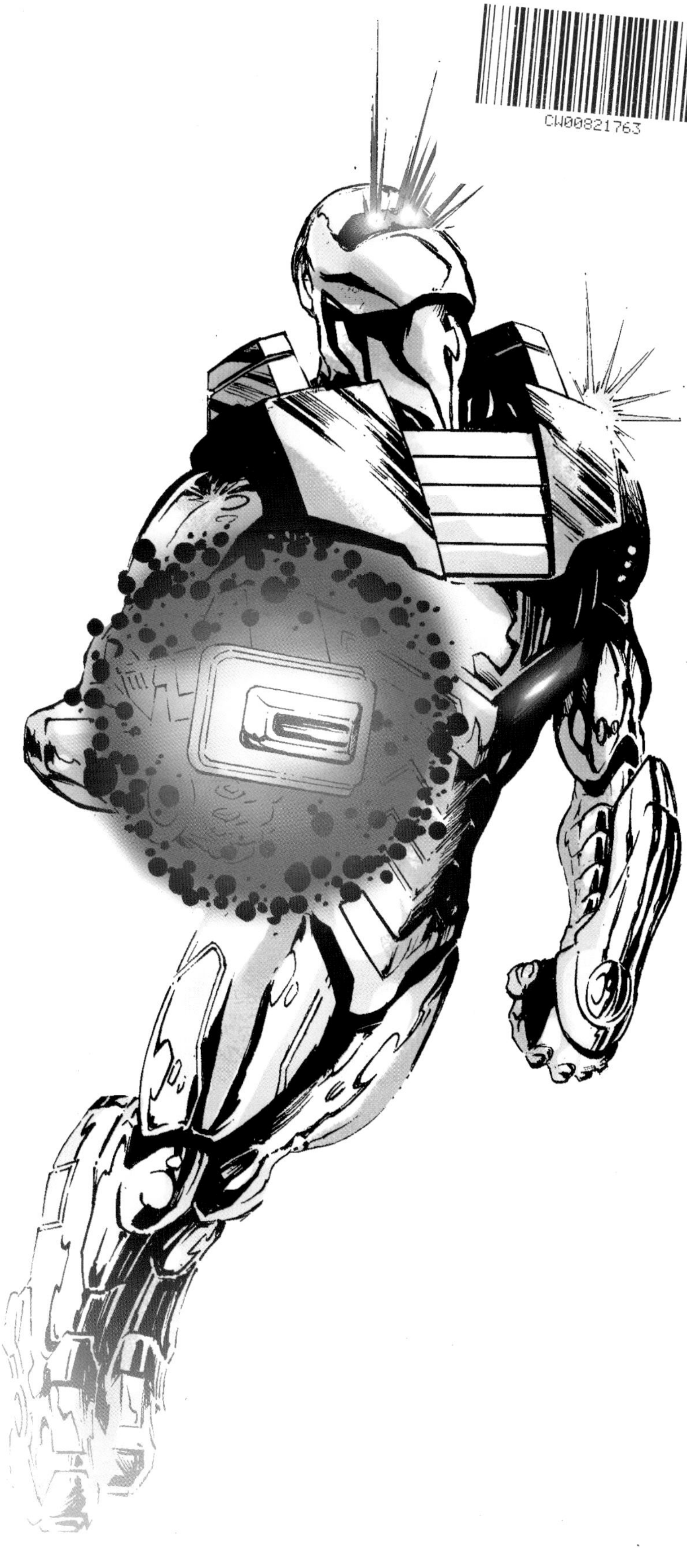

Facebook: **facebook.com/idwpublishing**
Twitter: **@idwpublishing**
YouTube: **youtube.com/idwpublishing**
Tumblr: **tumblr.idwpublishing.com**
Instagram: **instagram.com/idwpublishing**

Special Thanks to Derryl Depriest, David Erwin, Mark Weber, Ed Lane, Beth Artale, Josh Feldman, Michael Kelly, and Michael Mantlo.

ISBN: 978-1-63140-817-5   20 19 18 17   1 2 3 4

COVER ART BY
ZACH HOWARD

COVER COLORS BY
NELSON DÁNIEL

COLLECTION EDITS BY
JUSTIN EISINGER
AND ALONZO SIMON

COLLECTION DESIGN BY
JEFF POWELL

PUBLISHER
TED ADAMS

Originally published as ROM issues #0–4 and ROM: REVOLUTION.

Ted Adams, CEO & Publisher
Greg Goldstein, President & COO
Robbie Robbins, EVP/Sr. Graphic Artist
Chris Ryall, Chief Creative Officer
David Hedgecock, Editor-in-Chief
Laurie Windrow, Senior VP of Sales & Marketing
Matthew Ruzicka, CPA, Chief Financial Officer
Dirk Wood, VP of Marketing
Lorelei Bunjes, VP of Digital Services
Jeff Webber, VP of Digital and Subsidiary Rights
Jerry Bennington, VP of New Product Development

ROM
EARTHFALL

STORY BY
CHRIS RYALL & CHRISTOS GAGE

#0-4

PENCILS AND COLORS BY
DAVID MESSINA

INKS BY
MICHELE PASTA

COLOR ASSIST BY
ALESSANDRA ALEXAKIS

LETTERS BY
SHAWN LEE

REVOLUTION

ART BY
RON JOSEPH

COLORS BY
JAY FOTOS

LETTERS BY
SHAWN LEE
& CHRIS MOWRY

DEDICATED TO THE FIRST SPACE KNIGHTS,
BILL MANTLO AND SAL BUSCEMA

WHO'S WHO

ROM

A silver-suited space warrior and member of the galactic Solstar Order, Rom has fought the Dire Wraiths on different planets for over 200 years. Now, armed with his Wraith-detecting Analyzer and Wraith-slaying Neutralizer, he has pursued them to Earth in an attempt to stop them from doing what he's already witnessed too many times: destroying the planet and everyone on it.

DIRE WRAITHS

A space-faring race of aliens who can use their black magic-powered abilities to subsume or fully consume the identities of humans and other organic life, twisting it for their own nefarious purposes. The Wraiths have infiltrated and replaced many humans, some in key leadership positions.

D'RGE

One of the most powerful Wraith Sorcerers. Multi-armed and supremely powerful, his true abilities have yet to be seen.

CAMILLA BYERS

A police officer and survivor of a Wraith attack that occurred upon Rom's arrival on Earth. She was wounded by one of the Wraiths and, as her wound grows, she finds herself able to enter Wraiths' minds, even as they can do the same. Now she too is on the run even as the Wraiths take steps to track her down...

DARBY MASON

A war veteran who recently returned to her childhood home in Northern California to be with her family and get her head straight. Unfortunately, her entire town, including her family, was killed and replaced by Dire Wraiths. She was thus-far-inexplicably able to resist their initial attack and now she and ROM are on the run from a town gone mad.

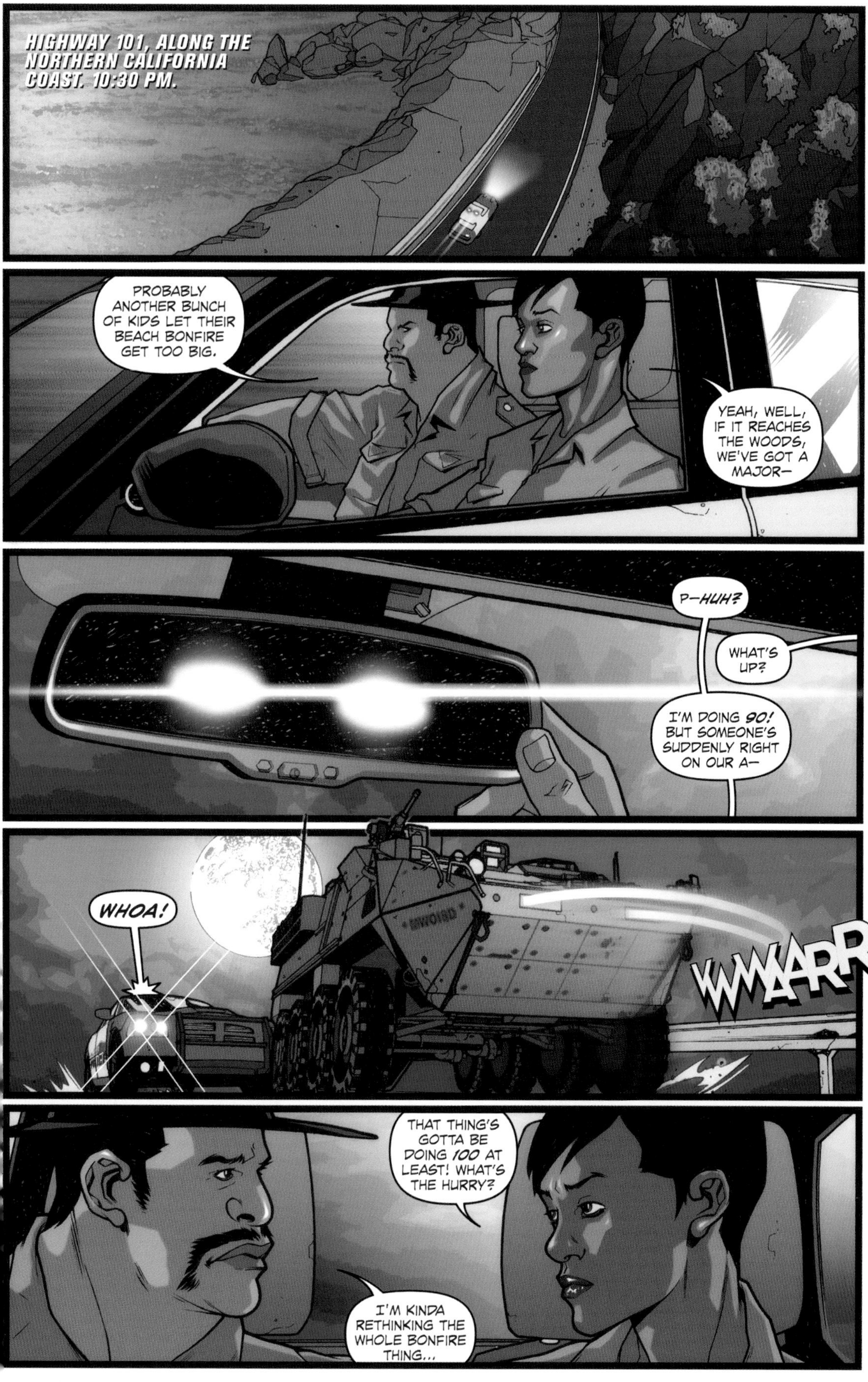

HIGHWAY 101, ALONG THE NORTHERN CALIFORNIA COAST. 10:30 PM.
PROBABLY ANOTHER BUNCH OF KIDS LET THEIR BEACH BONFIRE GET TOO BIG.
YEAH, WELL, IF IT REACHES THE WOODS, WE'VE GOT A MAJOR—
P—HUH?
WHAT'S UP?
I'M DOING 90! BUT SOMEONE'S SUDDENLY RIGHT ON OUR A—
WHOA!
WWAARR
THAT THING'S GOTTA BE DOING 100 AT LEAST! WHAT'S THE HURRY?
I'M KINDA RETHINKING THE WHOLE BONFIRE THING...

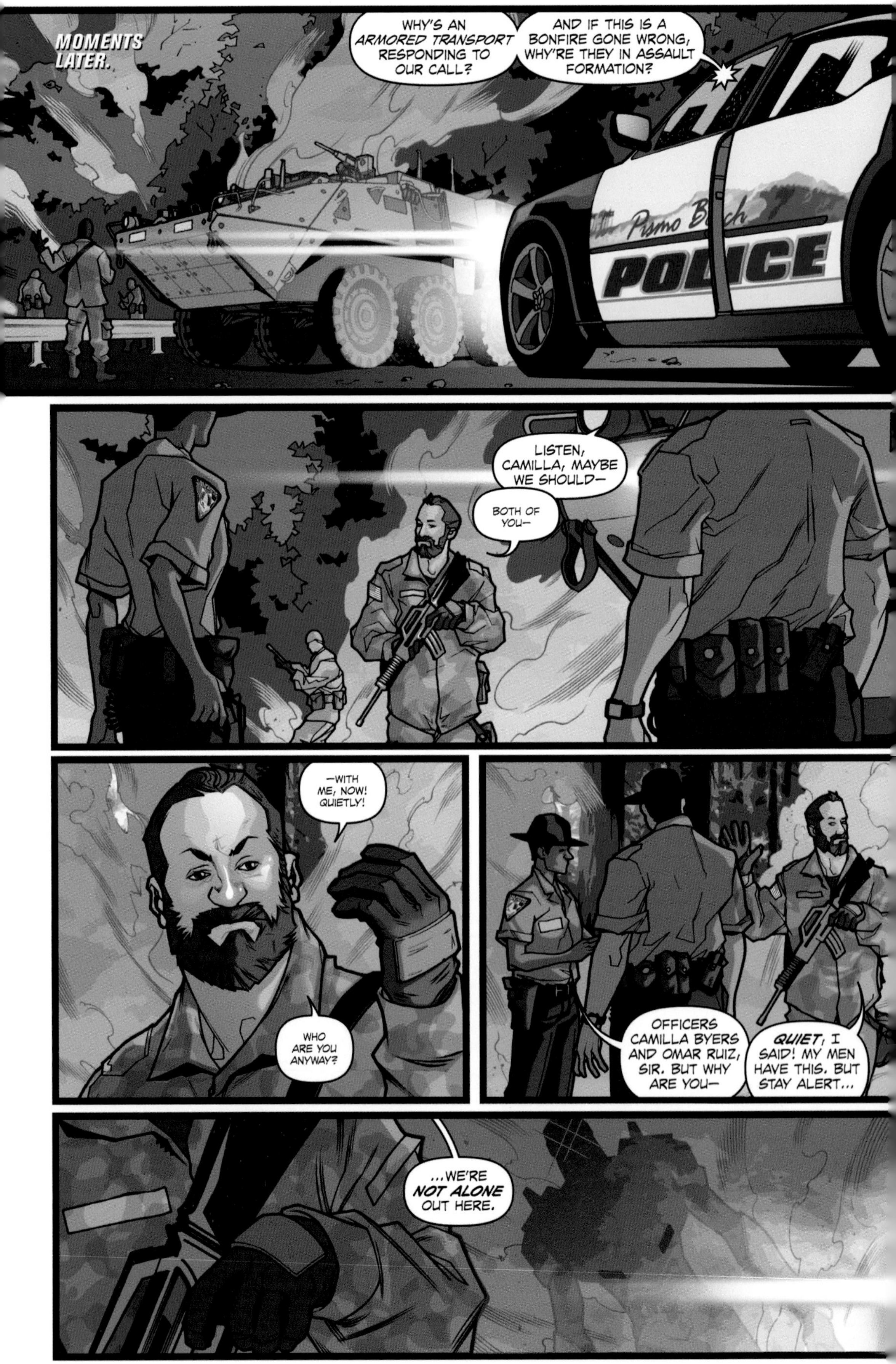
MOMENTS LATER.
WHY'S AN ARMORED TRANSPORT RESPONDING TO OUR CALL?
AND IF THIS IS A BONFIRE GONE WRONG, WHY'RE THEY IN ASSAULT FORMATION?
Pismo Beach
POLICE
LISTEN, CAMILLA, MAYBE WE SHOULD—
BOTH OF YOU—
—WITH ME, NOW! QUIETLY!
WHO ARE YOU ANYWAY?
OFFICERS CAMILLA BYERS AND OMAR RUIZ, SIR. BUT WHY ARE YOU—
QUIET, I SAID! MY MEN HAVE THIS. BUT STAY ALERT...
...WE'RE NOT ALONE OUT HERE.

IDW PUBLISHING AND HASBRO ENTERTAINMENT PROUDLY PRESENT
THE ARRIVAL OF ROM

EARTHFALL: PRELUDE

BY RYALL, GAGE & MESSINA

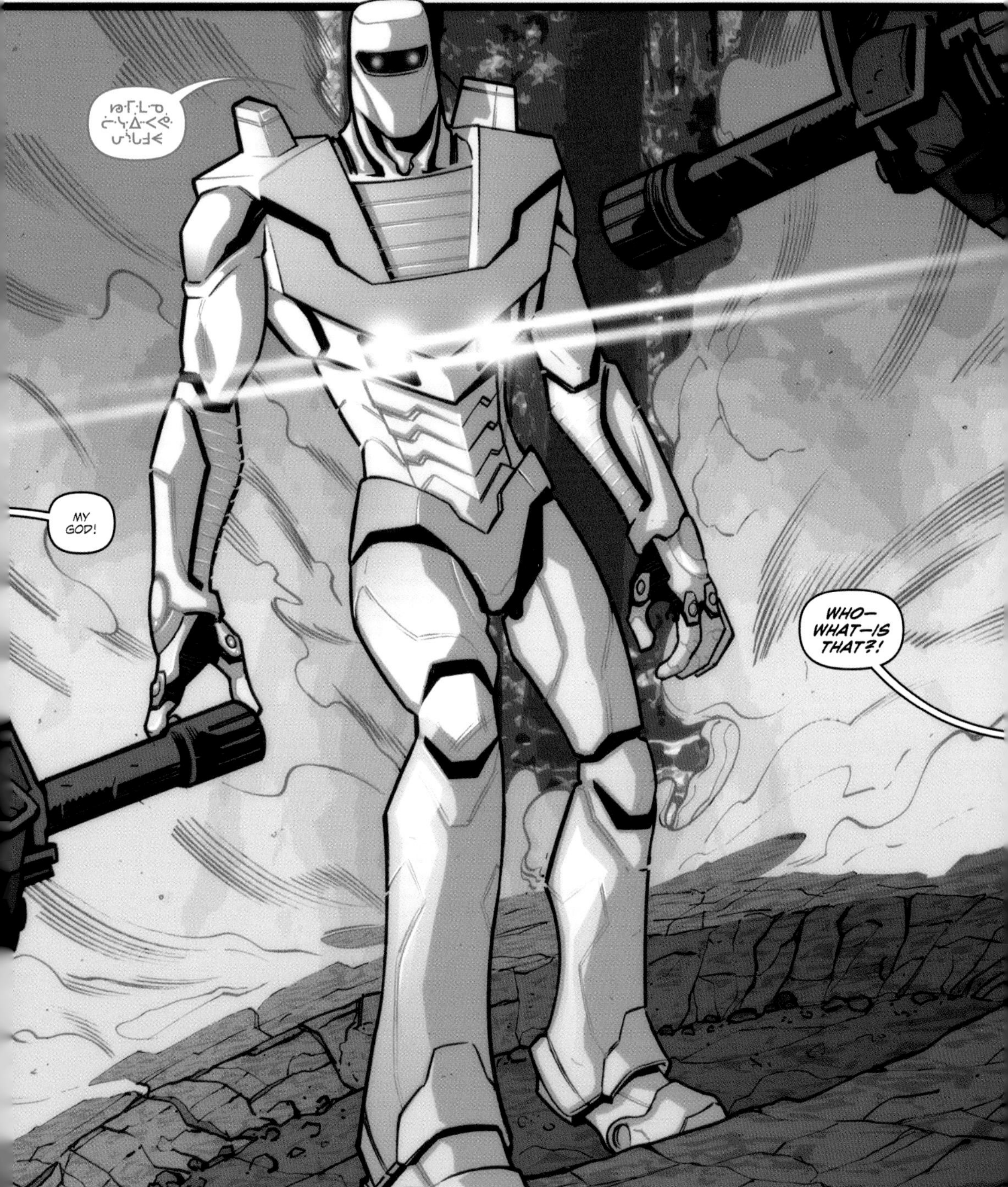
MY GOD!
WHO—WHAT—IS THAT?!

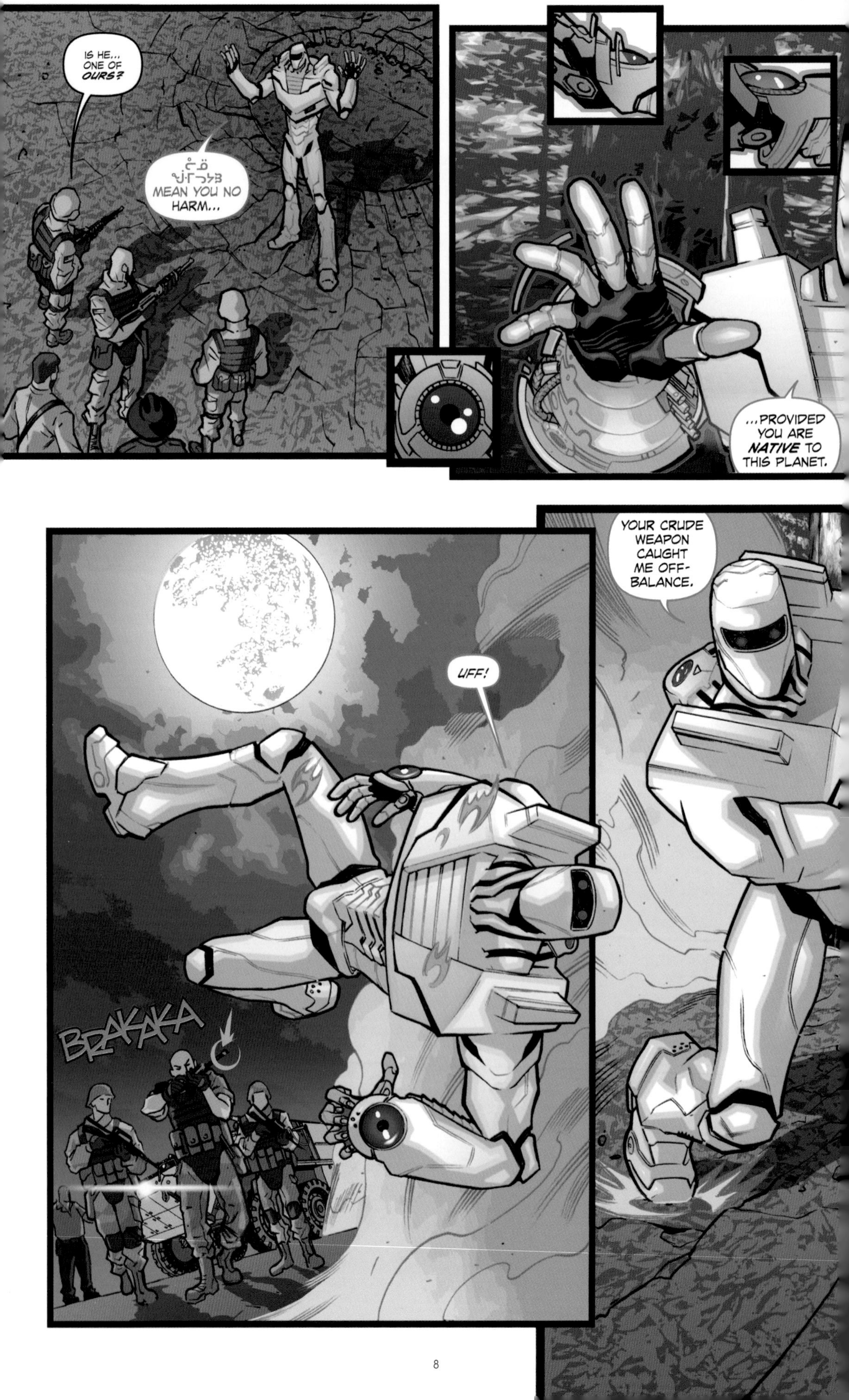
IS HE... ONE OF OURS?
MEAN YOU NO HARM...
...PROVIDED YOU ARE NATIVE TO THIS PLANET.
BRAKAKA
UFF!
YOUR CRUDE WEAPON CAUGHT ME OFF-BALANCE.

MY *ENERGY ANALYZER* WILL REVEAL ALL.

ARMOR'S ENERGIZING! *TAKE HIM DOWN!*

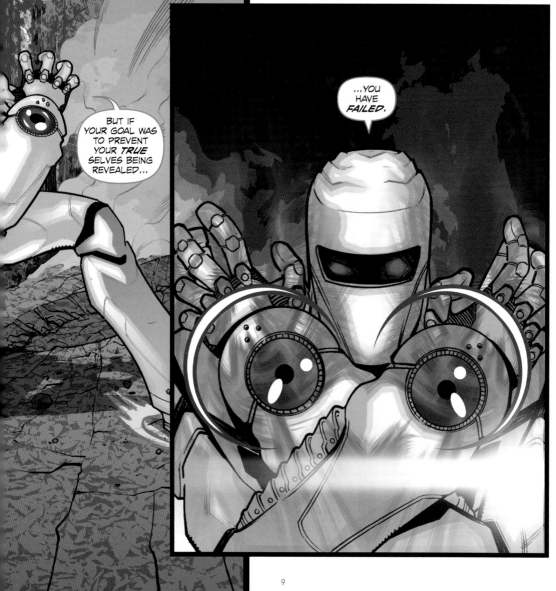

BUT IF YOUR GOAL WAS TO PREVENT YOUR *TRUE* SELVES BEING REVEALED...

...YOU HAVE *FAILED.*

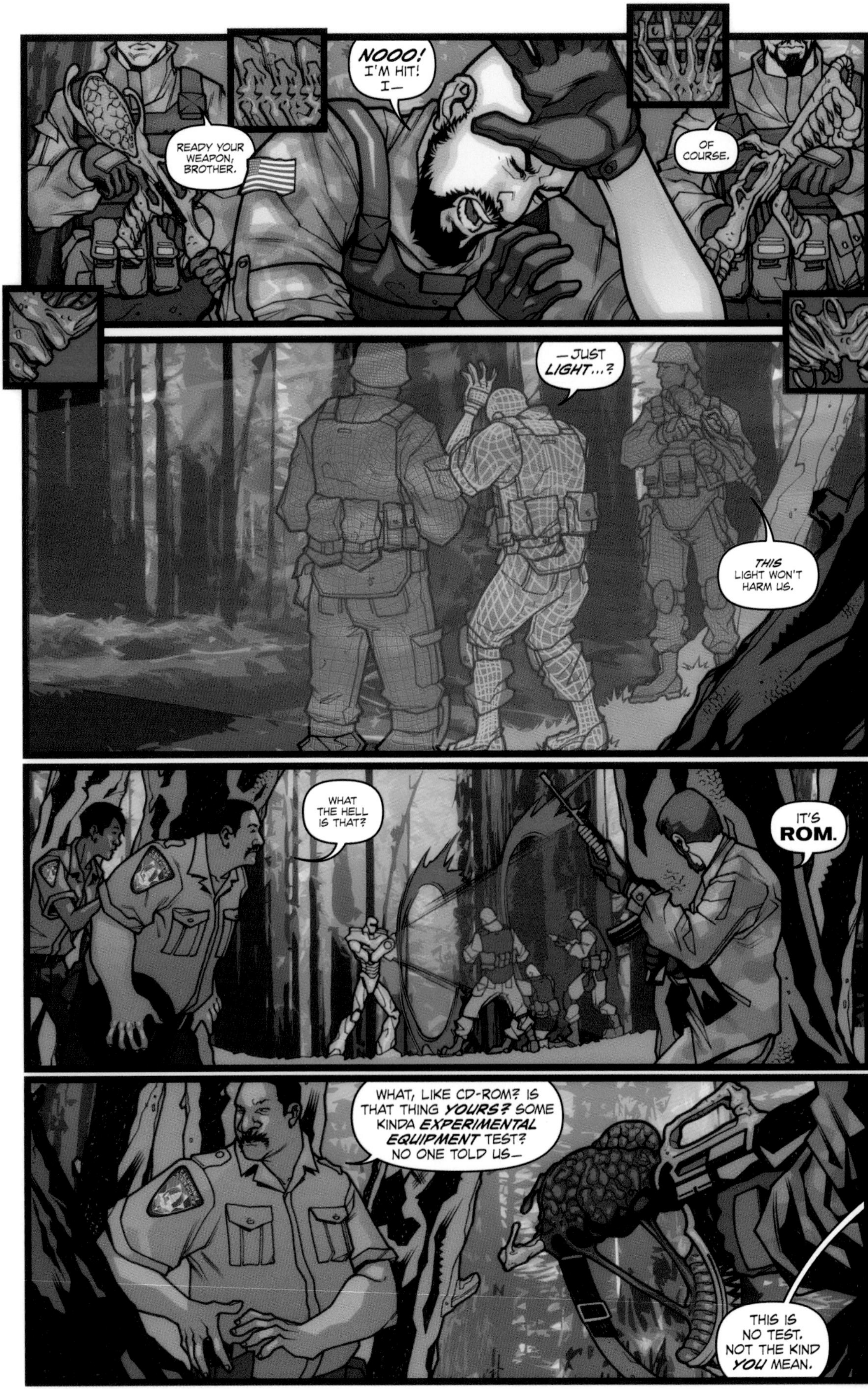
NOOO! I'M HIT! I—
READY YOUR WEAPON, BROTHER.
OF COURSE.
—JUST LIGHT...?
THIS LIGHT WON'T HARM US.
WHAT THE HELL IS THAT?
IT'S ROM.
WHAT, LIKE CD-ROM? IS THAT THING YOURS? SOME KINDA EXPERIMENTAL EQUIPMENT TEST? NO ONE TOLD US—
THIS IS NO TEST. NOT THE KIND YOU MEAN.

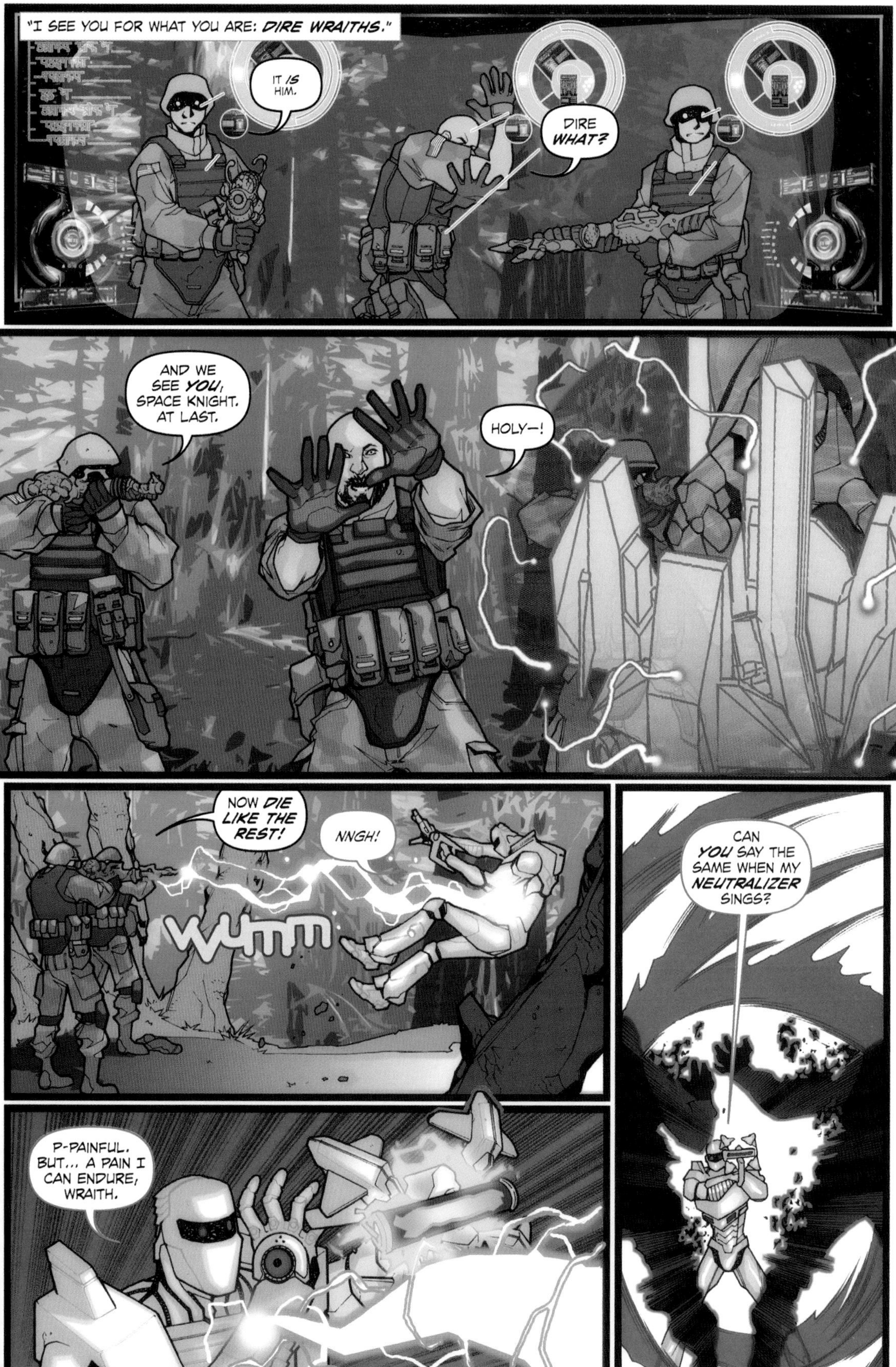

"I SEE YOU FOR WHAT YOU ARE: DIRE WRAITHS."
IT IS HIM.
DIRE WHAT?
AND WE SEE YOU, SPACE KNIGHT. AT LAST.
HOLY—!
NOW DIE LIKE THE REST!
NNGH!
WUMM
CAN YOU SAY THE SAME WHEN MY NEUTRALIZER SINGS?
P-PAINFUL. BUT... A PAIN I CAN ENDURE, WRAITH.

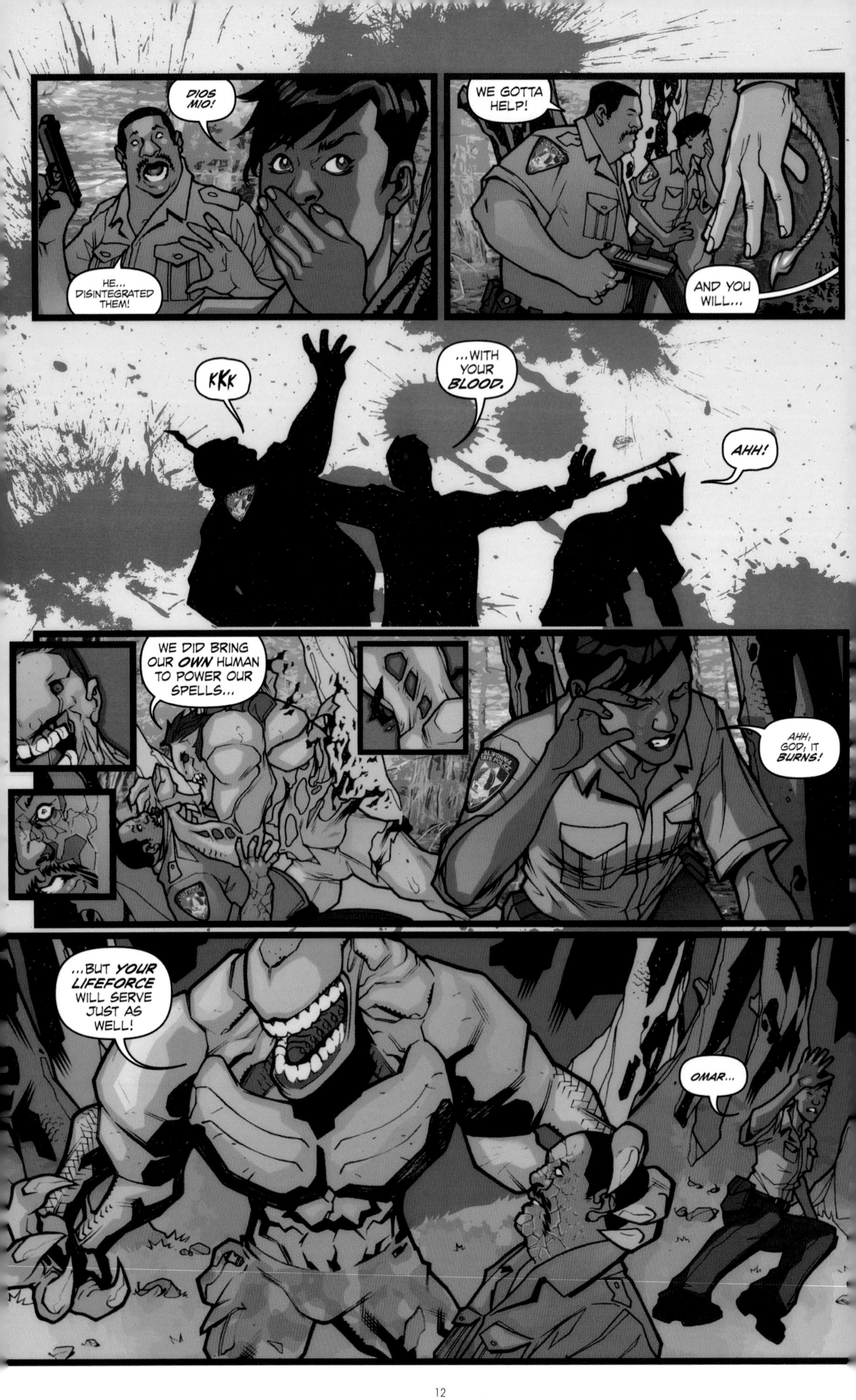
DIOS MIO!
HE... DISINTEGRATED THEM!
WE GOTTA HELP!
AND YOU WILL...
KKK
...WITH YOUR BLOOD.
AHH!
WE DID BRING OUR OWN HUMAN TO POWER OUR SPELLS...
AHH; GOD; IT BURNS!
...BUT YOUR LIFEFORCE WILL SERVE JUST AS WELL!
OMAR...

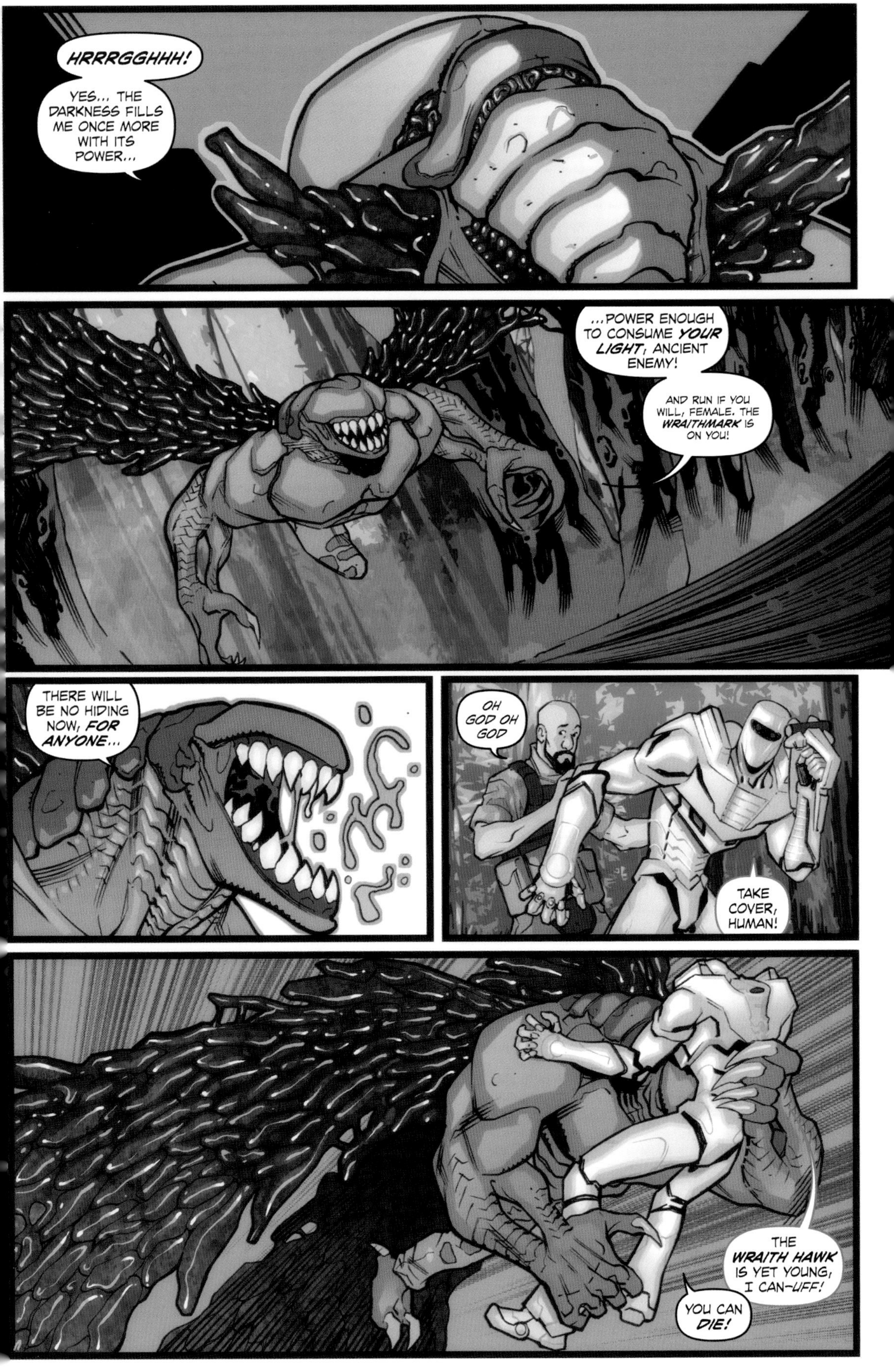
HRRRGGHHH!
YES... THE DARKNESS FILLS ME ONCE MORE WITH ITS POWER...
...POWER ENOUGH TO CONSUME YOUR LIGHT, ANCIENT ENEMY!
AND RUN IF YOU WILL, FEMALE. THE WRAITHMARK IS ON YOU!
THERE WILL BE NO HIDING NOW, FOR ANYONE...
OH GOD OH GOD
TAKE COVER, HUMAN!
THE WRAITH HAWK IS YET YOUNG, I CAN-UFF!
YOU CAN DIE!

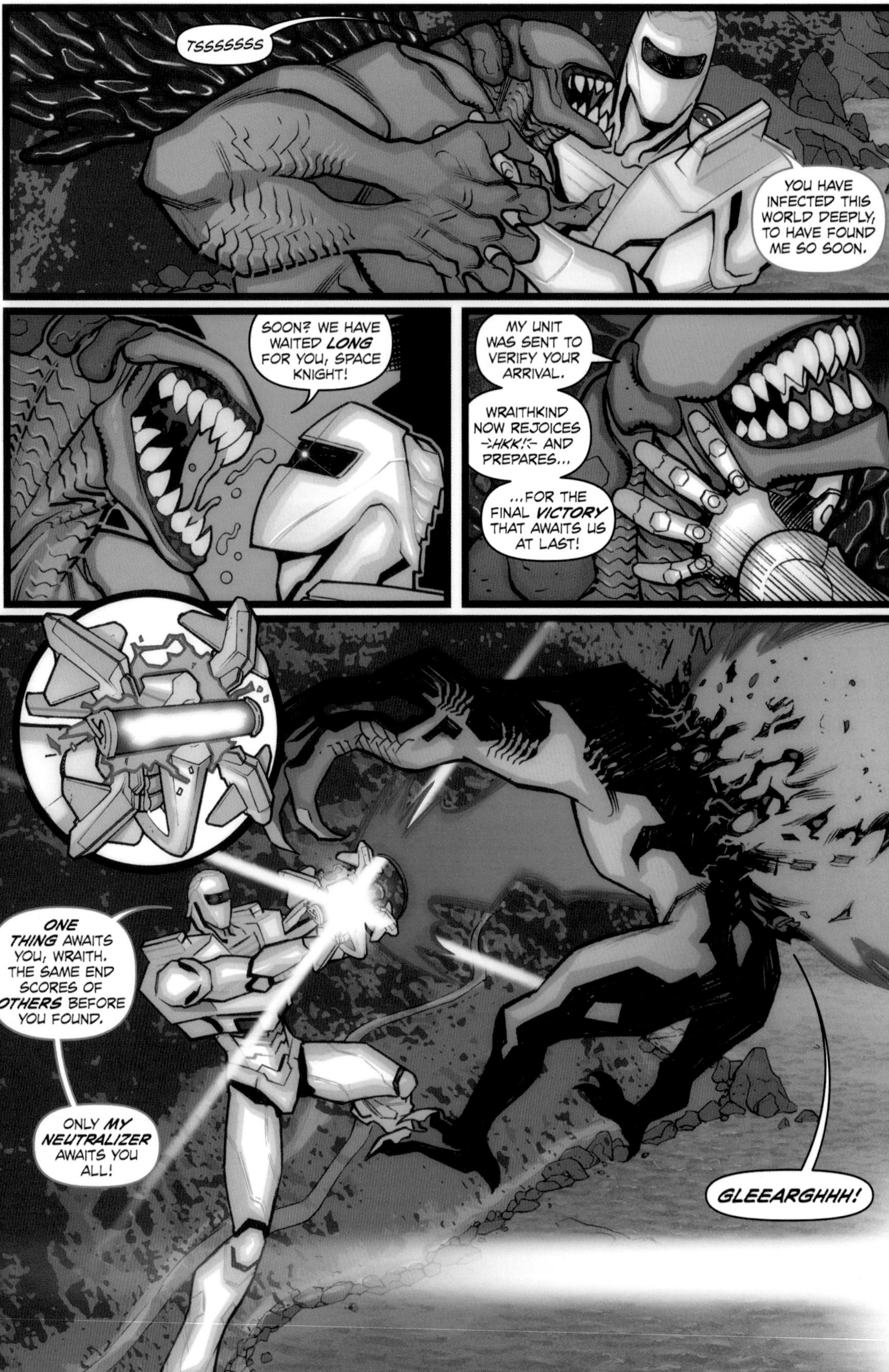
TSSSSSSS
YOU HAVE INFECTED THIS WORLD DEEPLY, TO HAVE FOUND ME SO SOON.
SOON? WE HAVE WAITED LONG FOR YOU, SPACE KNIGHT!
MY UNIT WAS SENT TO VERIFY YOUR ARRIVAL.
WRAITHKIND NOW REJOICES -HKK!- AND PREPARES...
...FOR THE FINAL VICTORY THAT AWAITS US AT LAST!
ONE THING AWAITS YOU, WRAITH. THE SAME END SCORES OF OTHERS BEFORE YOU FOUND.
ONLY MY NEUTRALIZER AWAITS YOU ALL!
GLEEARGHHH!

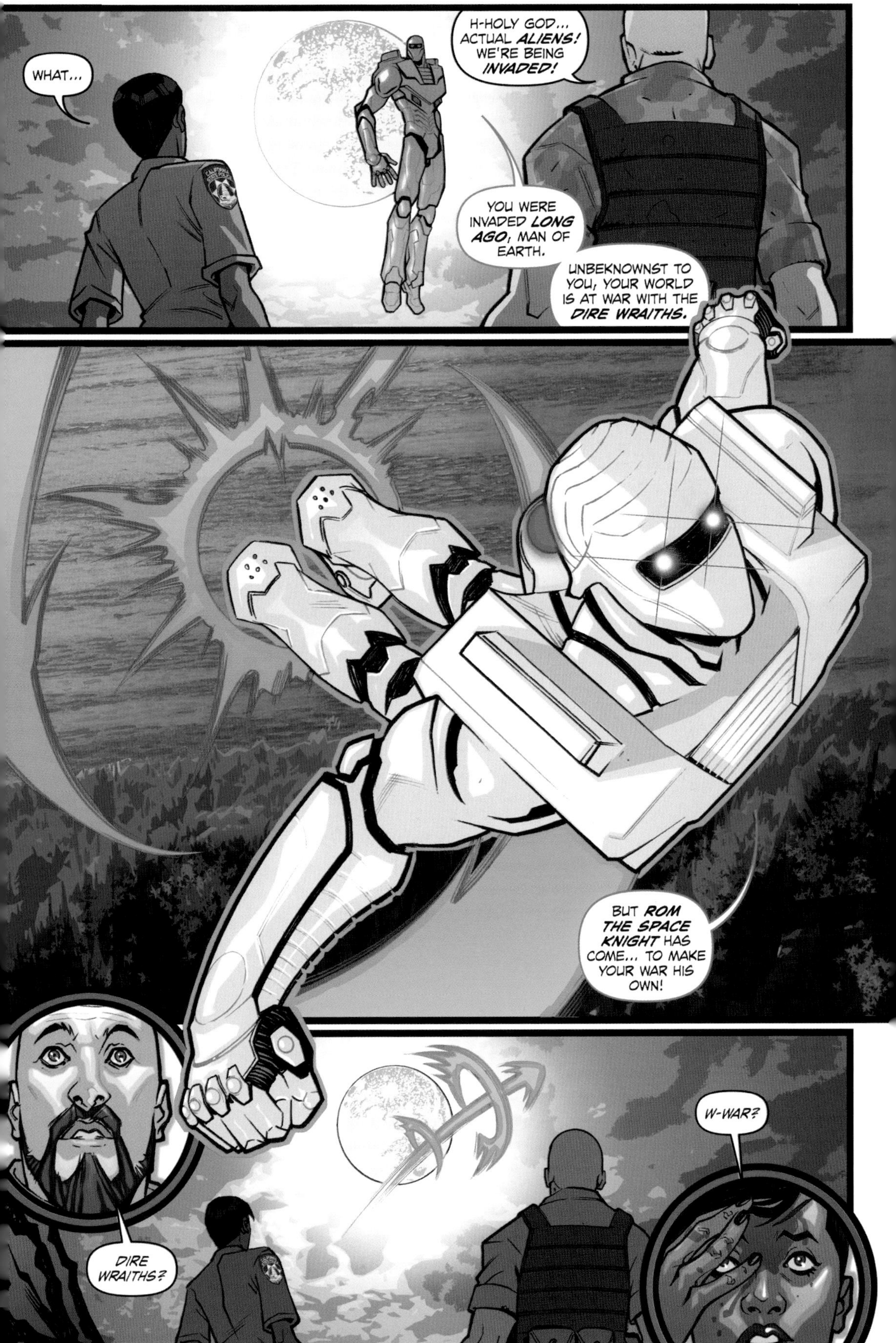

WHAT...
H-HOLY GOD... ACTUAL ALIENS! WE'RE BEING INVADED!
YOU WERE INVADED LONG AGO, MAN OF EARTH.
UNBEKNOWNST TO YOU, YOUR WORLD IS AT WAR WITH THE DIRE WRAITHS.
BUT ROM THE SPACE KNIGHT HAS COME... TO MAKE YOUR WAR HIS OWN!
DIRE WRAITHS?
W-WAR?

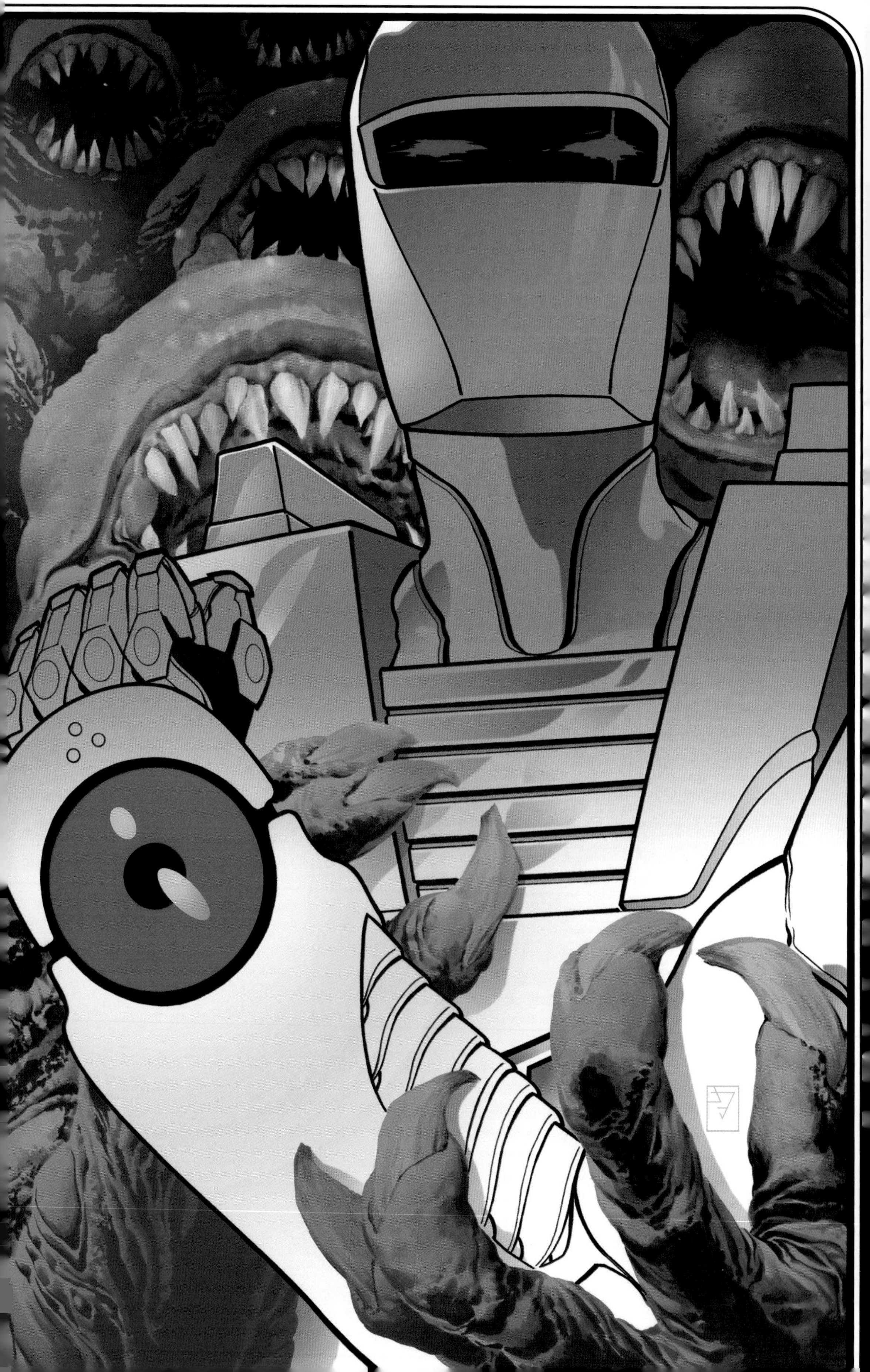

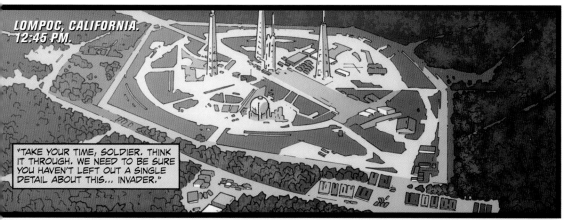

"TAKE YOUR TIME, SOLDIER. THINK IT THROUGH. WE NEED TO BE SURE YOU HAVEN'T LEFT OUT A SINGLE DETAIL ABOUT THIS... INVADER."

VANDENBERG
AIR FORCE BASE

"I'VE TOLD YOU WHAT I SAW, SIR. THE METAL SUIT, THE... MUTATION. THE MURDERS."

BUT YOU EARTH DEFENSE COMMAND FOLKS KEEP DODGING MY QUESTION.

WAS THAT THING ONE OF OURS?

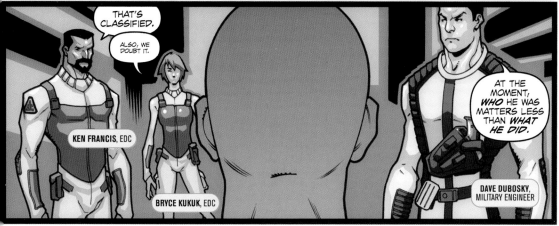

THAT'S CLASSIFIED.

ALSO, WE DOUBT IT.

KEN FRANCIS, EDC

BRYCE KUKUK, EDC

AT THE MOMENT, WHO HE WAS MATTERS LESS THAN WHAT HE DID.

DAVE DUBOSKY, MILITARY ENGINEER

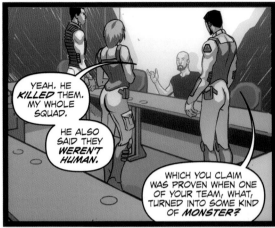

YEAH. HE *KILLED* THEM. MY WHOLE SQUAD.

HE ALSO SAID THEY *WEREN'T HUMAN.*

WHICH YOU CLAIM WAS PROVEN WHEN ONE OF YOUR TEAM, WHAT, TURNED INTO SOME KIND OF *MONSTER?*

MORE THAN THAT, SIR. HE... SUCKED ONE OF THE LOCAL COPS DRY.

USED HIM LIKE... LIKE *FUEL* OR SOMETHING.

GIANT ROBOTS IN DISTANT LANDS, THAT'S ONE THING. BUT A NEW PLAYER, KILLING TROOPS ON AMERICAN SOIL...

GO TELL THE BRASS. WE'LL FINISH HERE.

THE METAL GUY SAID THEY WERE ALL ALIENS, DISGUISED AS US. IS THAT KIND OF INFILTRATION EVEN POSSIBLE?

ALL THINGS ARE POSSIBLE.

SHLIK

POSSIBLE. AND IN SOME CASES, *HUMAN*—

SHLIK

"—INEVITABLE."

YEEEAAARGH!

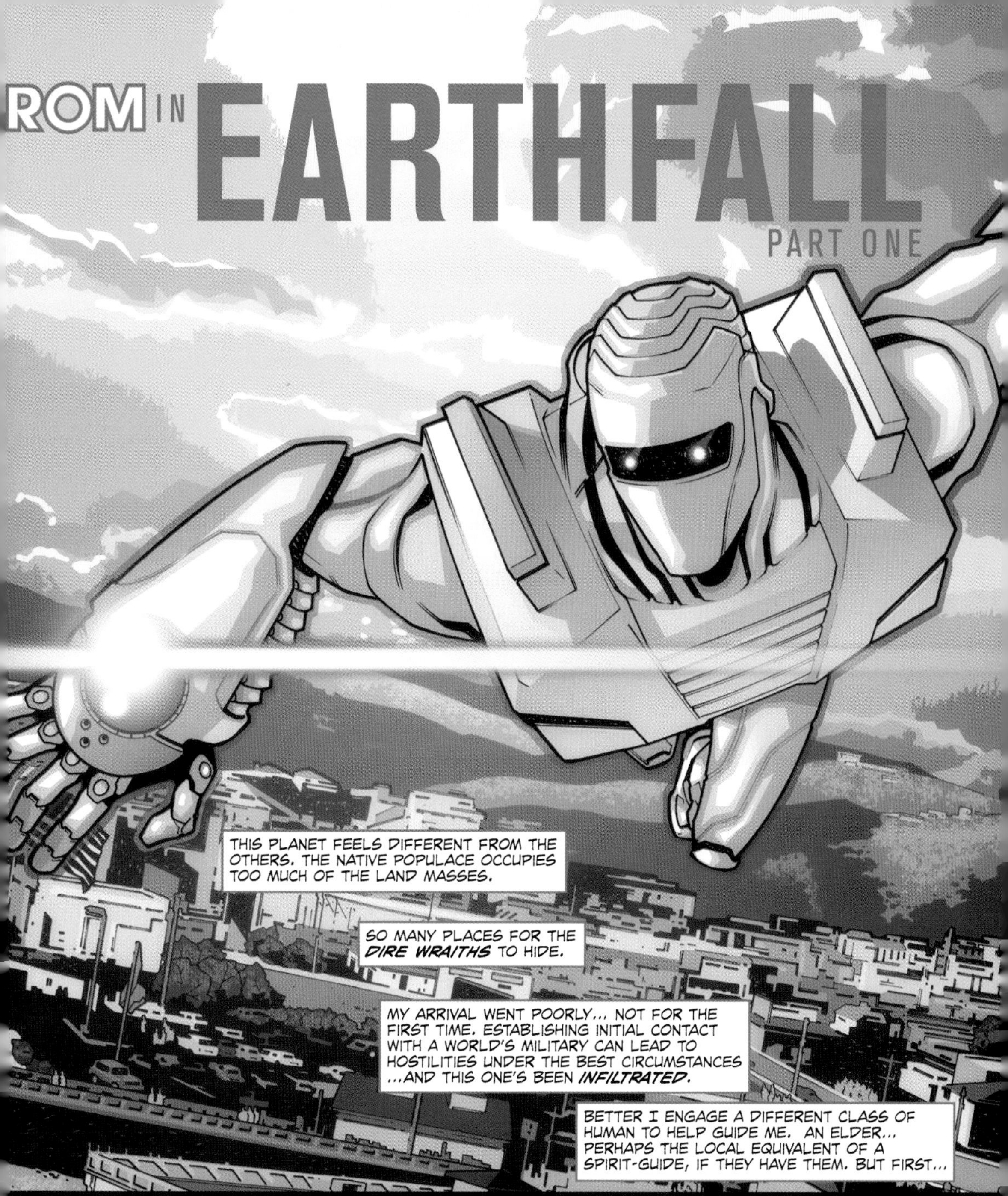
ROM IN EARTHFALL
PART ONE
THIS PLANET FEELS DIFFERENT FROM THE OTHERS. THE NATIVE POPULACE OCCUPIES TOO MUCH OF THE LAND MASSES.
SO MANY PLACES FOR THE DIRE WRAITHS TO HIDE.
MY ARRIVAL WENT POORLY... NOT FOR THE FIRST TIME. ESTABLISHING INITIAL CONTACT WITH A WORLD'S MILITARY CAN LEAD TO HOSTILITIES UNDER THE BEST CIRCUMSTANCES ...AND THIS ONE'S BEEN INFILTRATED.
BETTER I ENGAGE A DIFFERENT CLASS OF HUMAN TO HELP GUIDE ME. AN ELDER... PERHAPS THE LOCAL EQUIVALENT OF A SPIRIT-GUIDE, IF THEY HAVE THEM. BUT FIRST...

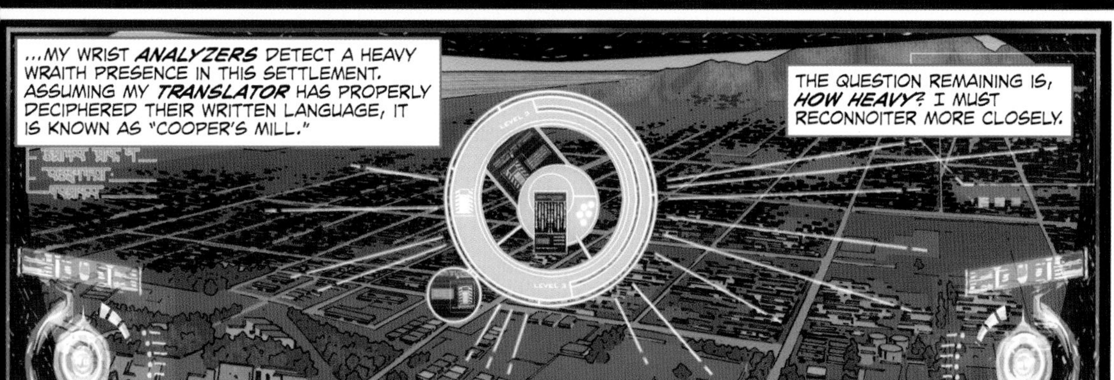
...MY WRIST ANALYZERS DETECT A HEAVY WRAITH PRESENCE IN THIS SETTLEMENT. ASSUMING MY TRANSLATOR HAS PROPERLY DECIPHERED THEIR WRITTEN LANGUAGE, IT IS KNOWN AS "COOPER'S MILL."
THE QUESTION REMAINING IS, HOW HEAVY? I MUST RECONNOITER MORE CLOSELY.

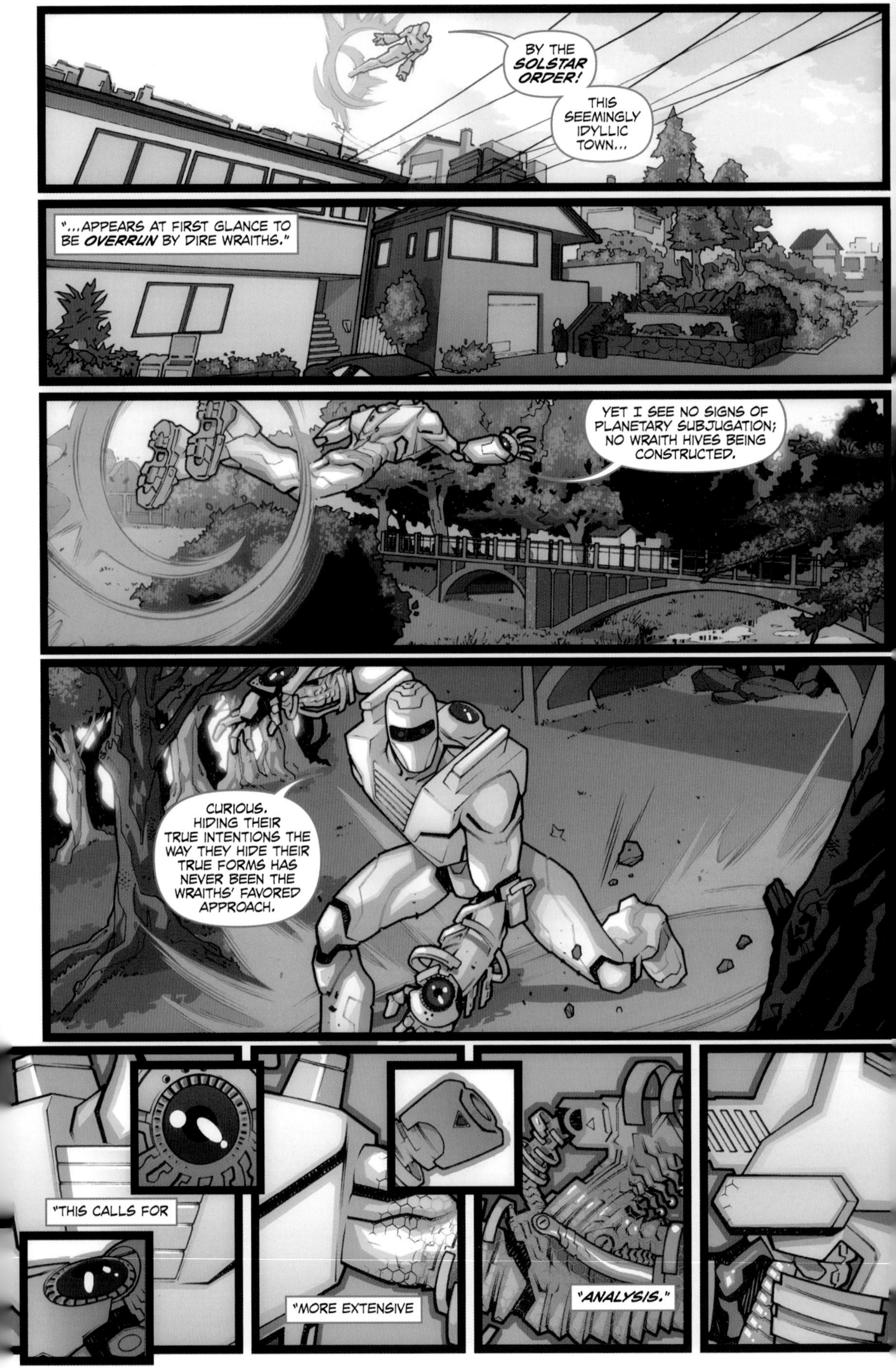
BY THE SOLSTAR ORDER!
THIS SEEMINGLY IDYLLIC TOWN...
"...APPEARS AT FIRST GLANCE TO BE OVERRUN BY DIRE WRAITHS."
YET I SEE NO SIGNS OF PLANETARY SUBJUGATION; NO WRAITH HIVES BEING CONSTRUCTED.
CURIOUS. HIDING THEIR TRUE INTENTIONS THE WAY THEY HIDE THEIR TRUE FORMS HAS NEVER BEEN THE WRAITHS' FAVORED APPROACH.
"THIS CALLS FOR
"MORE EXTENSIVE
"ANALYSIS."

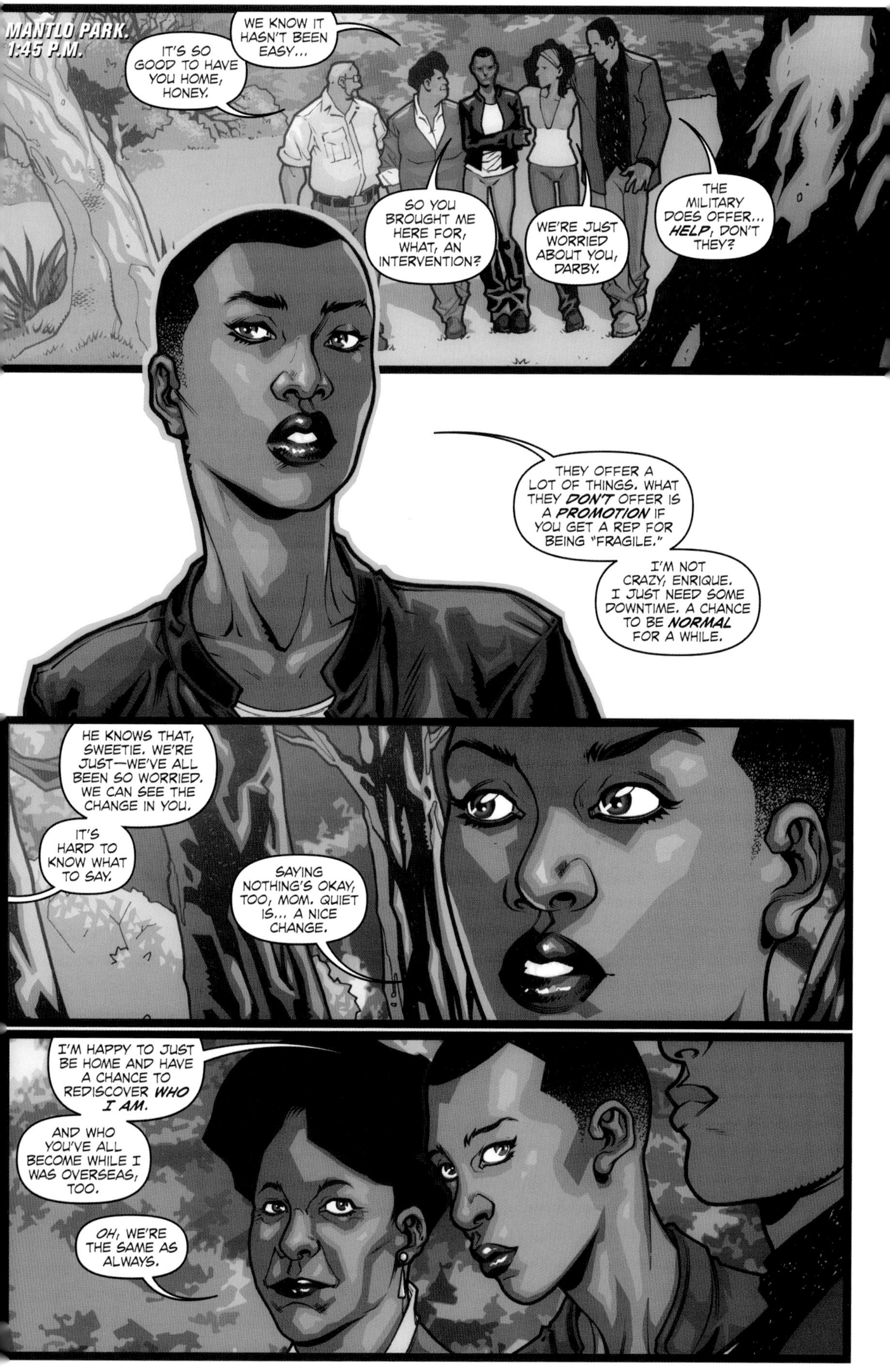
MANTLO PARK. 1:45 P.M.
IT'S SO GOOD TO HAVE YOU HOME, HONEY.
WE KNOW IT HASN'T BEEN EASY...
SO YOU BROUGHT ME HERE FOR, WHAT, AN INTERVENTION?
WE'RE JUST WORRIED ABOUT YOU, DARBY.
THE MILITARY DOES OFFER... HELP, DON'T THEY?
THEY OFFER A LOT OF THINGS. WHAT THEY DON'T OFFER IS A PROMOTION IF YOU GET A REP FOR BEING "FRAGILE."
I'M NOT CRAZY, ENRIQUE. I JUST NEED SOME DOWNTIME. A CHANCE TO BE NORMAL FOR A WHILE.
HE KNOWS THAT, SWEETIE. WE'RE JUST—WE'VE ALL BEEN SO WORRIED. WE CAN SEE THE CHANGE IN YOU.
IT'S HARD TO KNOW WHAT TO SAY.
SAYING NOTHING'S OKAY, TOO, MOM. QUIET IS... A NICE CHANGE.
I'M HAPPY TO JUST BE HOME AND HAVE A CHANCE TO REDISCOVER WHO I AM.
AND WHO YOU'VE ALL BECOME WHILE I WAS OVERSEAS, TOO.
OH, WE'RE THE SAME AS ALWAYS.

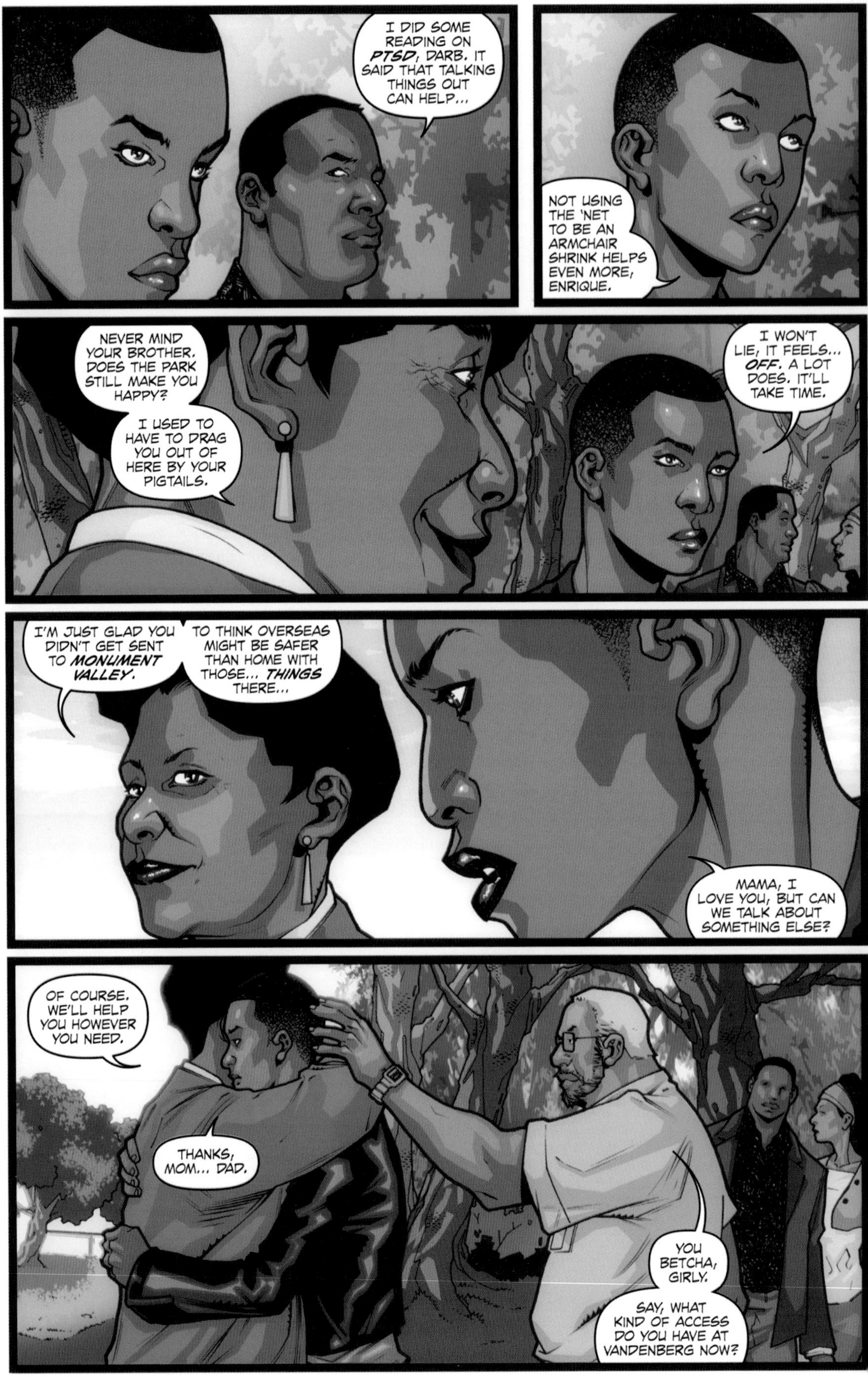

I DID SOME READING ON PTSD, DARB. IT SAID THAT TALKING THINGS OUT CAN HELP...
NOT USING THE 'NET TO BE AN ARMCHAIR SHRINK HELPS EVEN MORE, ENRIQUE.
NEVER MIND YOUR BROTHER. DOES THE PARK STILL MAKE YOU HAPPY?
I USED TO HAVE TO DRAG YOU OUT OF HERE BY YOUR PIGTAILS.
I WON'T LIE, IT FEELS... OFF. A LOT DOES. IT'LL TAKE TIME.
I'M JUST GLAD YOU DIDN'T GET SENT TO MONUMENT VALLEY.
TO THINK OVERSEAS MIGHT BE SAFER THAN HOME WITH THOSE... THINGS THERE...
MAMA, I LOVE YOU, BUT CAN WE TALK ABOUT SOMETHING ELSE?
OF COURSE. WE'LL HELP YOU HOWEVER YOU NEED.
THANKS, MOM... DAD.
YOU BETCHA, GIRLY.
SAY, WHAT KIND OF ACCESS DO YOU HAVE AT VANDENBERG NOW?

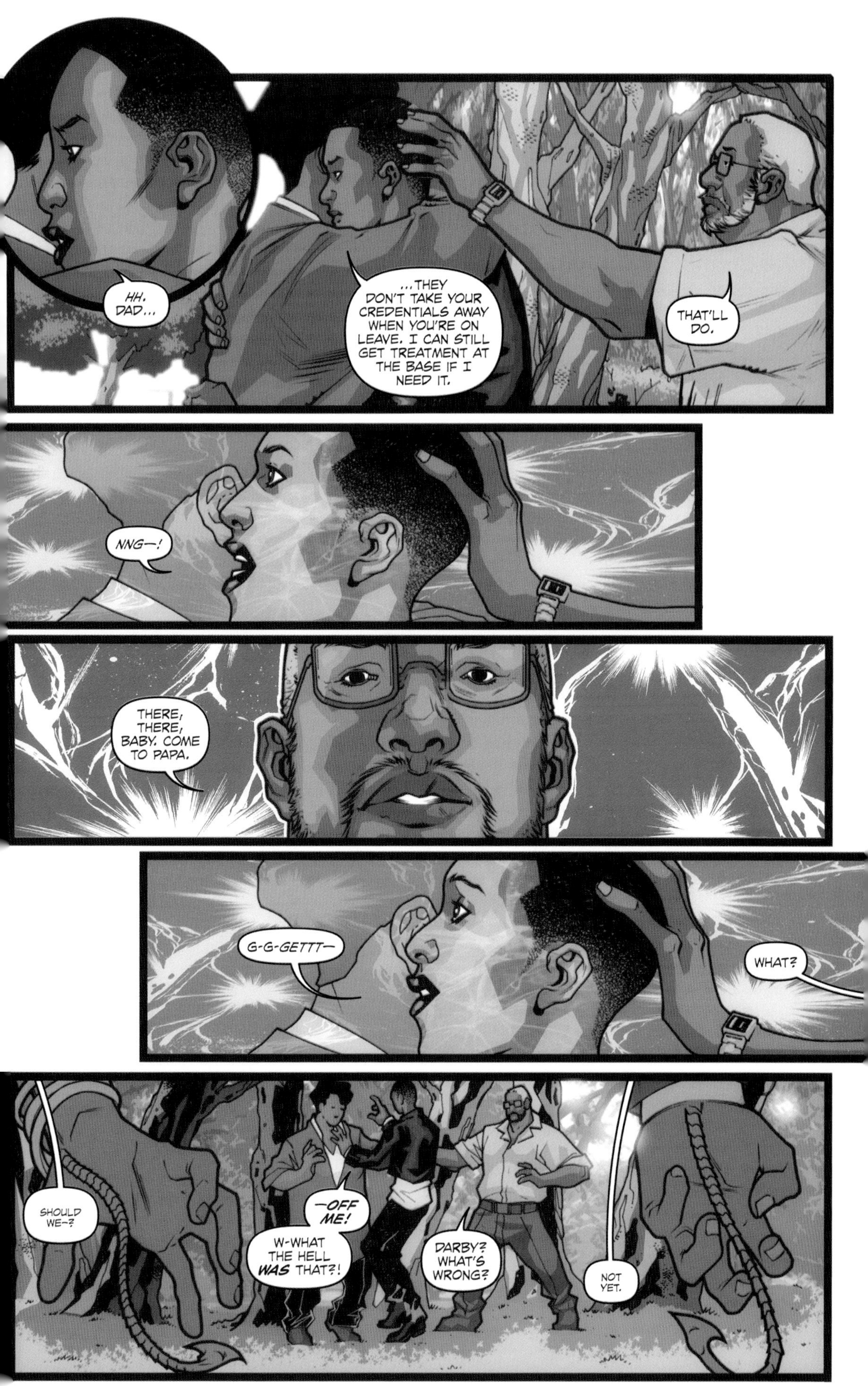
HH. DAD...
...THEY DON'T TAKE YOUR CREDENTIALS AWAY WHEN YOU'RE ON LEAVE. I CAN STILL GET TREATMENT AT THE BASE IF I NEED IT.
THAT'LL DO.
NNG—!
THERE, THERE, BABY. COME TO PAPA.
G-G-GETTT—
WHAT?
SHOULD WE-?
—OFF ME!
W-WHAT THE HELL WAS THAT?!
DARBY? WHAT'S WRONG?
NOT YET.

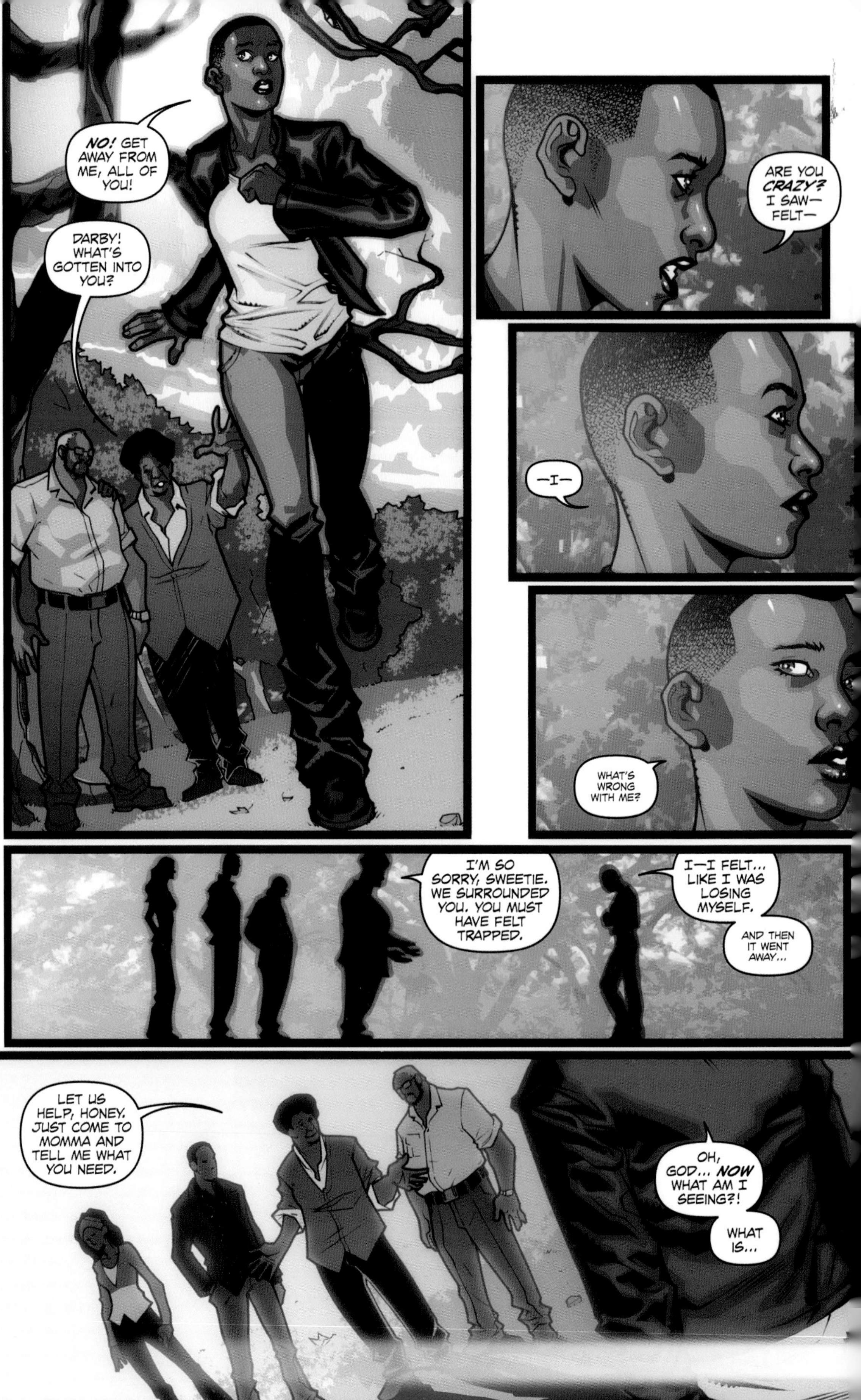
NO! GET AWAY FROM ME, ALL OF YOU!
DARBY! WHAT'S GOTTEN INTO YOU?
ARE YOU CRAZY? I SAW— FELT—
—I—
WHAT'S WRONG WITH ME?
I'M SO SORRY, SWEETIE. WE SURROUNDED YOU. YOU MUST HAVE FELT TRAPPED.
I—I FELT... LIKE I WAS LOSING MYSELF.
AND THEN IT WENT AWAY...
LET US HELP, HONEY. JUST COME TO MOMMA AND TELL ME WHAT YOU NEED.
OH, GOD... NOW WHAT AM I SEEING?!
WHAT IS...

"...THAT?"

I AM *ROM*.

STEP AWAY, HUMAN. THESE OTHERS...

"...STAND REVEALED AS *DIRE WRAITHS* ONE AND ALL."

DIRE *WHAT?!* WHAT ARE *YOU?!*

BACK AWAY FROM THEM!

DOES ANYONE ELSE SEE THIS?

MOVE *ASIDE* WHILE MY *ANALYZER* GIVES WAY...

...TO MY *NEUTRALIZER.*

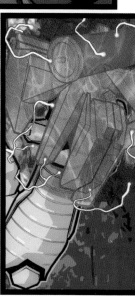

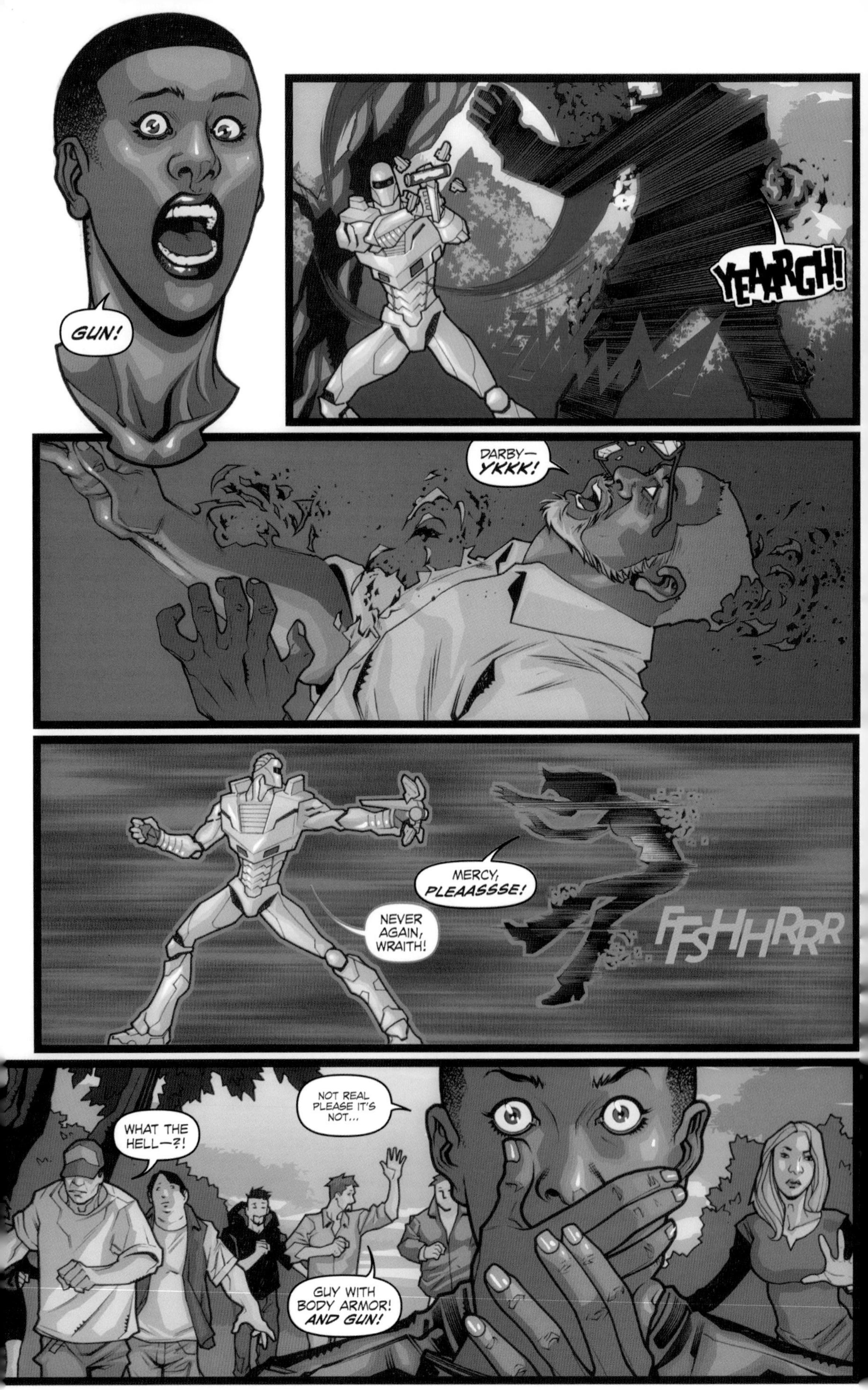
GUN!
YEAARGH!
ZWAMM
DARBY—
YKKK!
MERCY,
PLEAASSSE!
NEVER AGAIN, WRAITH!
FFSHHRRR
WHAT THE HELL—?!
NOT REAL PLEASE IT'S NOT...
GUY WITH BODY ARMOR! AND GUN!

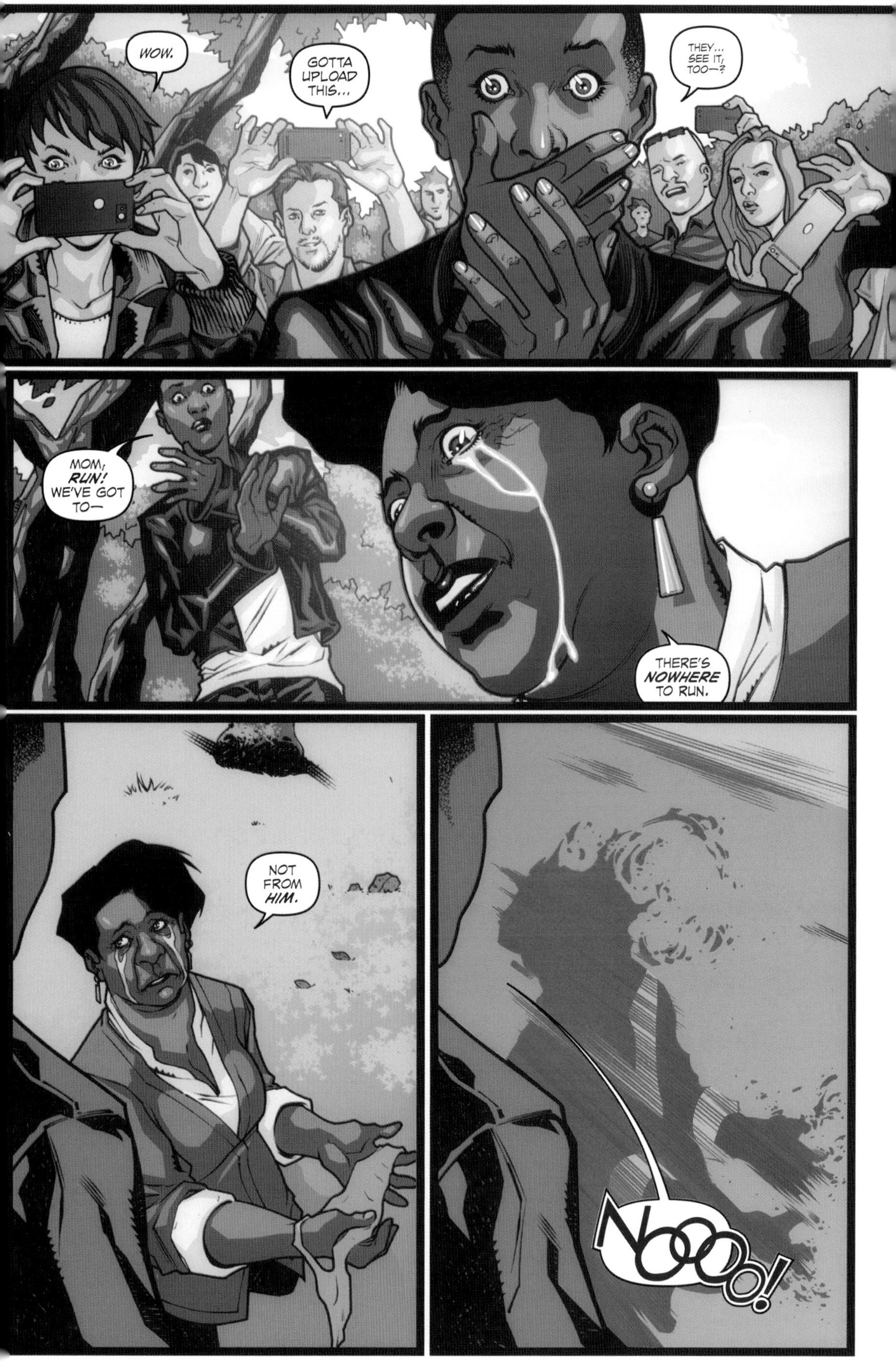
WOW.
GOTTA UPLOAD THIS...
THEY... SEE IT, TOO—?
MOM, RUN! WE'VE GOT TO—
THERE'S NOWHERE TO RUN.
NOT FROM HIM.
NOOOO!

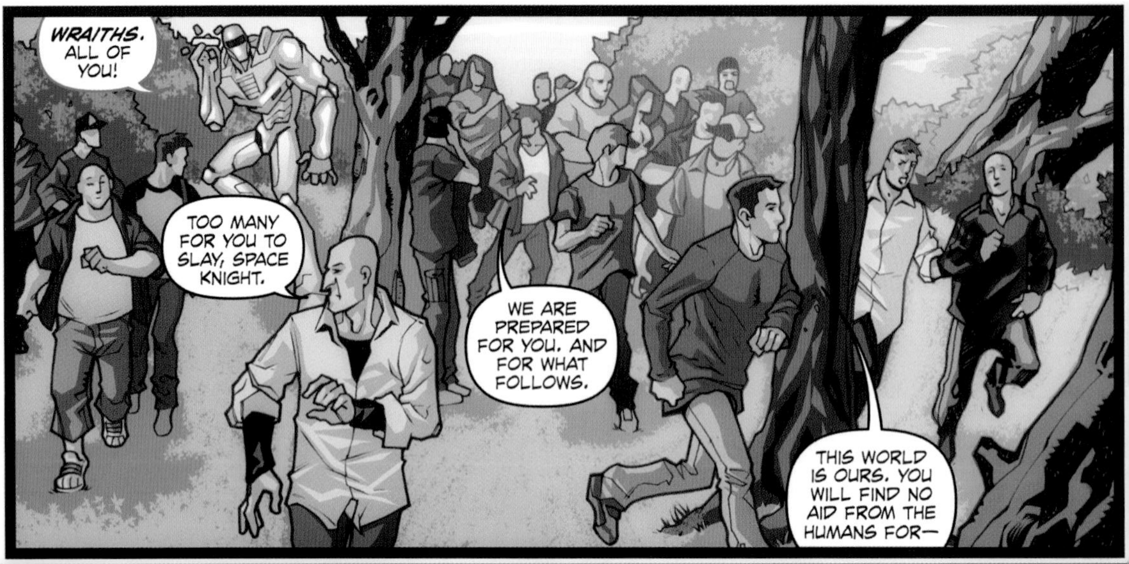
WRAITHS. ALL OF YOU!
TOO MANY FOR YOU TO SLAY, SPACE KNIGHT.
WE ARE PREPARED FOR YOU. AND FOR WHAT FOLLOWS.
THIS WORLD IS OURS. YOU WILL FIND NO AID FROM THE HUMANS FOR—

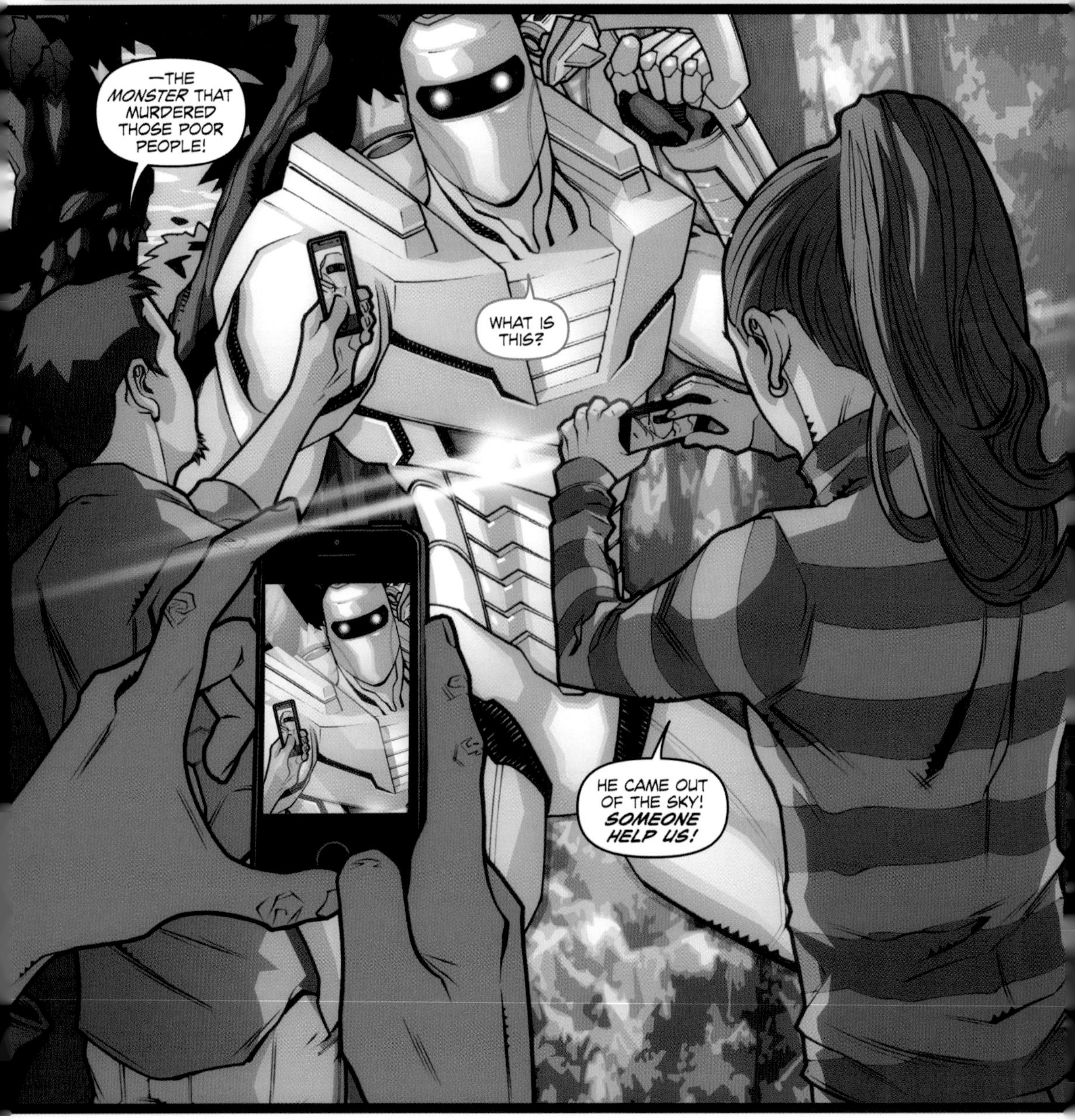
—THE MONSTER THAT MURDERED THOSE POOR PEOPLE!
WHAT IS THIS?
HE CAME OUT OF THE SKY! SOMEONE HELP US!

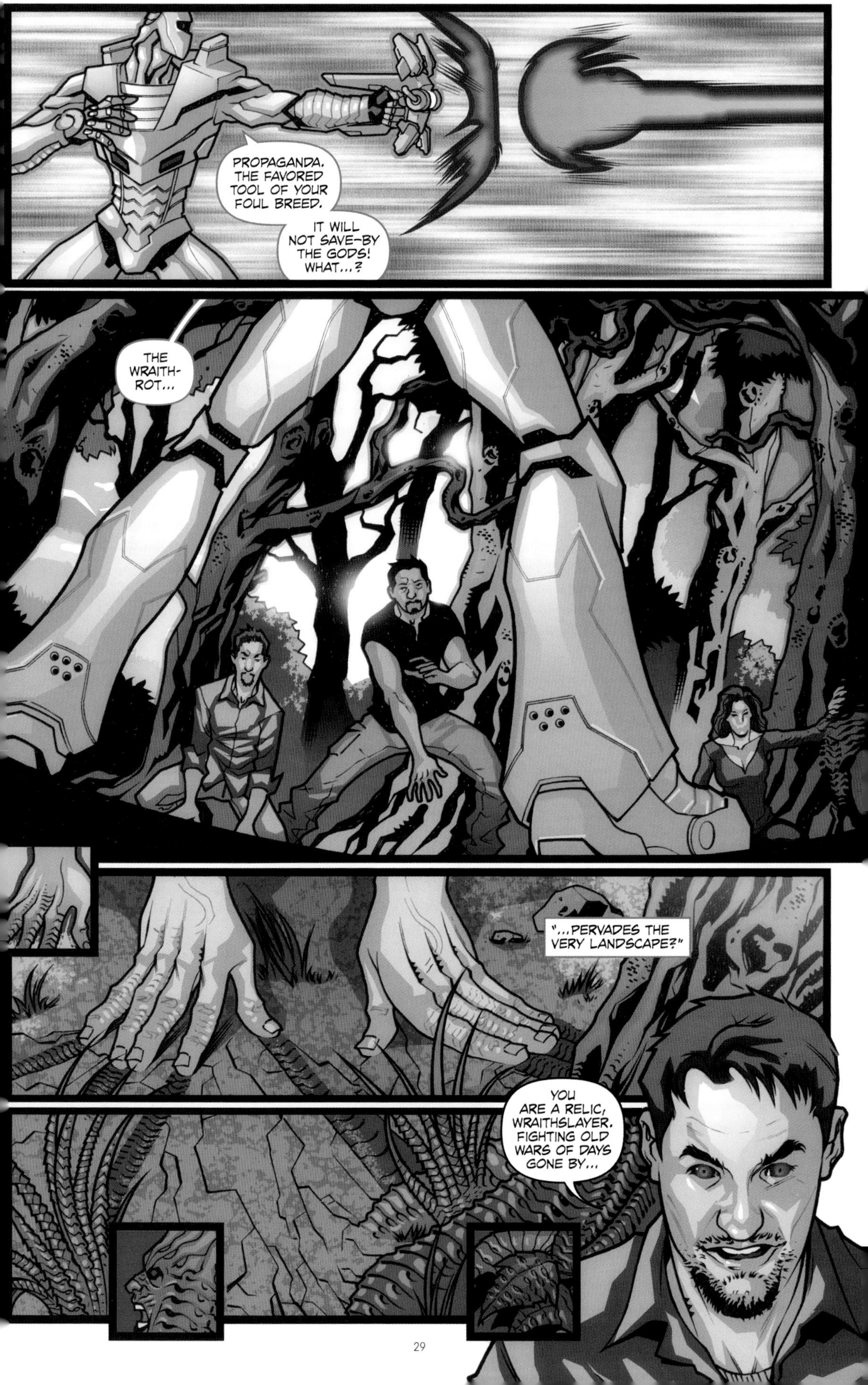

PROPAGANDA. THE FAVORED TOOL OF YOUR FOUL BREED.
IT WILL NOT SAVE--BY THE GODS! WHAT...?
THE WRAITH-ROT...
"...PERVADES THE VERY LANDSCAPE?"
YOU ARE A RELIC, WRAITHSLAYER. FIGHTING OLD WARS OF DAYS GONE BY...

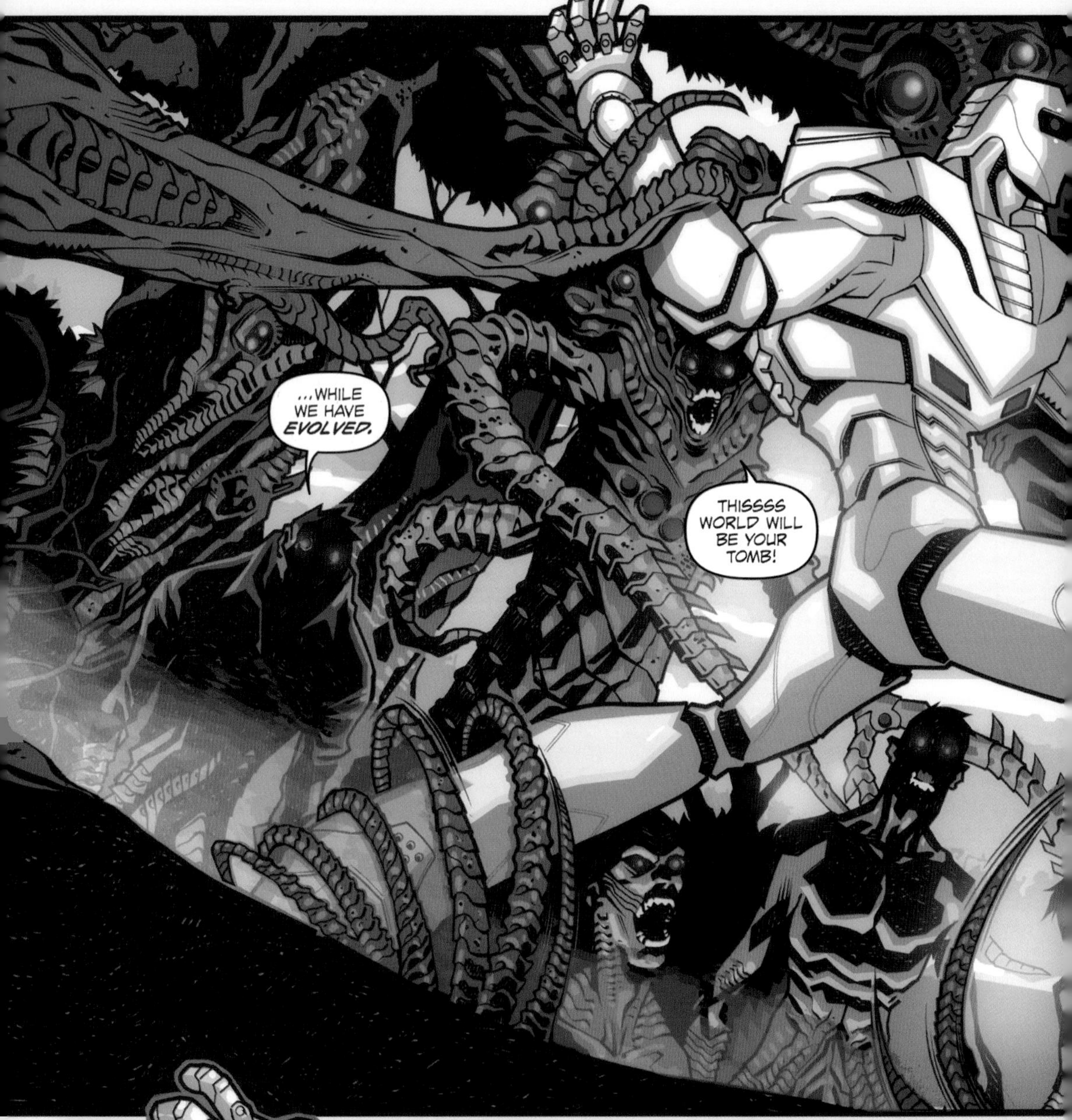
...WHILE WE HAVE EVOLVED.
THISSSS WORLD WILL BE YOUR TOMB!

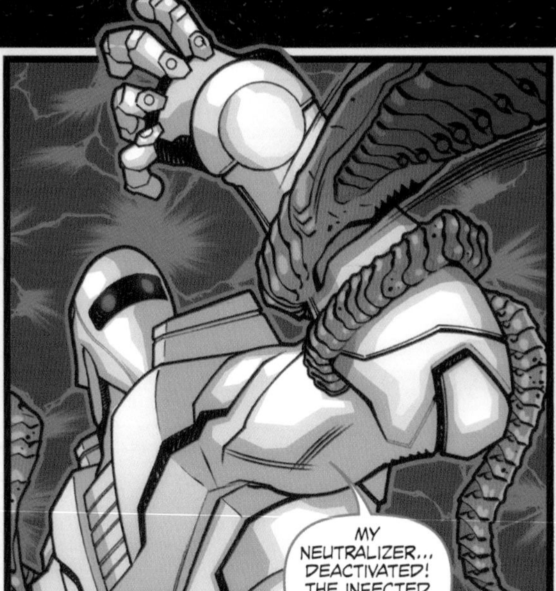
MY NEUTRALIZER... DEACTIVATED! THE INFECTED VEGETATION...

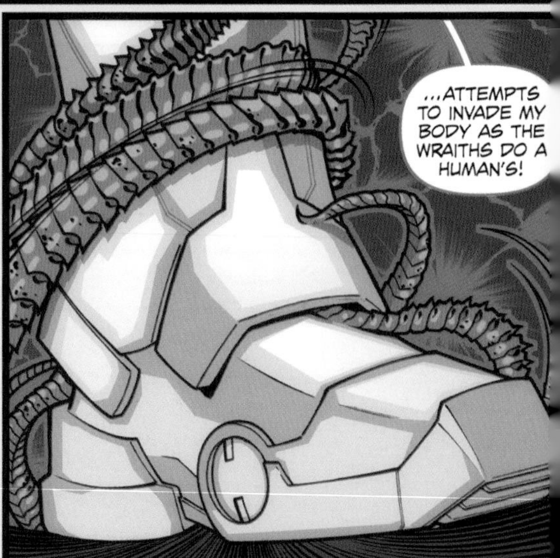
...ATTEMPTS TO INVADE MY BODY AS THE WRAITHS DO A HUMAN'S!

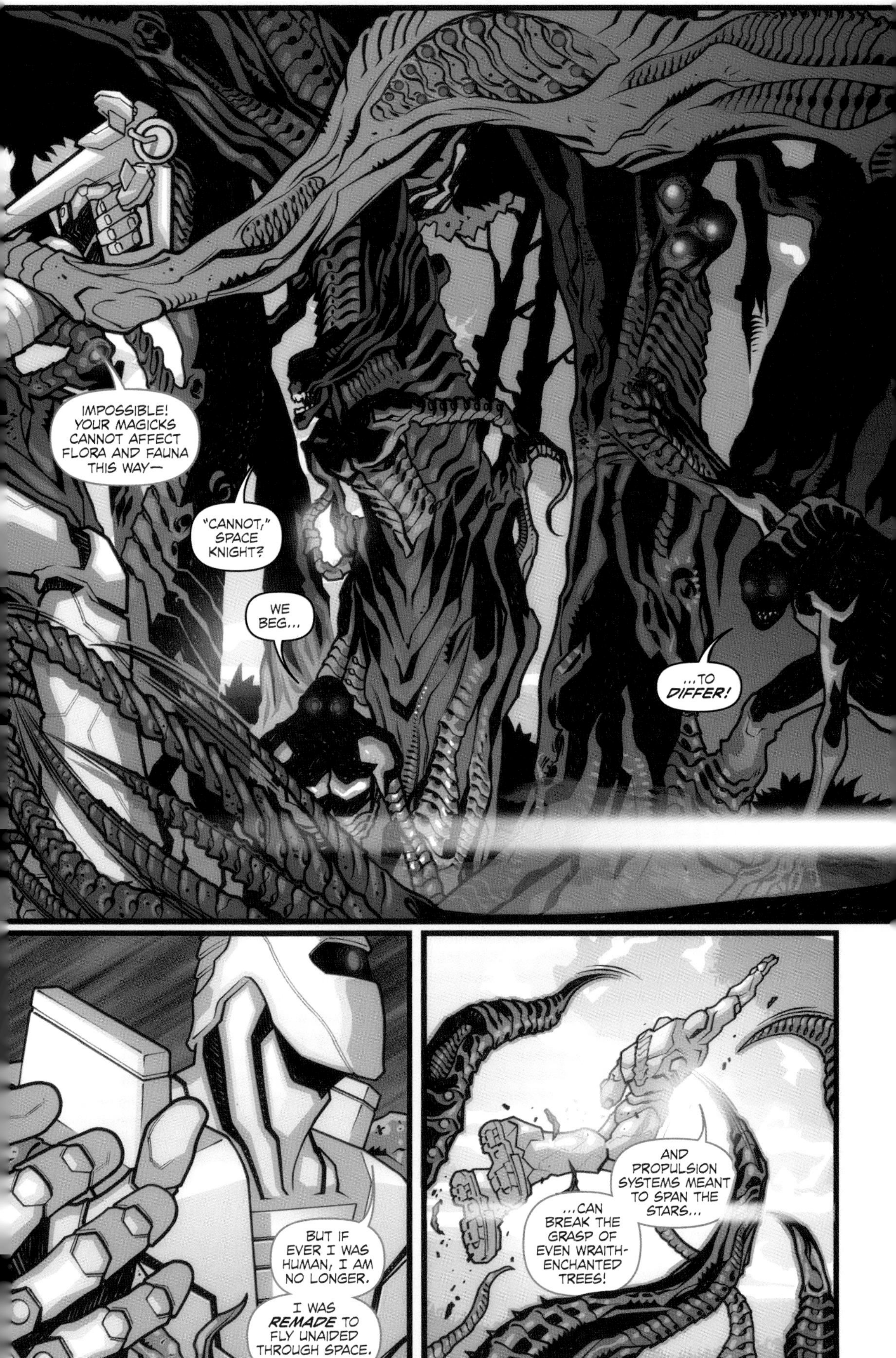
IMPOSSIBLE! YOUR MAGICKS CANNOT AFFECT FLORA AND FAUNA THIS WAY—
"CANNOT," SPACE KNIGHT?
WE BEG...
...TO DIFFER!
BUT IF EVER I WAS HUMAN, I AM NO LONGER.
I WAS REMADE TO FLY UNAIDED THROUGH SPACE.
AND PROPULSION SYSTEMS MEANT TO SPAN THE STARS...
...CAN BREAK THE GRASP OF EVEN WRAITH-ENCHANTED TREES!

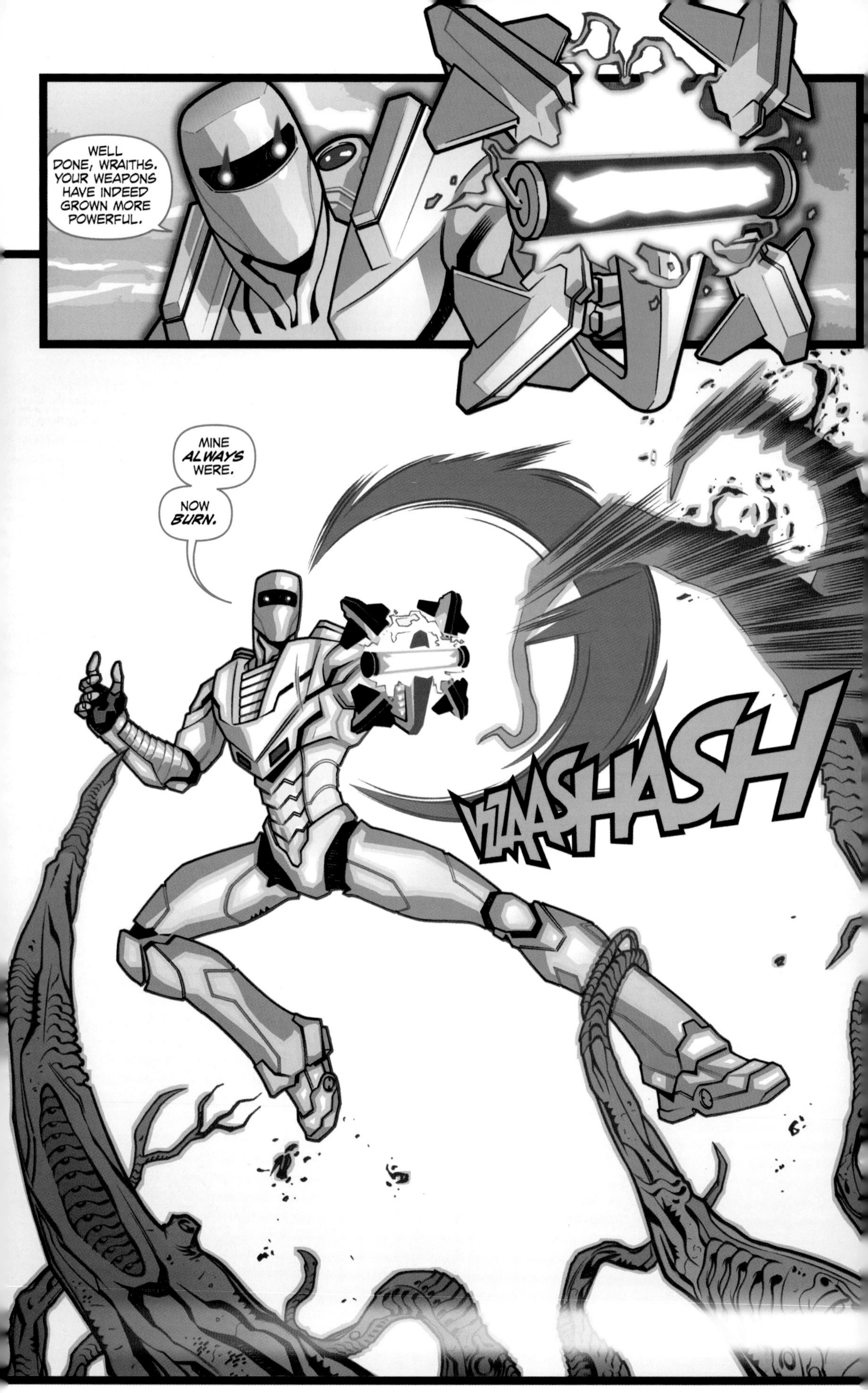
WELL DONE, WRAITHS. YOUR WEAPONS HAVE INDEED GROWN MORE POWERFUL.
MINE *ALWAYS* WERE.
NOW *BURN.*
VZAASHASH

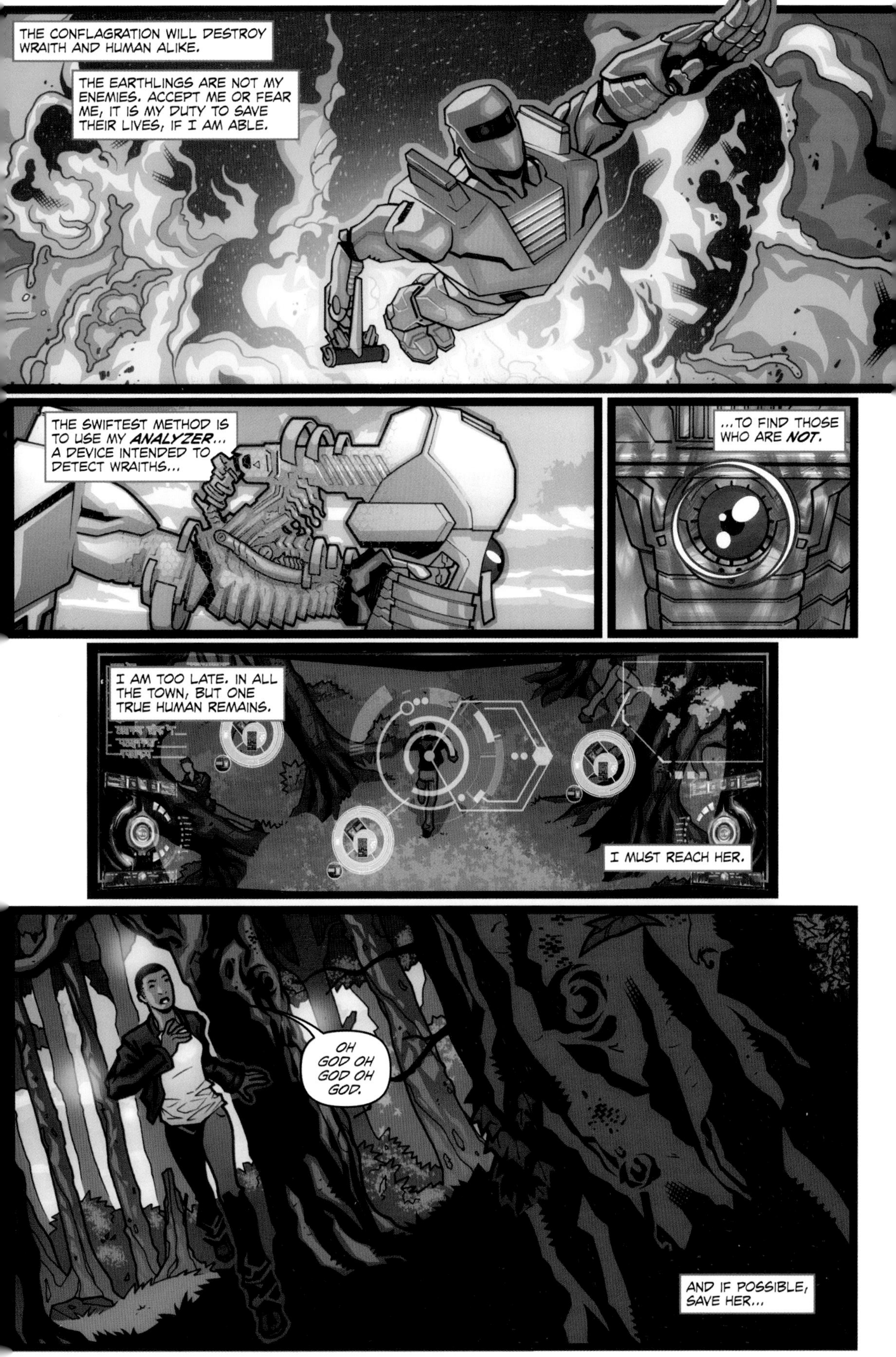
THE CONFLAGRATION WILL DESTROY WRAITH AND HUMAN ALIKE.
THE EARTHLINGS ARE NOT MY ENEMIES. ACCEPT ME OR FEAR ME, IT IS MY DUTY TO SAVE THEIR LIVES, IF I AM ABLE.
THE SWIFTEST METHOD IS TO USE MY ***ANALYZER***... A DEVICE INTENDED TO DETECT WRAITHS...
...TO FIND THOSE WHO ARE ***NOT***.
I AM TOO LATE. IN ALL THE TOWN, BUT ONE TRUE HUMAN REMAINS.
I MUST REACH HER.
OH GOD OH GOD OH GOD.
AND IF POSSIBLE, SAVE HER...

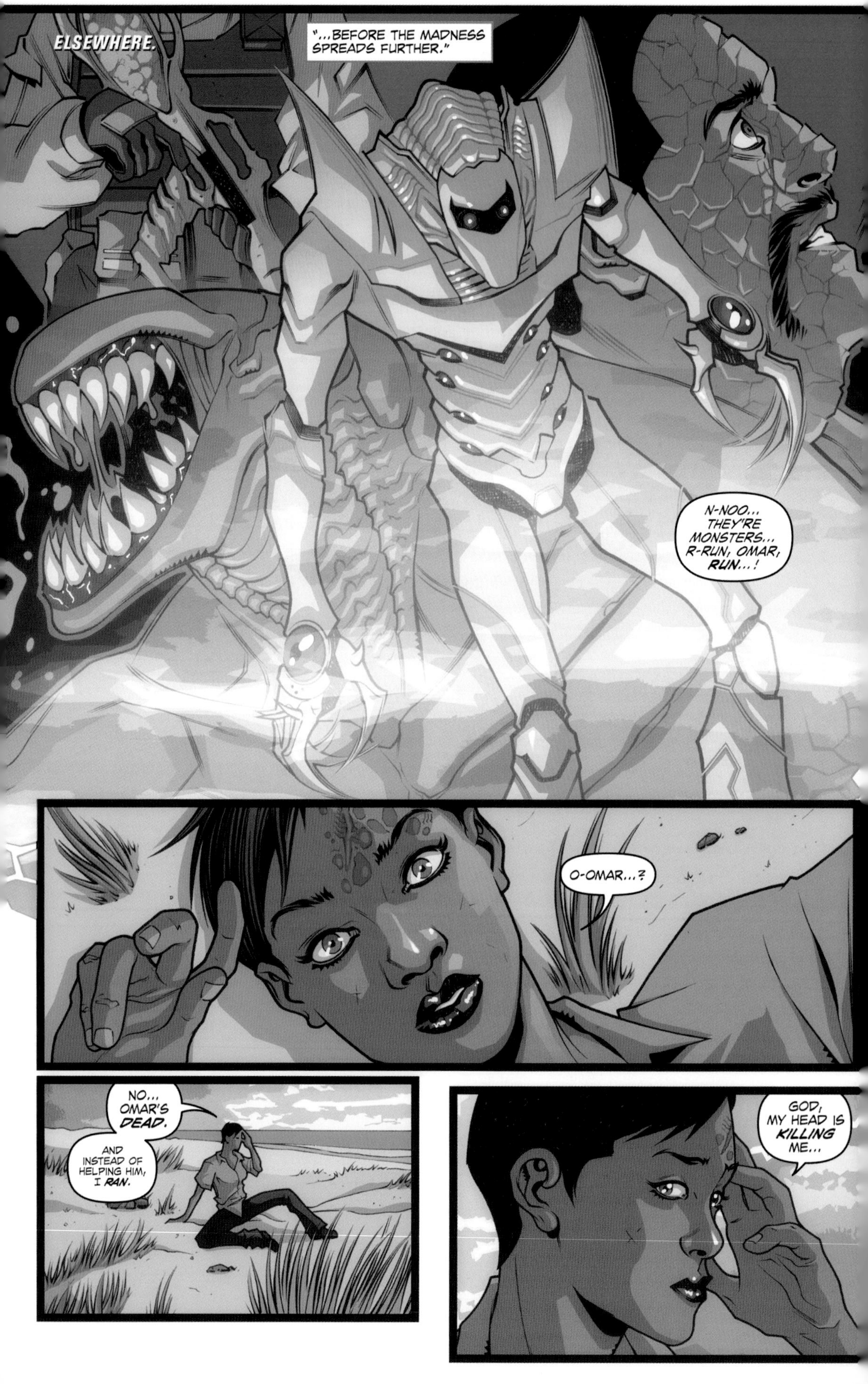
ELSEWHERE.
"...BEFORE THE MADNESS SPREADS FURTHER."
N-NOO... THEY'RE MONSTERS... R-RUN, OMAR, RUN...!
O-OMAR...?
NO... OMAR'S DEAD.
AND INSTEAD OF HELPING HIM, I RAN.
GOD, MY HEAD IS KILLING ME...

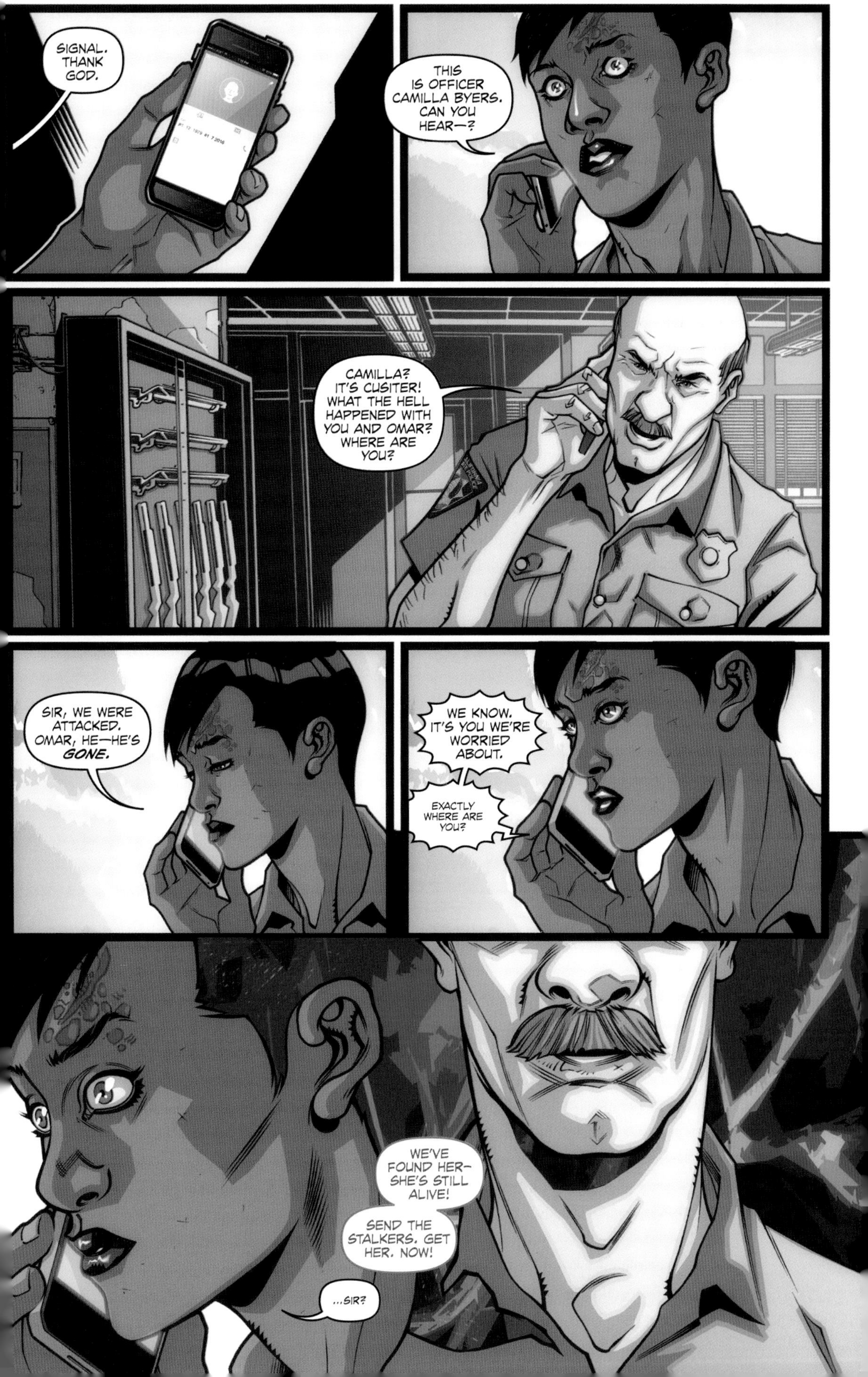
SIGNAL. THANK GOD.
THIS IS OFFICER CAMILLA BYERS. CAN YOU HEAR—?
CAMILLA? IT'S CUSITER! WHAT THE HELL HAPPENED WITH YOU AND OMAR? WHERE ARE YOU?
SIR, WE WERE ATTACKED. OMAR, HE—HE'S *GONE.*
WE KNOW. IT'S YOU WE'RE WORRIED ABOUT.
EXACTLY WHERE ARE YOU?
WE'VE FOUND HER—SHE'S STILL ALIVE!
SEND THE STALKERS. GET HER. NOW!
...SIR?

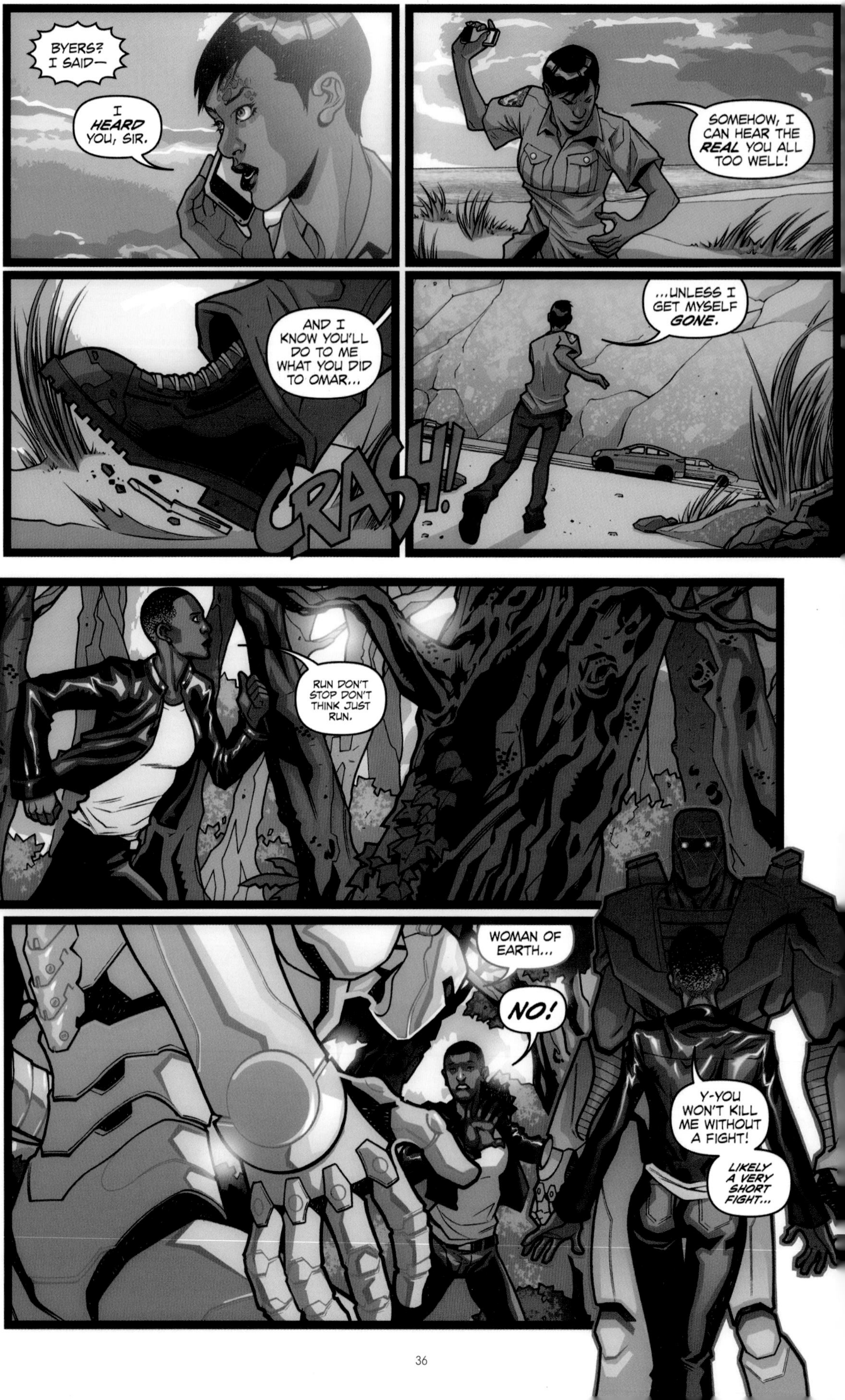

BYERS? I SAID—
I HEARD YOU, SIR.
SOMEHOW, I CAN HEAR THE REAL YOU ALL TOO WELL!
AND I KNOW YOU'LL DO TO ME WHAT YOU DID TO OMAR...
CRASH!
...UNLESS I GET MYSELF GONE.
RUN DON'T STOP DON'T THINK JUST RUN.
WOMAN OF EARTH...
NO!
Y-YOU WON'T KILL ME WITHOUT A FIGHT!
LIKELY A VERY SHORT FIGHT...

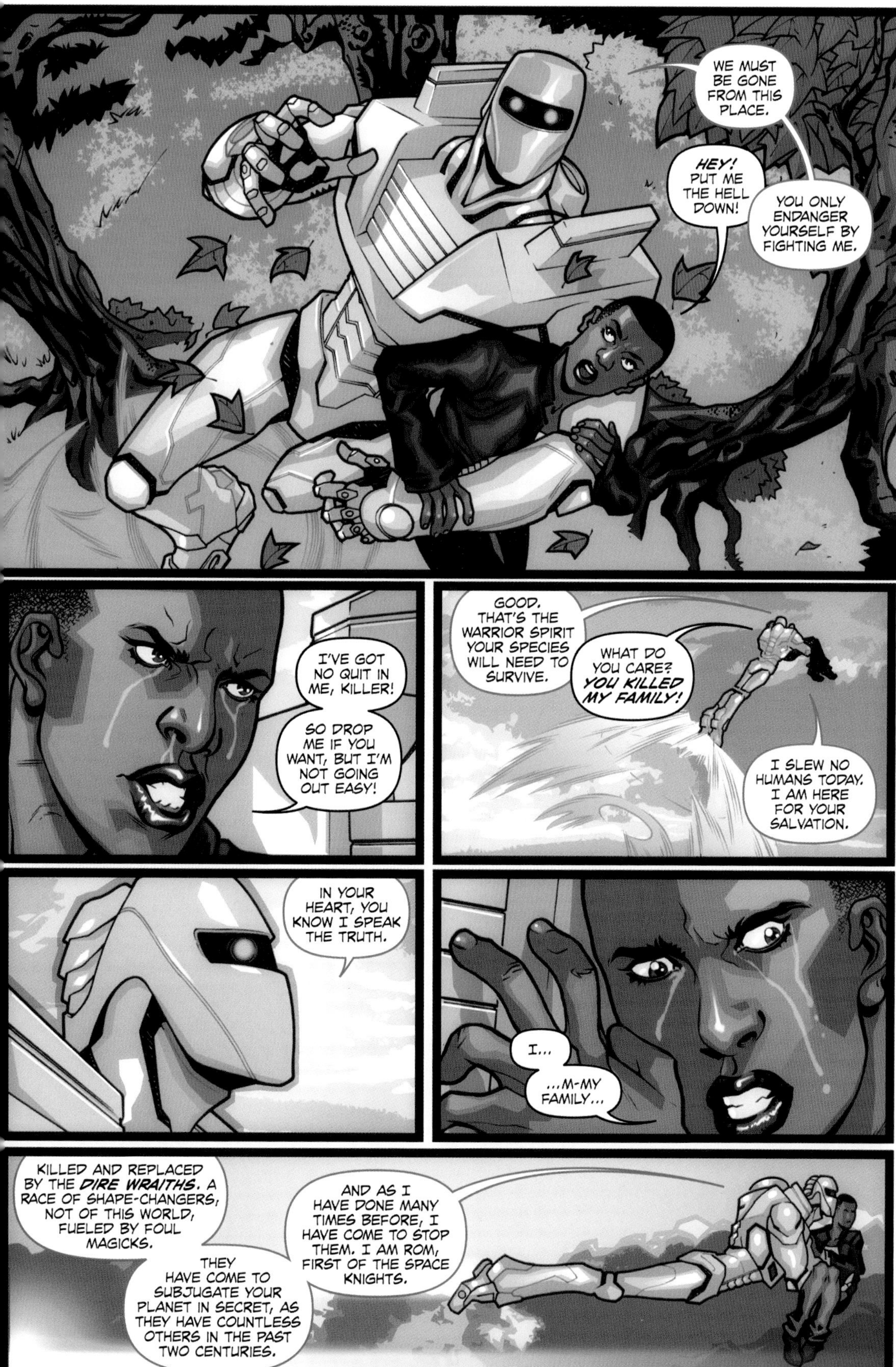

WE MUST BE GONE FROM THIS PLACE.
HEY! PUT ME THE HELL DOWN!
YOU ONLY ENDANGER YOURSELF BY FIGHTING ME.
I'VE GOT NO QUIT IN ME, KILLER!
SO DROP ME IF YOU WANT, BUT I'M NOT GOING OUT EASY!
GOOD. THAT'S THE WARRIOR SPIRIT YOUR SPECIES WILL NEED TO SURVIVE.
WHAT DO YOU CARE? YOU KILLED MY FAMILY!
I SLEW NO HUMANS TODAY. I AM HERE FOR YOUR SALVATION.
IN YOUR HEART, YOU KNOW I SPEAK THE TRUTH.
I...
...M-MY FAMILY...
KILLED AND REPLACED BY THE DIRE WRAITHS. A RACE OF SHAPE-CHANGERS, NOT OF THIS WORLD, FUELED BY FOUL MAGICKS.
THEY HAVE COME TO SUBJUGATE YOUR PLANET IN SECRET, AS THEY HAVE COUNTLESS OTHERS IN THE PAST TWO CENTURIES.
AND AS I HAVE DONE MANY TIMES BEFORE, I HAVE COME TO STOP THEM. I AM ROM, FIRST OF THE SPACE KNIGHTS.

TH-THEN... MY FAMILY... THEY'RE REALLY DEAD?

I FEAR SO. MY CONDOLENCES, WOMAN OF EARTH. I... UNDERSTAND YOUR SORROW.

THEY... KILLED YOUR FAMILY, TOO?

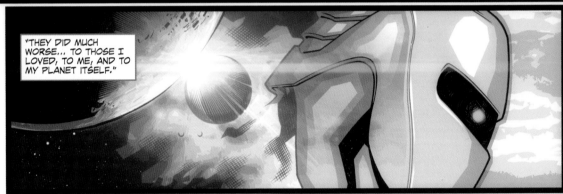

"THEY DID MUCH WORSE... TO THOSE I LOVED, TO ME, AND TO MY PLANET ITSELF."

I GUESS AFTER THE PAST FEW YEARS, THE IDEA OF A KNIGHT FROM SPACE ISN'T AS NUTS AS IT USED TO BE.

BUT THAT FIRE YOU STARTED... THE PEOPLE... THIS IS MY HOME-TOWN.

NO LONGER. IT HAS BEEN OVERRUN AND SUBSUMED BY THE WRAITHS. ONLY YOU RESISTED THEIR CONTAGION. I MUST KNOW WHY.

THIS AND OTHER ANSWERS I REQUIRE BEFORE I CAN WIPE THE SCOURGE FROM THIS REGION.

HOLD UP. YOU'D KILL MY *ENTIRE TOWN?*

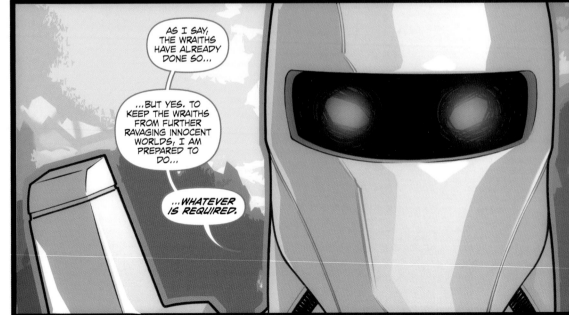

AS I SAY, THE WRAITHS HAVE ALREADY DONE SO...

...BUT YES. TO KEEP THE WRAITHS FROM FURTHER RAVAGING INNOCENT WORLDS, I AM PREPARED TO DO...

...*WHATEVER IS REQUIRED.*

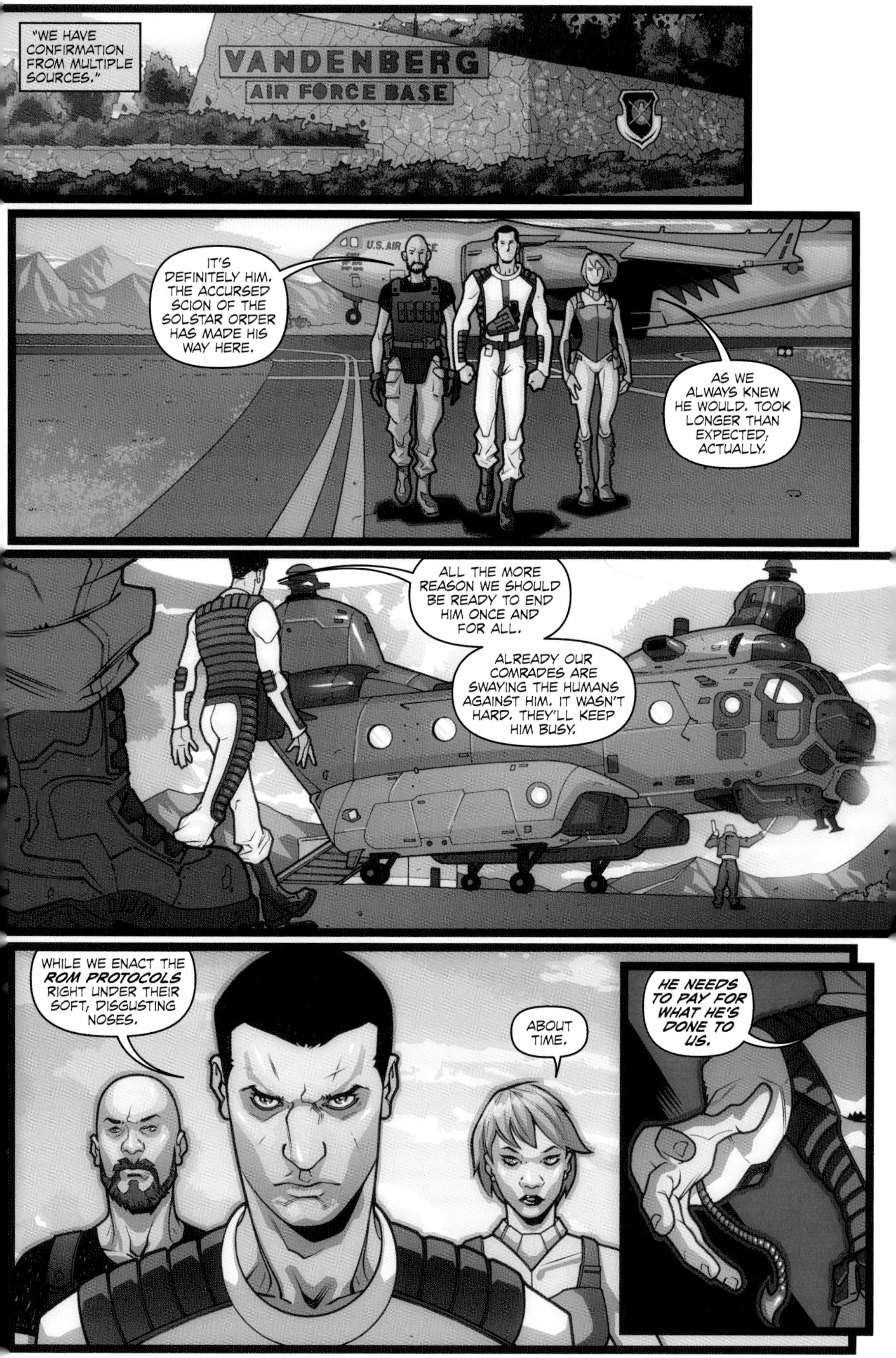
"WE HAVE CONFIRMATION FROM MULTIPLE SOURCES."
VANDENBERG
AIR FORCE BASE
U.S. AIR
IT'S DEFINITELY HIM. THE ACCURSED SCION OF THE SOLSTAR ORDER HAS MADE HIS WAY HERE.
AS WE ALWAYS KNEW HE WOULD. TOOK LONGER THAN EXPECTED, ACTUALLY.
ALL THE MORE REASON WE SHOULD BE READY TO END HIM ONCE AND FOR ALL.
ALREADY OUR COMRADES ARE SWAYING THE HUMANS AGAINST HIM. IT WASN'T HARD. THEY'LL KEEP HIM BUSY.
WHILE WE ENACT THE ROM PROTOCOLS RIGHT UNDER THEIR SOFT, DISGUSTING NOSES.
ABOUT TIME.
HE NEEDS TO PAY FOR WHAT HE'S DONE TO US.

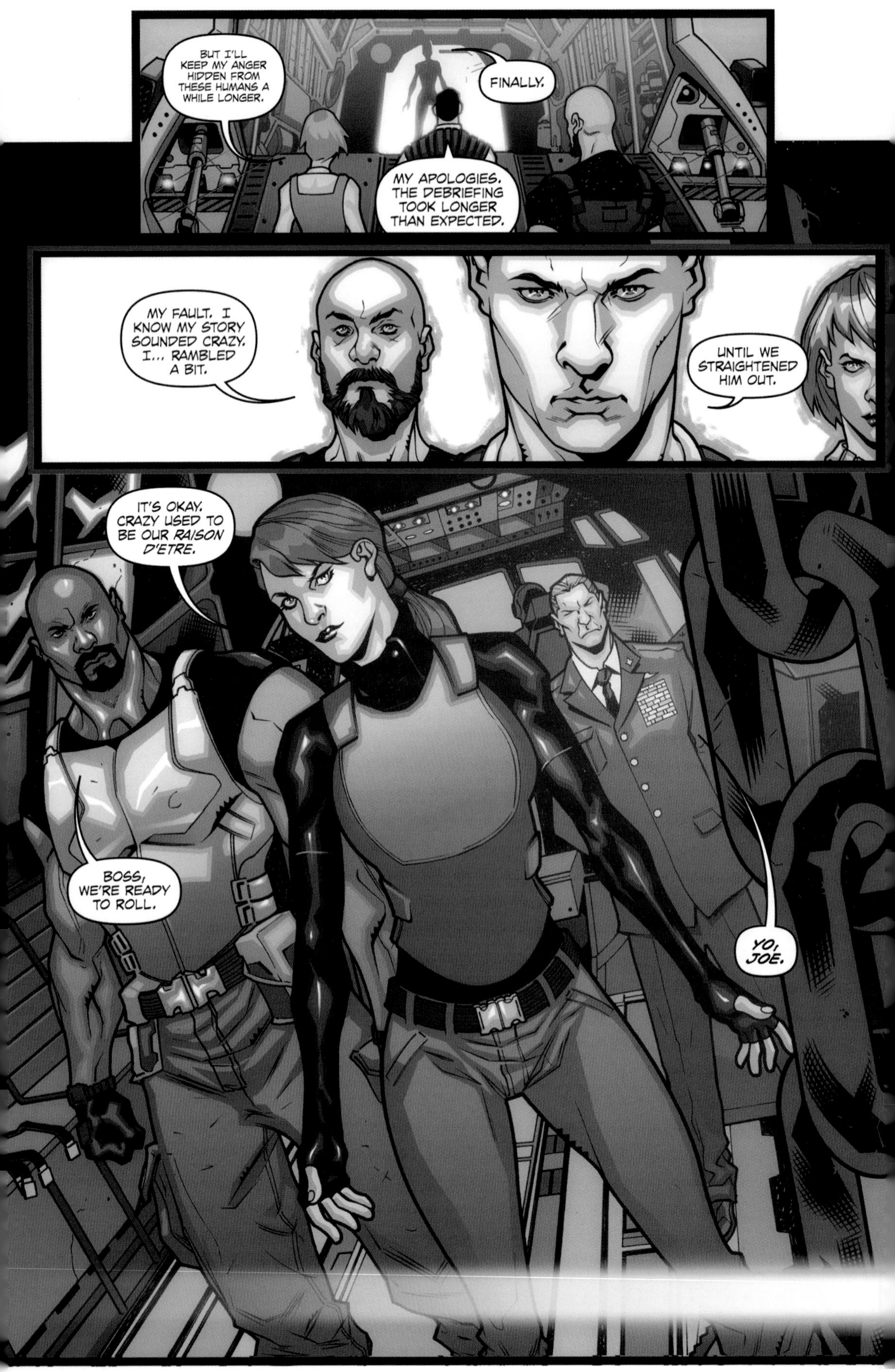
BUT I'LL KEEP MY ANGER HIDDEN FROM THESE HUMANS A WHILE LONGER.
FINALLY.
MY APOLOGIES. THE DEBRIEFING TOOK LONGER THAN EXPECTED.
MY FAULT. I KNOW MY STORY SOUNDED CRAZY. I... RAMBLED A BIT.
UNTIL WE STRAIGHTENED HIM OUT.
IT'S OKAY. CRAZY USED TO BE OUR *RAISON D'ETRE*.
BOSS, WE'RE READY TO ROLL.
YO, JOE.

ART BY **SAL BUSCEMA**, COLORS BY **MIKE CAVALLARO**

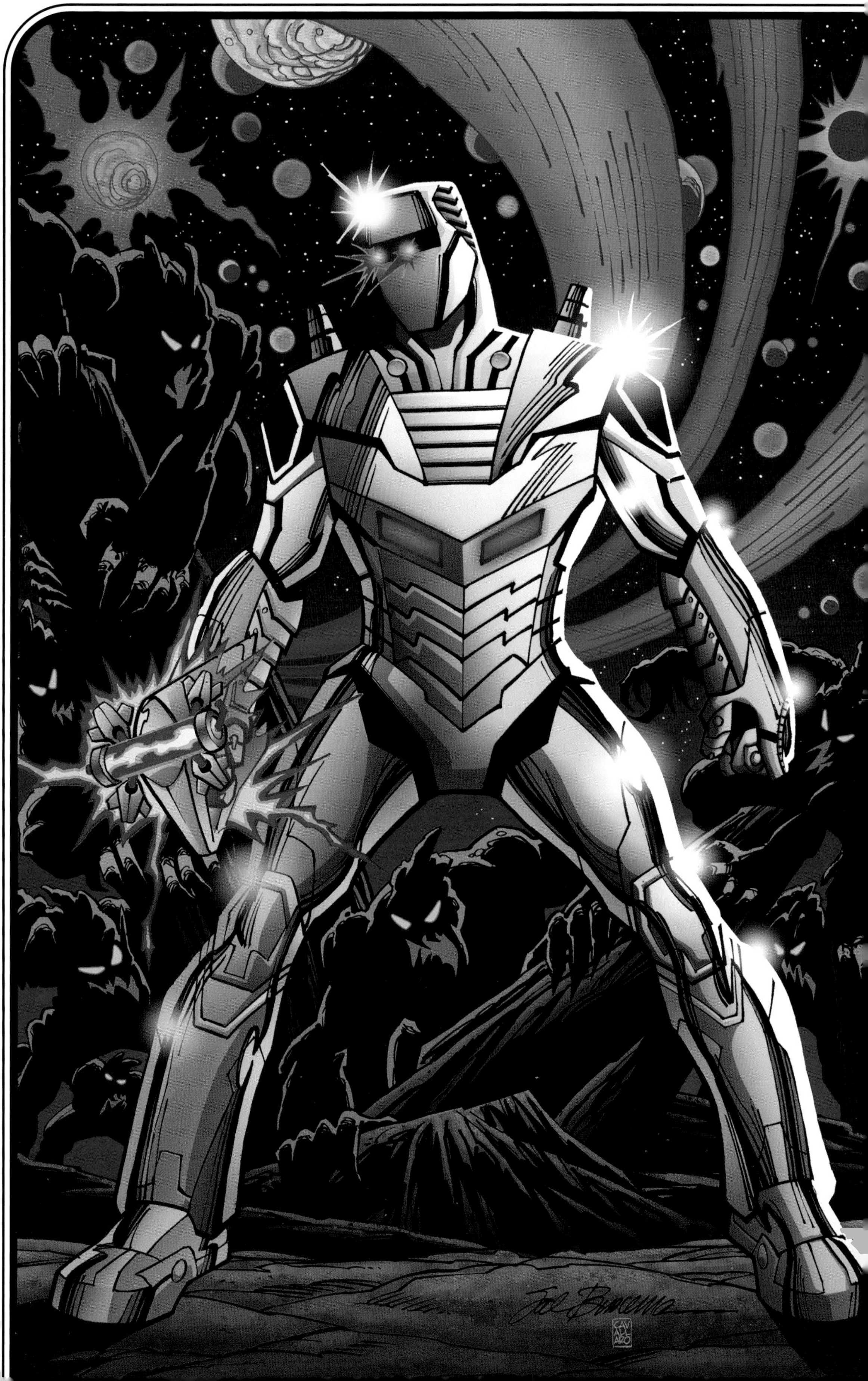

ART BY **ZACH HOWARD**, COLORS BY **NELSON DÁNIEL**

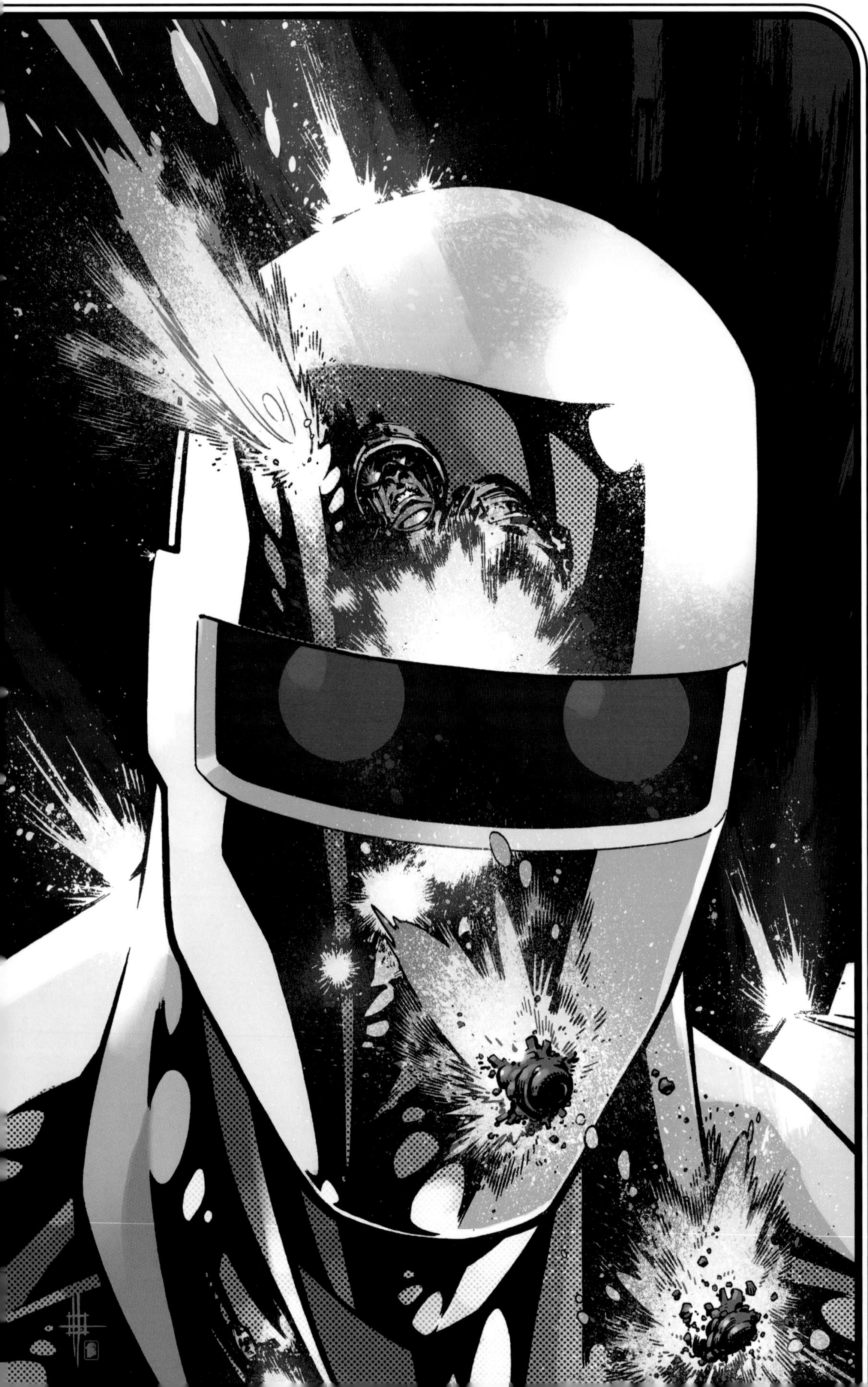

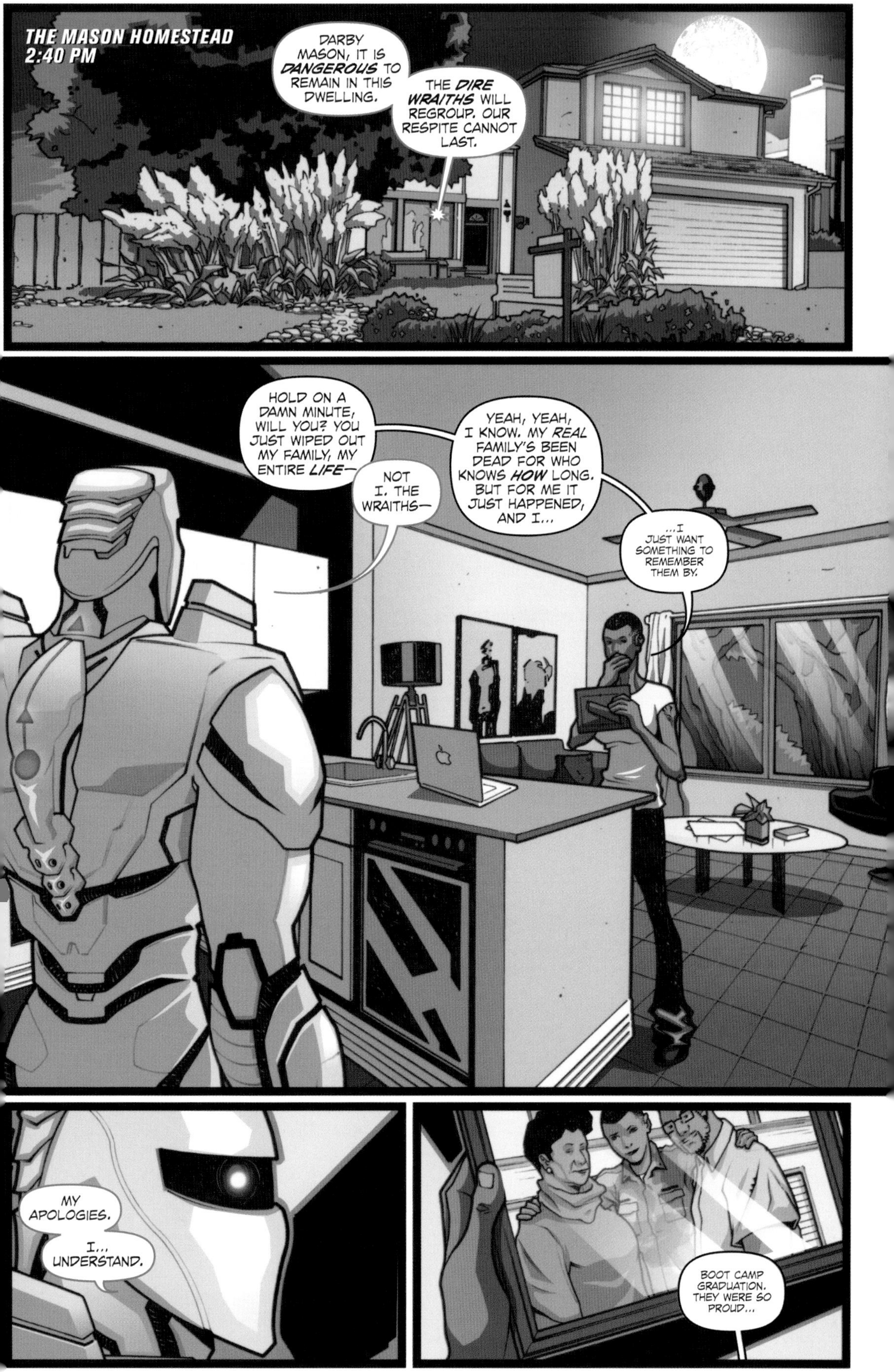
THE MASON HOMESTEAD
2:40 PM
DARBY MASON, IT IS DANGEROUS TO REMAIN IN THIS DWELLING.
THE DIRE WRAITHS WILL REGROUP. OUR RESPITE CANNOT LAST.
HOLD ON A DAMN MINUTE, WILL YOU? YOU JUST WIPED OUT MY FAMILY, MY ENTIRE LIFE—
NOT I. THE WRAITHS—
YEAH, YEAH, I KNOW. MY REAL FAMILY'S BEEN DEAD FOR WHO KNOWS HOW LONG. BUT FOR ME IT JUST HAPPENED, AND I...
...I JUST WANT SOMETHING TO REMEMBER THEM BY.
MY APOLOGIES.
I... UNDERSTAND.
BOOT CAMP GRADUATION. THEY WERE SO PROUD...

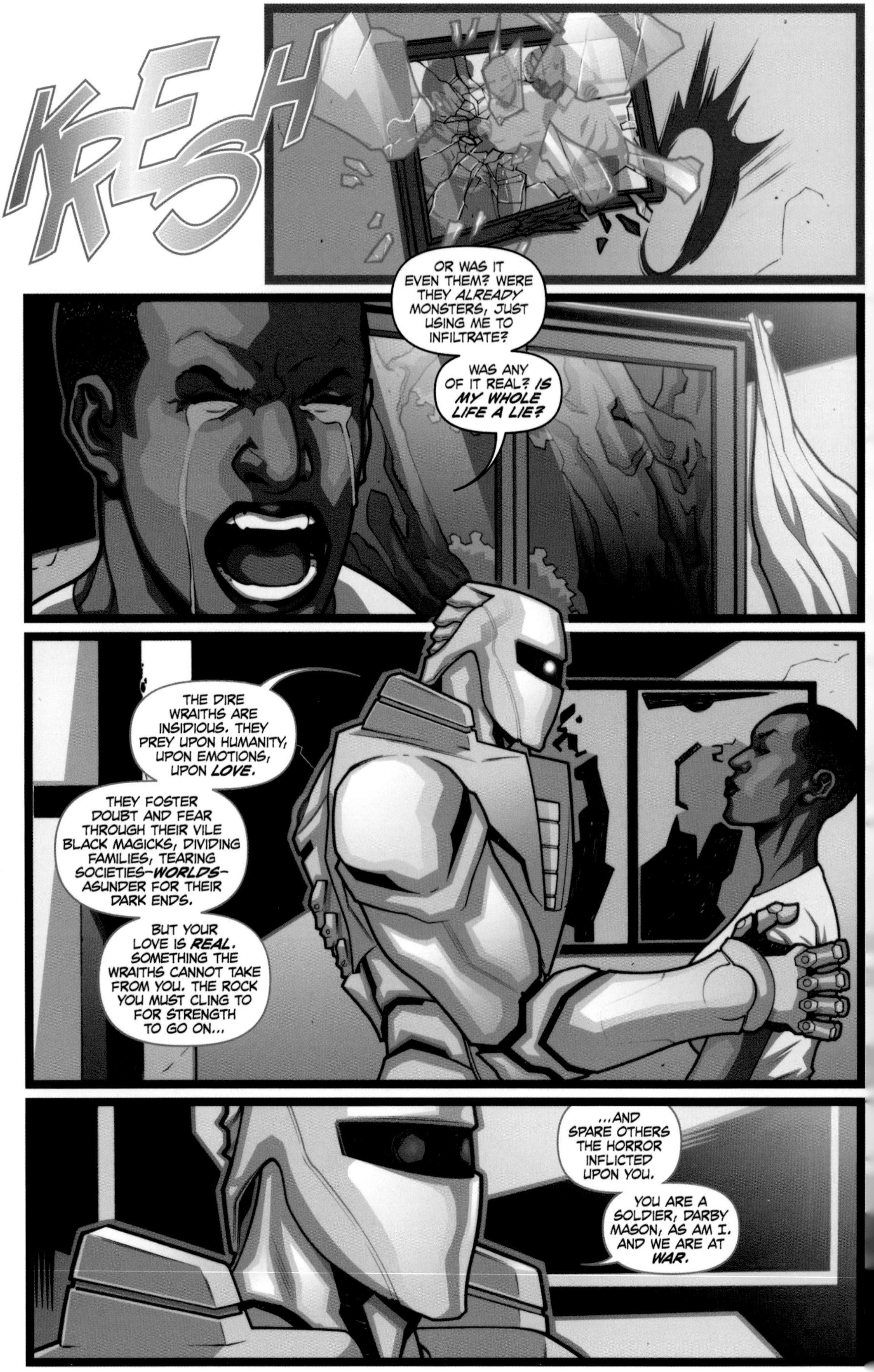
KRESH
OR WAS IT EVEN THEM? WERE THEY ALREADY MONSTERS, JUST USING ME TO INFILTRATE?
WAS ANY OF IT REAL? IS MY WHOLE LIFE A LIE?
THE DIRE WRAITHS ARE INSIDIOUS. THEY PREY UPON HUMANITY, UPON EMOTIONS, UPON LOVE.
THEY FOSTER DOUBT AND FEAR THROUGH THEIR VILE BLACK MAGICKS, DIVIDING FAMILIES, TEARING SOCIETIES--WORLDS--ASUNDER FOR THEIR DARK ENDS.
BUT YOUR LOVE IS REAL. SOMETHING THE WRAITHS CANNOT TAKE FROM YOU. THE ROCK YOU MUST CLING TO FOR STRENGTH TO GO ON...
...AND SPARE OTHERS THE HORROR INFLICTED UPON YOU.
YOU ARE A SOLDIER, DARBY MASON, AS AM I. AND WE ARE AT WAR.

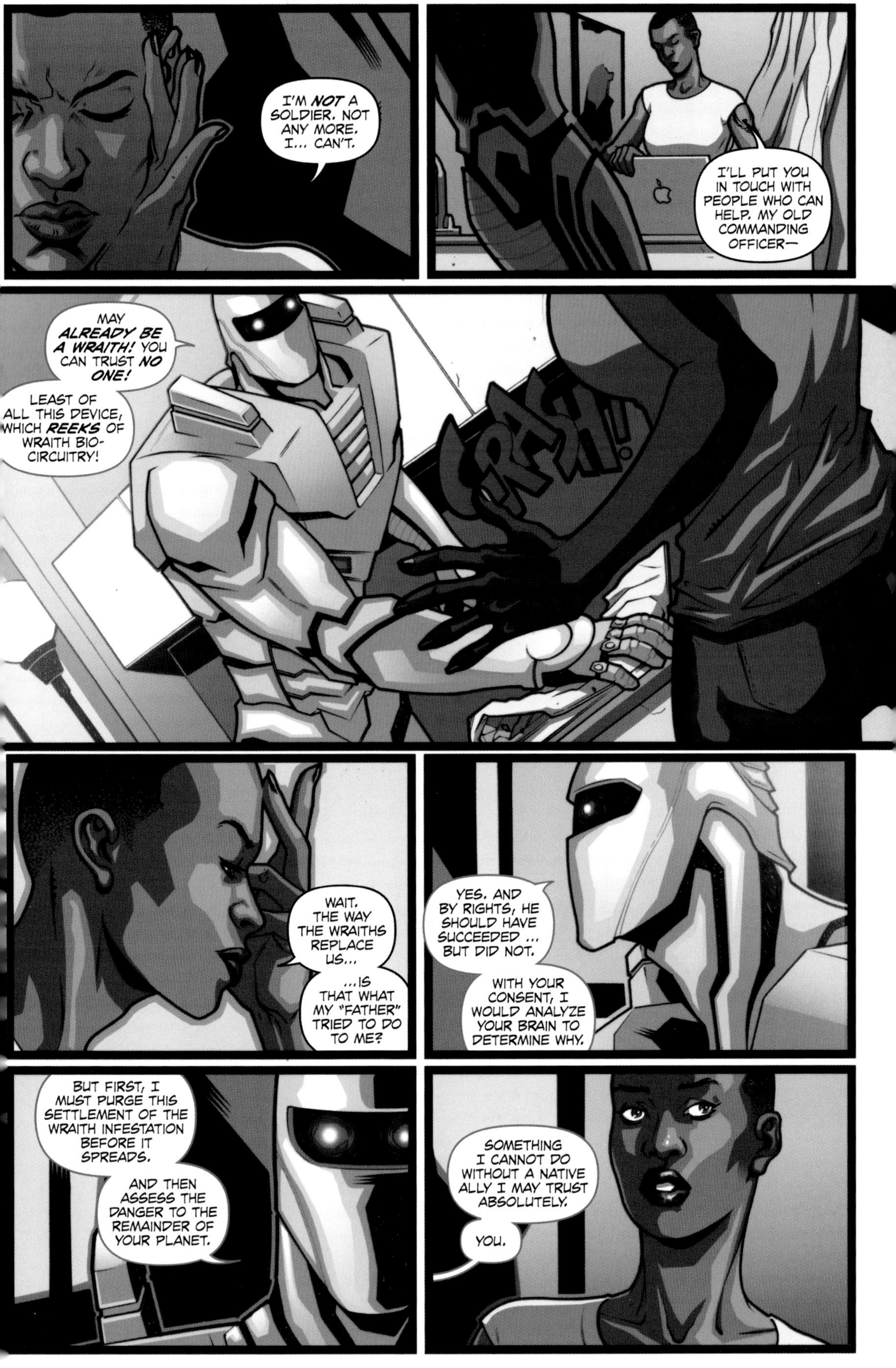
I'M NOT A SOLDIER. NOT ANY MORE. I... CAN'T.
I'LL PUT YOU IN TOUCH WITH PEOPLE WHO CAN HELP. MY OLD COMMANDING OFFICER—
MAY ALREADY BE A WRAITH! YOU CAN TRUST NO ONE!
LEAST OF ALL THIS DEVICE, WHICH REEKS OF WRAITH BIO-CIRCUITRY!
CRASH!
WAIT. THE WAY THE WRAITHS REPLACE US...
...IS THAT WHAT MY "FATHER" TRIED TO DO TO ME?
YES. AND BY RIGHTS, HE SHOULD HAVE SUCCEEDED ... BUT DID NOT.
WITH YOUR CONSENT, I WOULD ANALYZE YOUR BRAIN TO DETERMINE WHY.
BUT FIRST, I MUST PURGE THIS SETTLEMENT OF THE WRAITH INFESTATION BEFORE IT SPREADS.
AND THEN ASSESS THE DANGER TO THE REMAINDER OF YOUR PLANET.
SOMETHING I CANNOT DO WITHOUT A NATIVE ALLY I MAY TRUST ABSOLUTELY.
YOU.

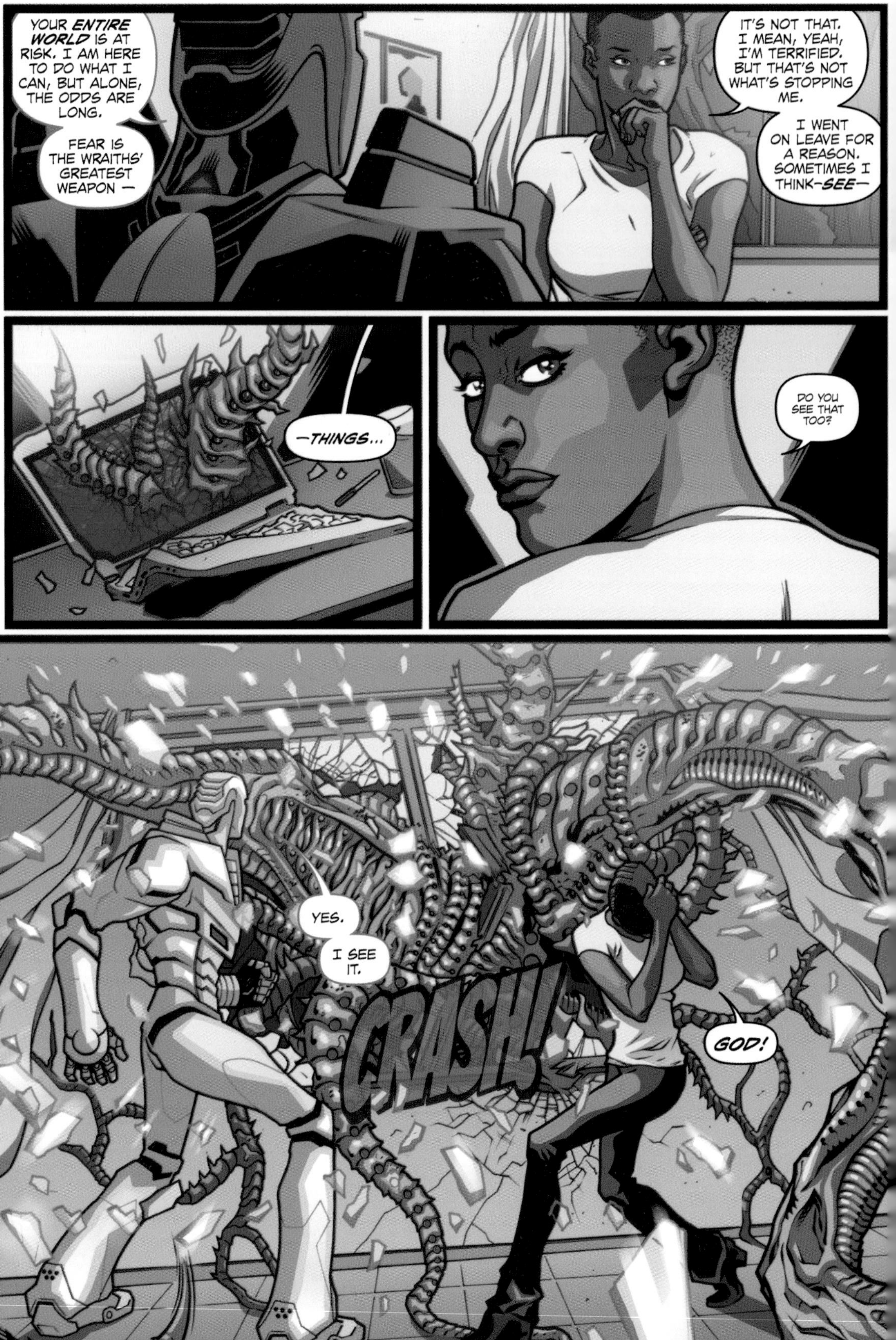
YOUR ENTIRE WORLD IS AT RISK. I AM HERE TO DO WHAT I CAN, BUT ALONE, THE ODDS ARE LONG.
FEAR IS THE WRAITHS' GREATEST WEAPON —
IT'S NOT THAT. I MEAN, YEAH, I'M TERRIFIED. BUT THAT'S NOT WHAT'S STOPPING ME.
I WENT ON LEAVE FOR A REASON. SOMETIMES I THINK—SEE—
—THINGS...
DO YOU SEE THAT TOO?
YES.
I SEE IT.
CRASH!
GOD!

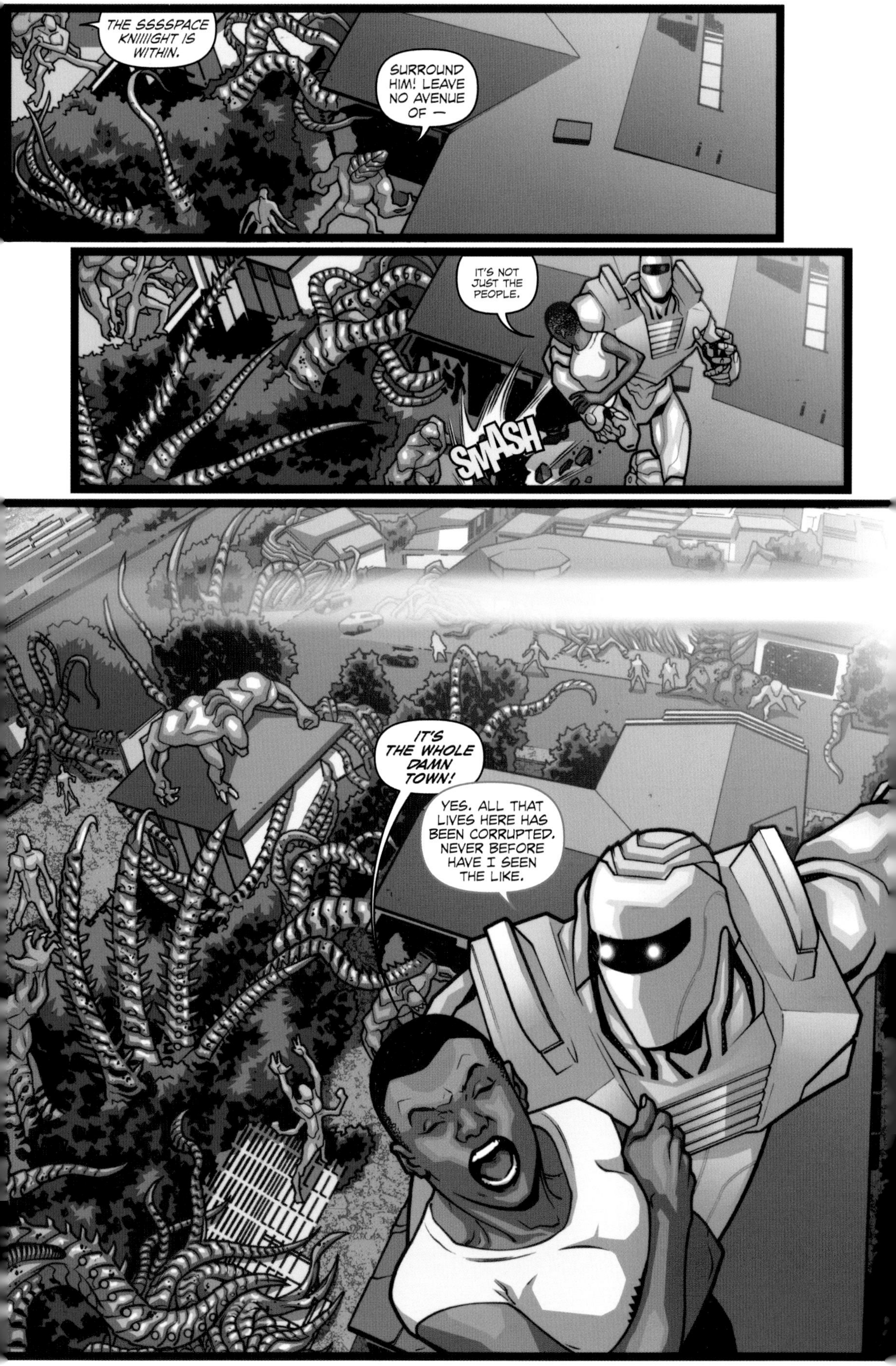
THE SSSSPACE KNIIIIGHT IS WITHIN.
SURROUND HIM! LEAVE NO AVENUE OF —
IT'S NOT JUST THE PEOPLE.
SMASH
IT'S THE WHOLE DAMN TOWN!
YES. ALL THAT LIVES HERE HAS BEEN CORRUPTED. NEVER BEFORE HAVE I SEEN THE LIKE.

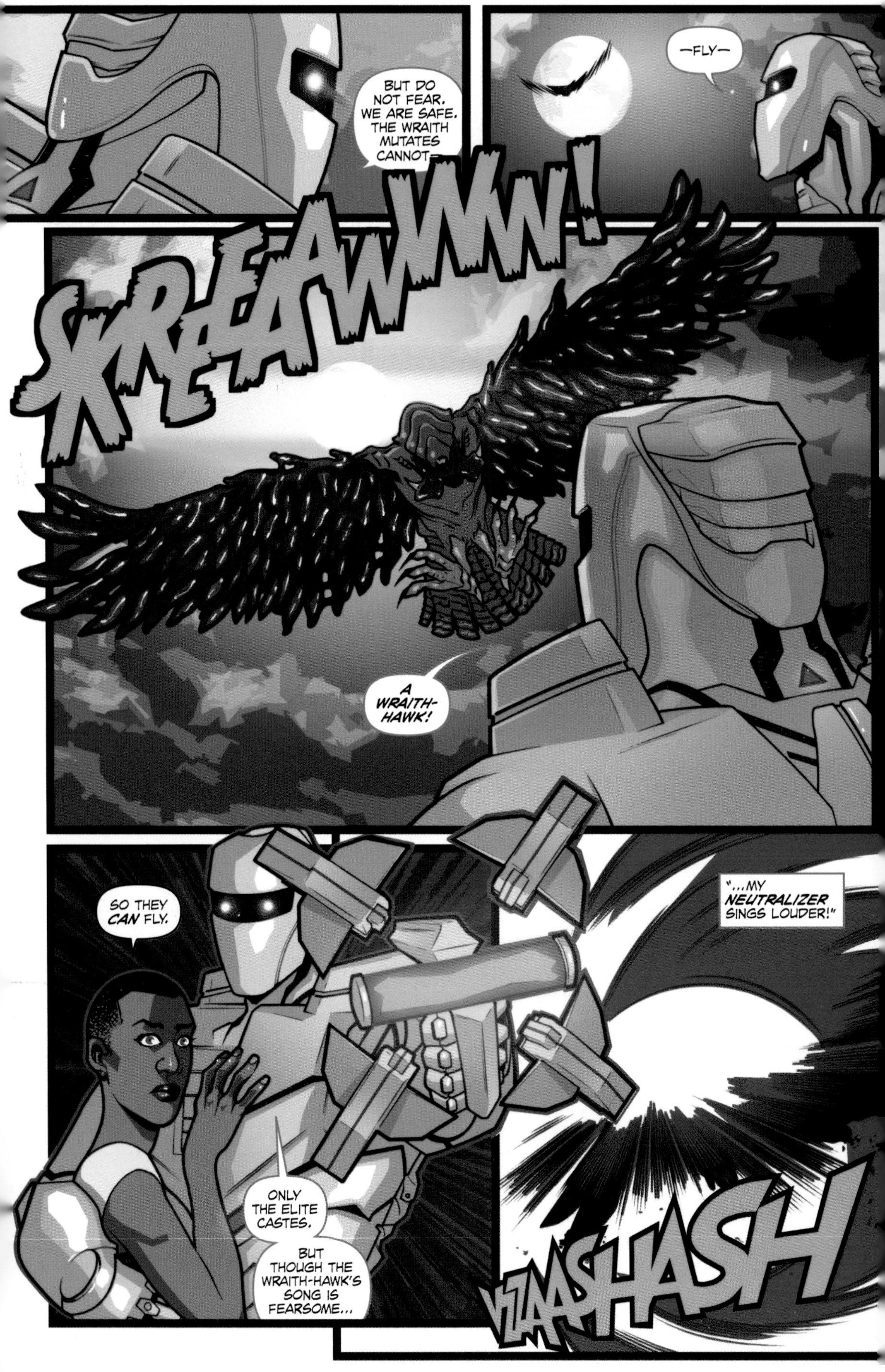
BUT DO NOT FEAR. WE ARE SAFE. THE WRAITH MUTATES CANNOT—
—FLY—
SKREEAWWWW!
A WRAITH-HAWK!
SO THEY CAN FLY.
ONLY THE ELITE CASTES.
BUT THOUGH THE WRAITH-HAWK'S SONG IS FEARSOME...
"...MY NEUTRALIZER SINGS LOUDER!"
VZAASHASH

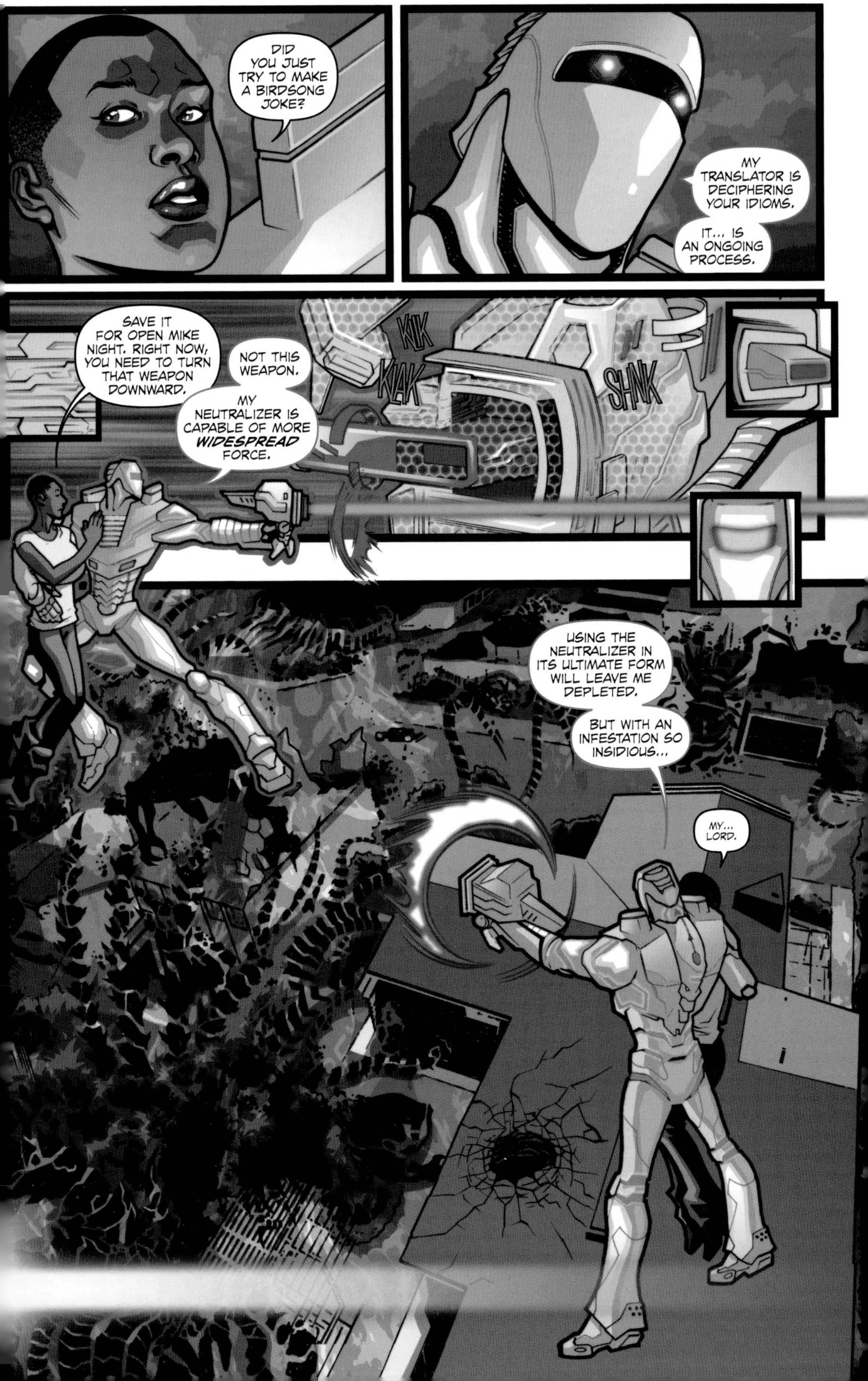
DID YOU JUST TRY TO MAKE A BIRDSONG JOKE?
MY TRANSLATOR IS DECIPHERING YOUR IDIOMS.
IT... IS AN ONGOING PROCESS.
SAVE IT FOR OPEN MIKE NIGHT. RIGHT NOW, YOU NEED TO TURN THAT WEAPON DOWNWARD.
NOT THIS WEAPON.
MY NEUTRALIZER IS CAPABLE OF MORE *WIDESPREAD* FORCE.
KLIK
KLAK
SHNK
USING THE NEUTRALIZER IN ITS ULTIMATE FORM WILL LEAVE ME DEPLETED.
BUT WITH AN INFESTATION SO INSIDIOUS...
MY... LORD.

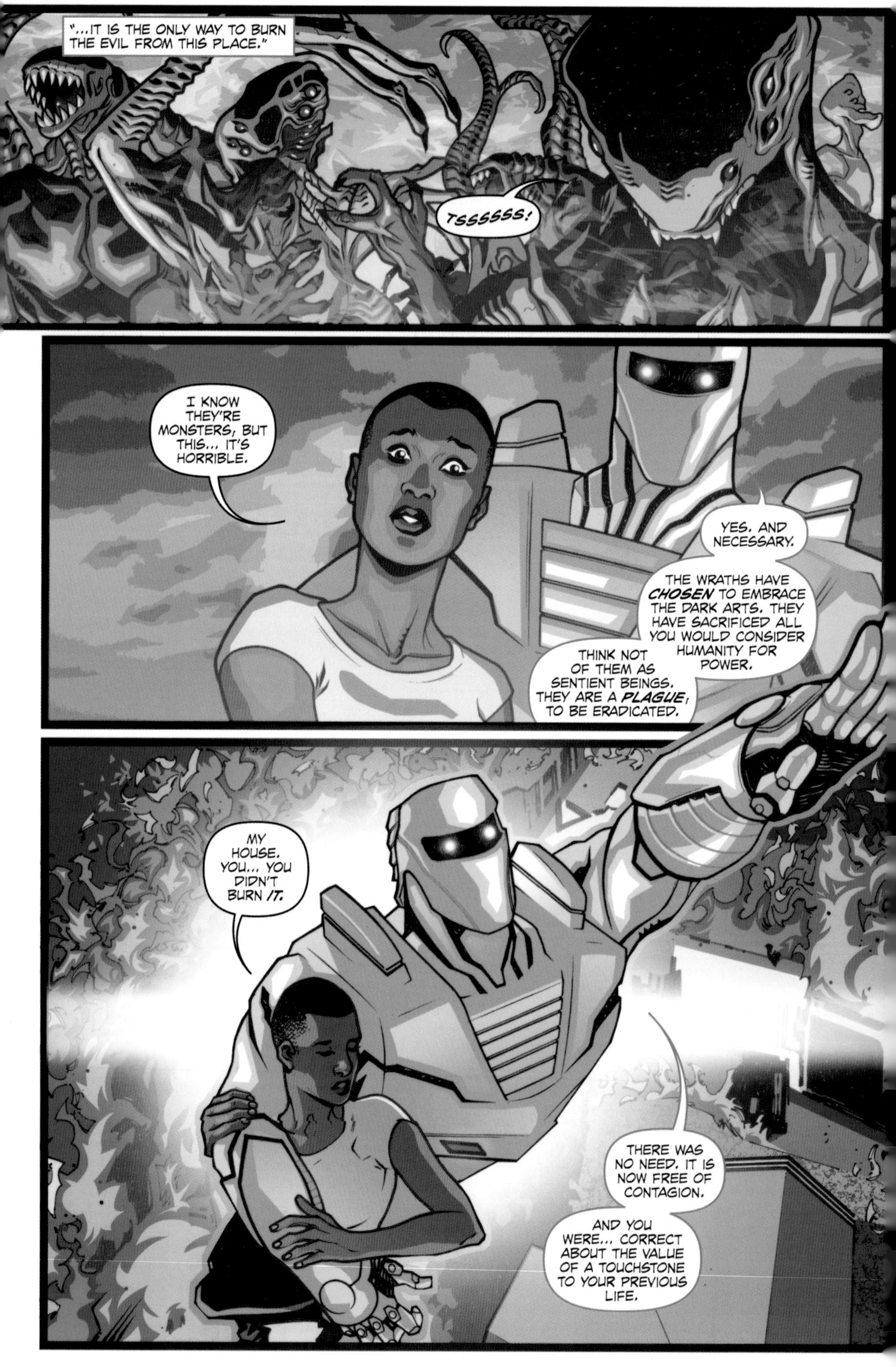

"...IT IS THE ONLY WAY TO BURN THE EVIL FROM THIS PLACE."
TSSSSSS!
I KNOW THEY'RE MONSTERS, BUT THIS... IT'S HORRIBLE.
YES. AND NECESSARY.
THE WRATHS HAVE CHOSEN TO EMBRACE THE DARK ARTS. THEY HAVE SACRIFICED ALL YOU WOULD CONSIDER HUMANITY FOR POWER.
THINK NOT OF THEM AS SENTIENT BEINGS. THEY ARE A PLAGUE, TO BE ERADICATED.
MY HOUSE. YOU... YOU DIDN'T BURN IT.
THERE WAS NO NEED. IT IS NOW FREE OF CONTAGION.
AND YOU WERE... CORRECT ABOUT THE VALUE OF A TOUCHSTONE TO YOUR PREVIOUS LIFE.

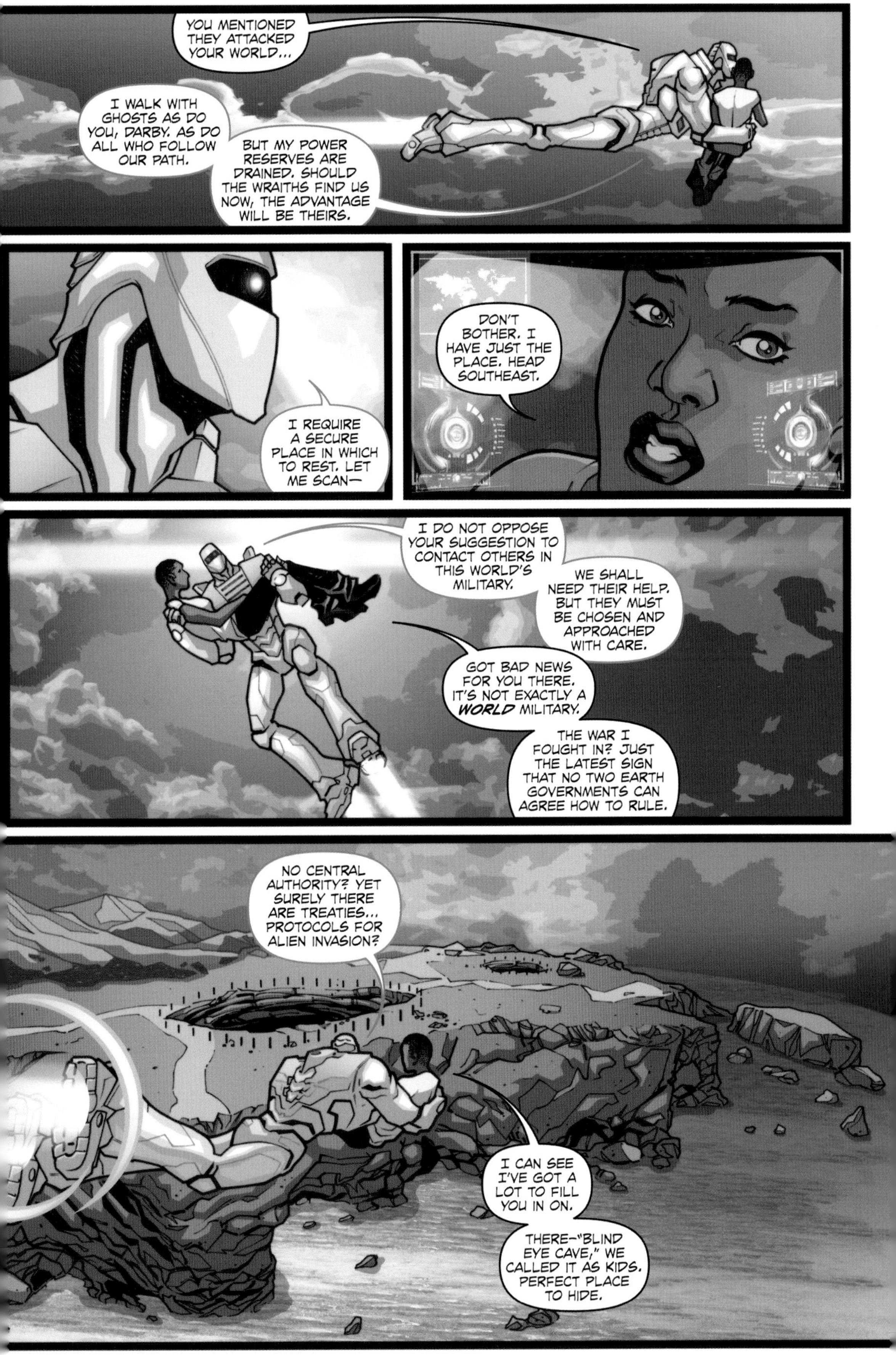

YOU MENTIONED THEY ATTACKED YOUR WORLD...
I WALK WITH GHOSTS AS DO YOU, DARBY. AS DO ALL WHO FOLLOW OUR PATH.
BUT MY POWER RESERVES ARE DRAINED. SHOULD THE WRAITHS FIND US NOW, THE ADVANTAGE WILL BE THEIRS.
I REQUIRE A SECURE PLACE IN WHICH TO REST. LET ME SCAN—
DON'T BOTHER. I HAVE JUST THE PLACE. HEAD SOUTHEAST.
I DO NOT OPPOSE YOUR SUGGESTION TO CONTACT OTHERS IN THIS WORLD'S MILITARY.
WE SHALL NEED THEIR HELP. BUT THEY MUST BE CHOSEN AND APPROACHED WITH CARE.
GOT BAD NEWS FOR YOU THERE. IT'S NOT EXACTLY A ***WORLD*** MILITARY.
THE WAR I FOUGHT IN? JUST THE LATEST SIGN THAT NO TWO EARTH GOVERNMENTS CAN AGREE HOW TO RULE.
NO CENTRAL AUTHORITY? YET SURELY THERE ARE TREATIES... PROTOCOLS FOR ALIEN INVASION?
I CAN SEE I'VE GOT A LOT TO FILL YOU IN ON.
THERE—"BLIND EYE CAVE," WE CALLED IT AS KIDS. PERFECT PLACE TO HIDE.

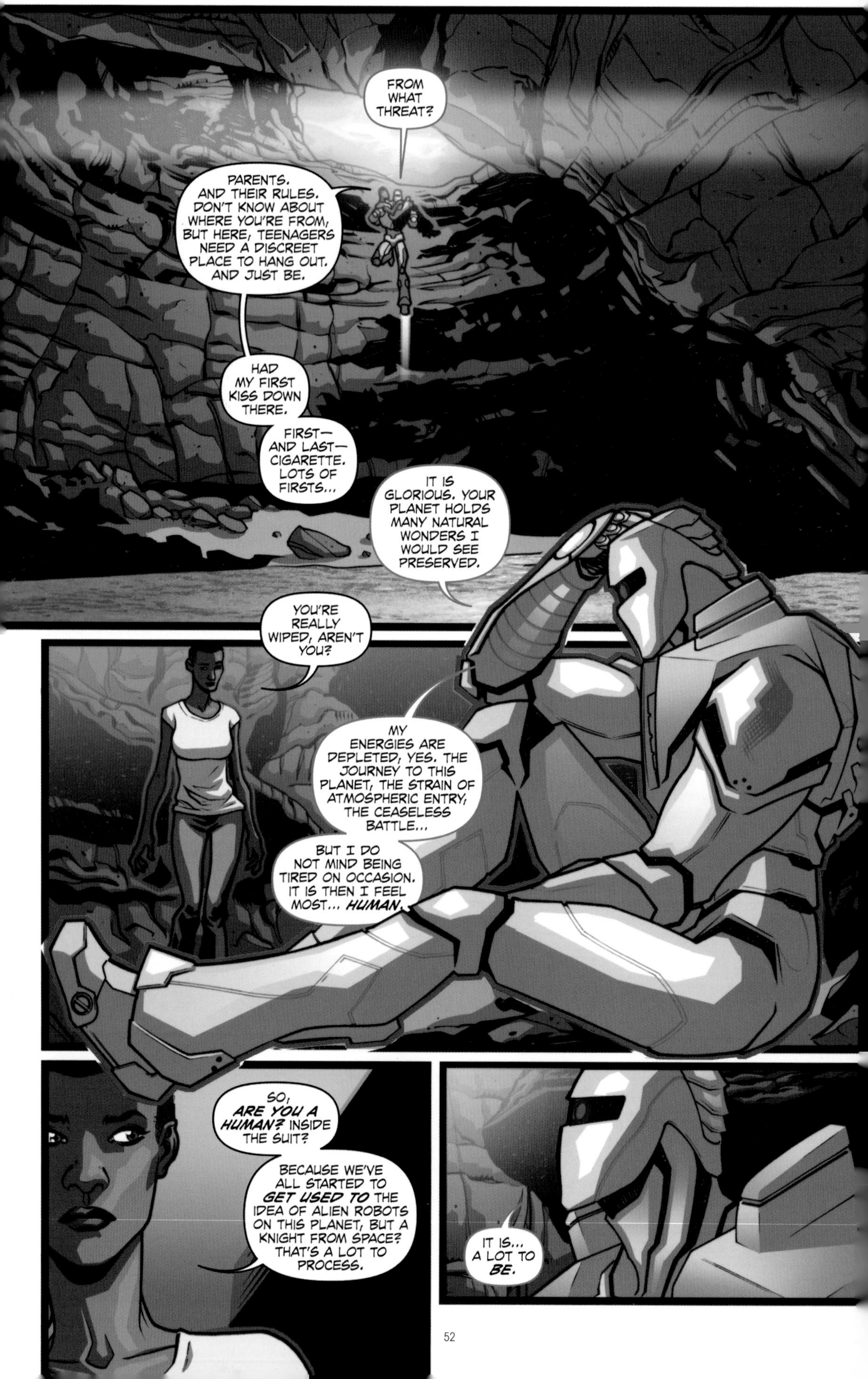

FROM WHAT THREAT?
PARENTS. AND THEIR RULES. DON'T KNOW ABOUT WHERE YOU'RE FROM, BUT HERE, TEENAGERS NEED A DISCREET PLACE TO HANG OUT. AND JUST BE.
HAD MY FIRST KISS DOWN THERE.
FIRST— AND LAST— CIGARETTE. LOTS OF FIRSTS...
IT IS GLORIOUS. YOUR PLANET HOLDS MANY NATURAL WONDERS I WOULD SEE PRESERVED.
YOU'RE REALLY WIPED, AREN'T YOU?
MY ENERGIES ARE DEPLETED, YES. THE JOURNEY TO THIS PLANET, THE STRAIN OF ATMOSPHERIC ENTRY, THE CEASELESS BATTLE...
BUT I DO NOT MIND BEING TIRED ON OCCASION. IT IS THEN I FEEL MOST... HUMAN.
SO, ARE YOU A HUMAN? INSIDE THE SUIT?
BECAUSE WE'VE ALL STARTED TO GET USED TO THE IDEA OF ALIEN ROBOTS ON THIS PLANET, BUT A KNIGHT FROM SPACE? THAT'S A LOT TO PROCESS.
IT IS... A LOT TO BE.

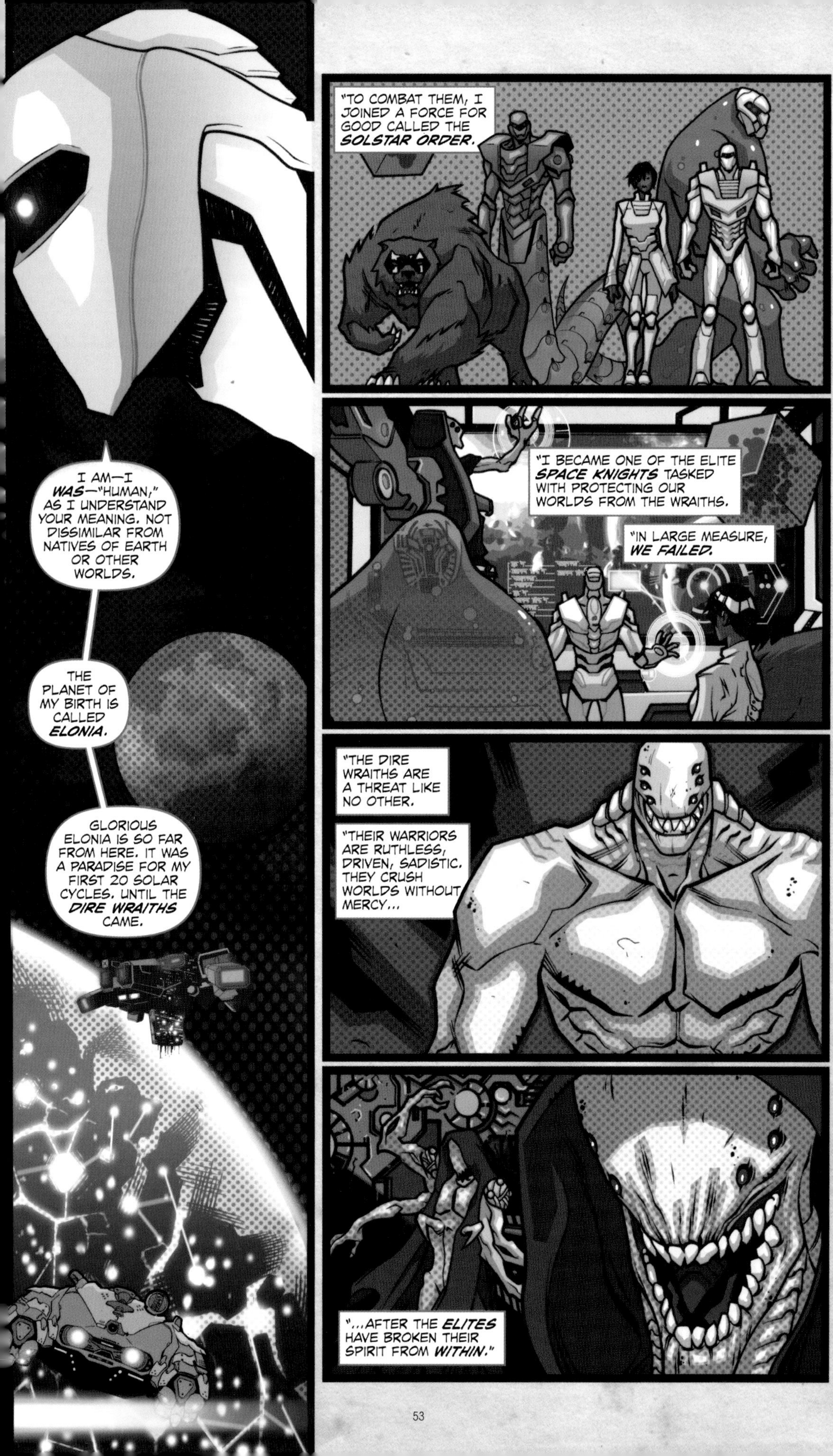
I AM—I WAS—"HUMAN," AS I UNDERSTAND YOUR MEANING. NOT DISSIMILAR FROM NATIVES OF EARTH OR OTHER WORLDS.
THE PLANET OF MY BIRTH IS CALLED ELONIA.
GLORIOUS ELONIA IS SO FAR FROM HERE. IT WAS A PARADISE FOR MY FIRST 20 SOLAR CYCLES. UNTIL THE DIRE WRAITHS CAME.
"TO COMBAT THEM, I JOINED A FORCE FOR GOOD CALLED THE SOLSTAR ORDER.
"I BECAME ONE OF THE ELITE SPACE KNIGHTS TASKED WITH PROTECTING OUR WORLDS FROM THE WRAITHS.
"IN LARGE MEASURE, WE FAILED.
"THE DIRE WRAITHS ARE A THREAT LIKE NO OTHER.
"THEIR WARRIORS ARE RUTHLESS, DRIVEN, SADISTIC. THEY CRUSH WORLDS WITHOUT MERCY...
"...AFTER THE ELITES HAVE BROKEN THEIR SPIRIT FROM WITHIN."

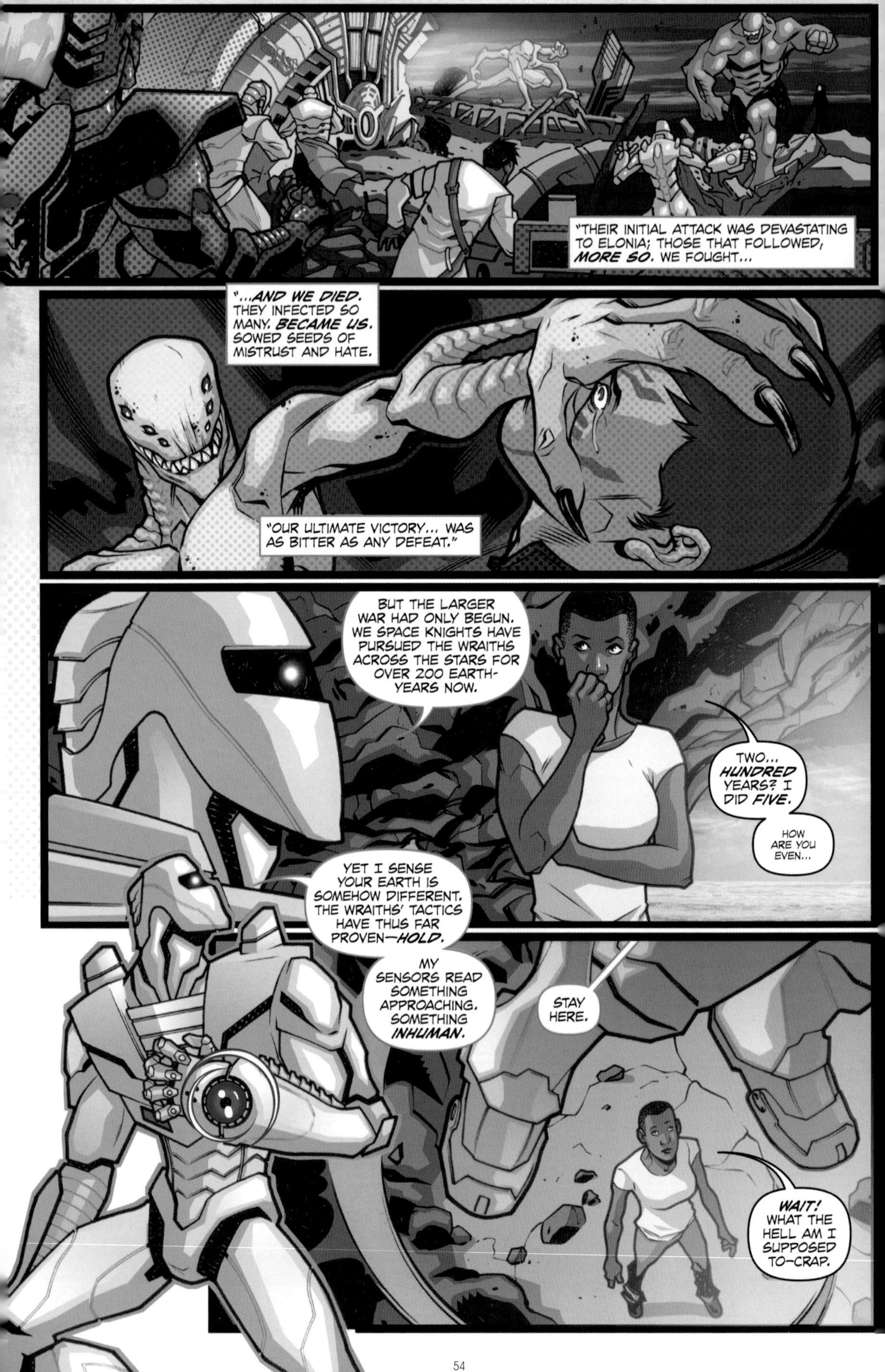
"THEIR INITIAL ATTACK WAS DEVASTATING TO ELONIA; THOSE THAT FOLLOWED, MORE SO. WE FOUGHT...
"...AND WE DIED. THEY INFECTED SO MANY. BECAME US. SOWED SEEDS OF MISTRUST AND HATE.
"OUR ULTIMATE VICTORY... WAS AS BITTER AS ANY DEFEAT."
BUT THE LARGER WAR HAD ONLY BEGUN. WE SPACE KNIGHTS HAVE PURSUED THE WRAITHS ACROSS THE STARS FOR OVER 200 EARTH-YEARS NOW.
TWO... HUNDRED YEARS? I DID FIVE.
HOW ARE YOU EVEN...
YET I SENSE YOUR EARTH IS SOMEHOW DIFFERENT. THE WRAITHS' TACTICS HAVE THUS FAR PROVEN—HOLD.
MY SENSORS READ SOMETHING APPROACHING. SOMETHING INHUMAN.
STAY HERE.
WAIT! WHAT THE HELL AM I SUPPOSED TO—CRAP.

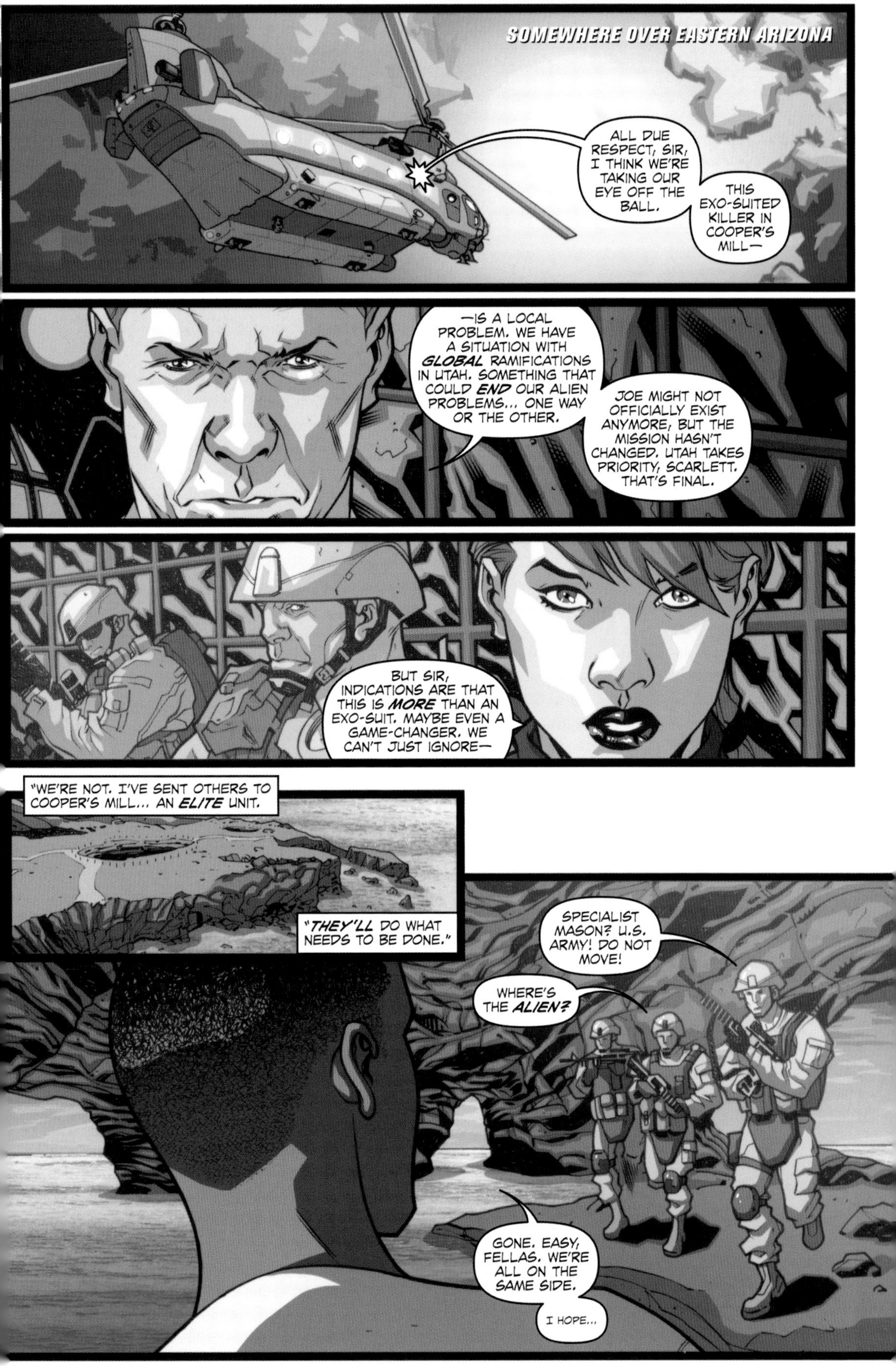
SOMEWHERE OVER EASTERN ARIZONA
ALL DUE RESPECT, SIR, I THINK WE'RE TAKING OUR EYE OFF THE BALL.
THIS EXO-SUITED KILLER IN COOPER'S MILL—
—IS A LOCAL PROBLEM. WE HAVE A SITUATION WITH GLOBAL RAMIFICATIONS IN UTAH. SOMETHING THAT COULD END OUR ALIEN PROBLEMS... ONE WAY OR THE OTHER.
JOE MIGHT NOT OFFICIALLY EXIST ANYMORE, BUT THE MISSION HASN'T CHANGED. UTAH TAKES PRIORITY, SCARLETT. THAT'S FINAL.
BUT SIR, INDICATIONS ARE THAT THIS IS MORE THAN AN EXO-SUIT. MAYBE EVEN A GAME-CHANGER. WE CAN'T JUST IGNORE—
"WE'RE NOT. I'VE SENT OTHERS TO COOPER'S MILL... AN ELITE UNIT.
"THEY'LL DO WHAT NEEDS TO BE DONE."
SPECIALIST MASON? U.S. ARMY! DO NOT MOVE!
WHERE'S THE ALIEN?
GONE. EASY, FELLAS. WE'RE ALL ON THE SAME SIDE.
I HOPE...

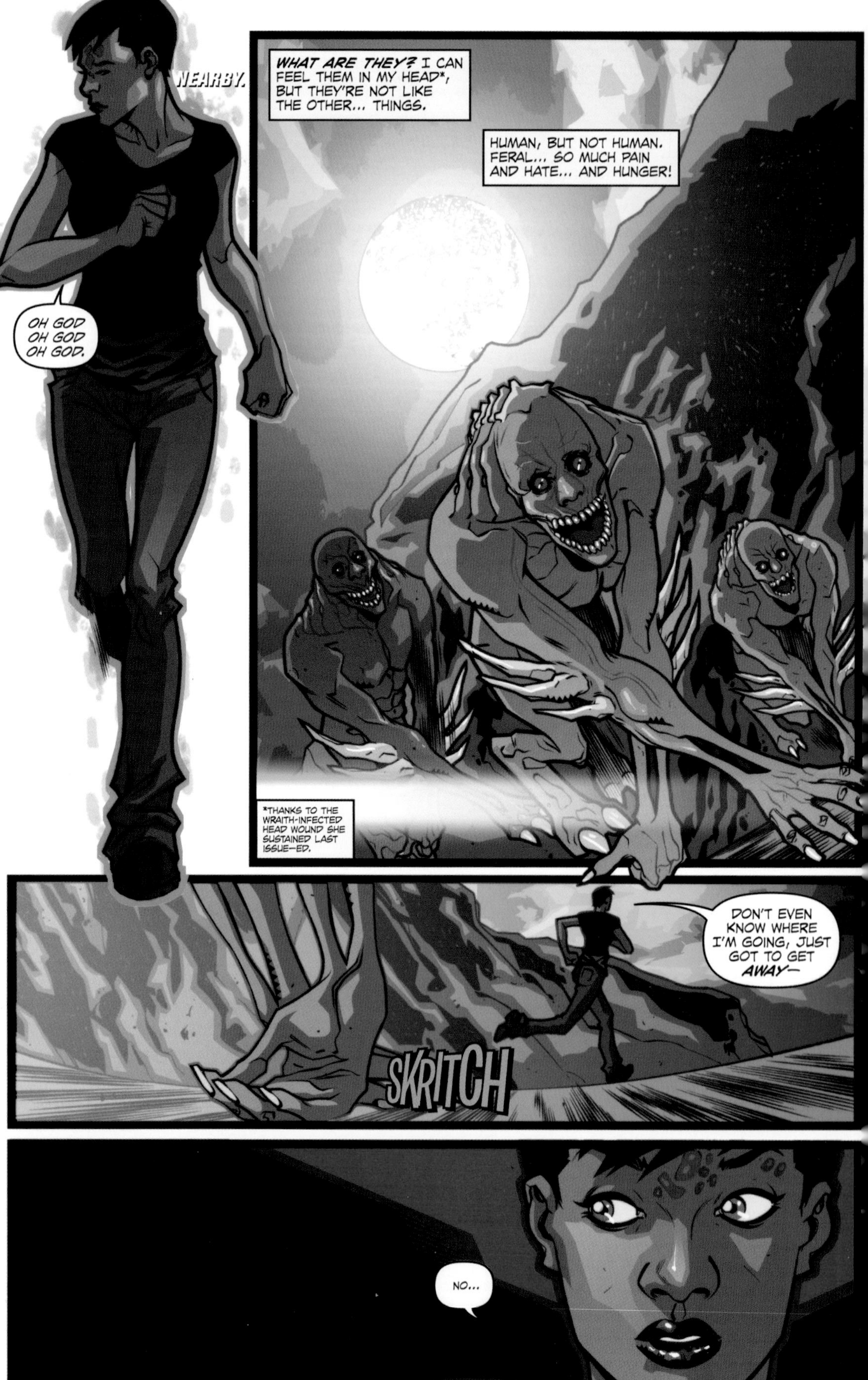
NEARBY.
OH GOD OH GOD OH GOD.
WHAT ARE THEY? I CAN FEEL THEM IN MY HEAD*, BUT THEY'RE NOT LIKE THE OTHER... THINGS.
HUMAN, BUT NOT HUMAN. FERAL... SO MUCH PAIN AND HATE... AND HUNGER!
*THANKS TO THE WRAITH-INFECTED HEAD WOUND SHE SUSTAINED LAST ISSUE—ED.
DON'T EVEN KNOW WHERE I'M GOING, JUST GOT TO GET AWAY—
SKRITCH
NO...

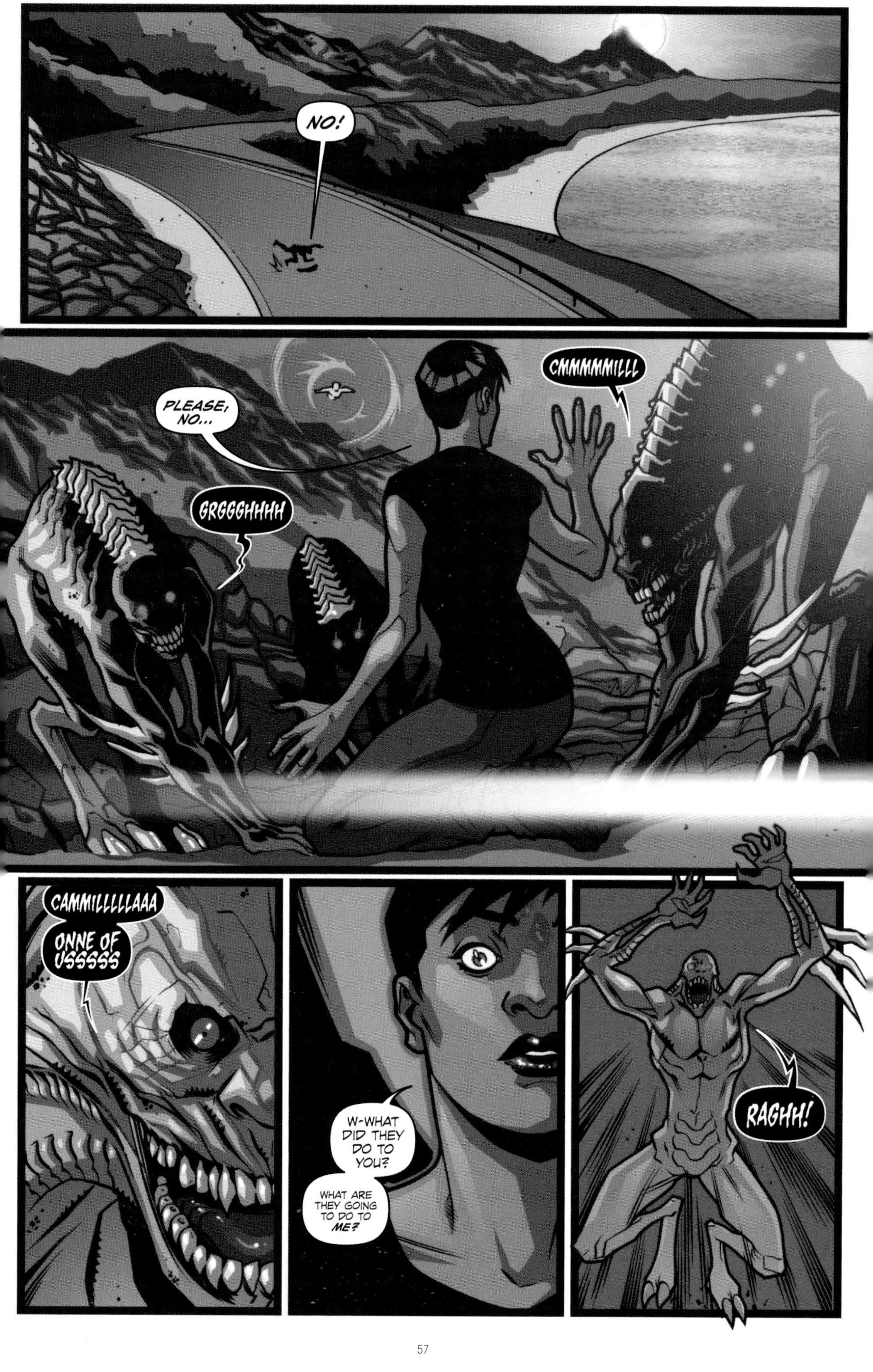
NO!
PLEASE, NO...
CMMMMMILLL
GRGGGHHHH
CAMMILLLLLAAA
ONNE OF USSSSS
W-WHAT DID THEY DO TO YOU?
WHAT ARE THEY GOING TO DO TO ME?
RAGHH!

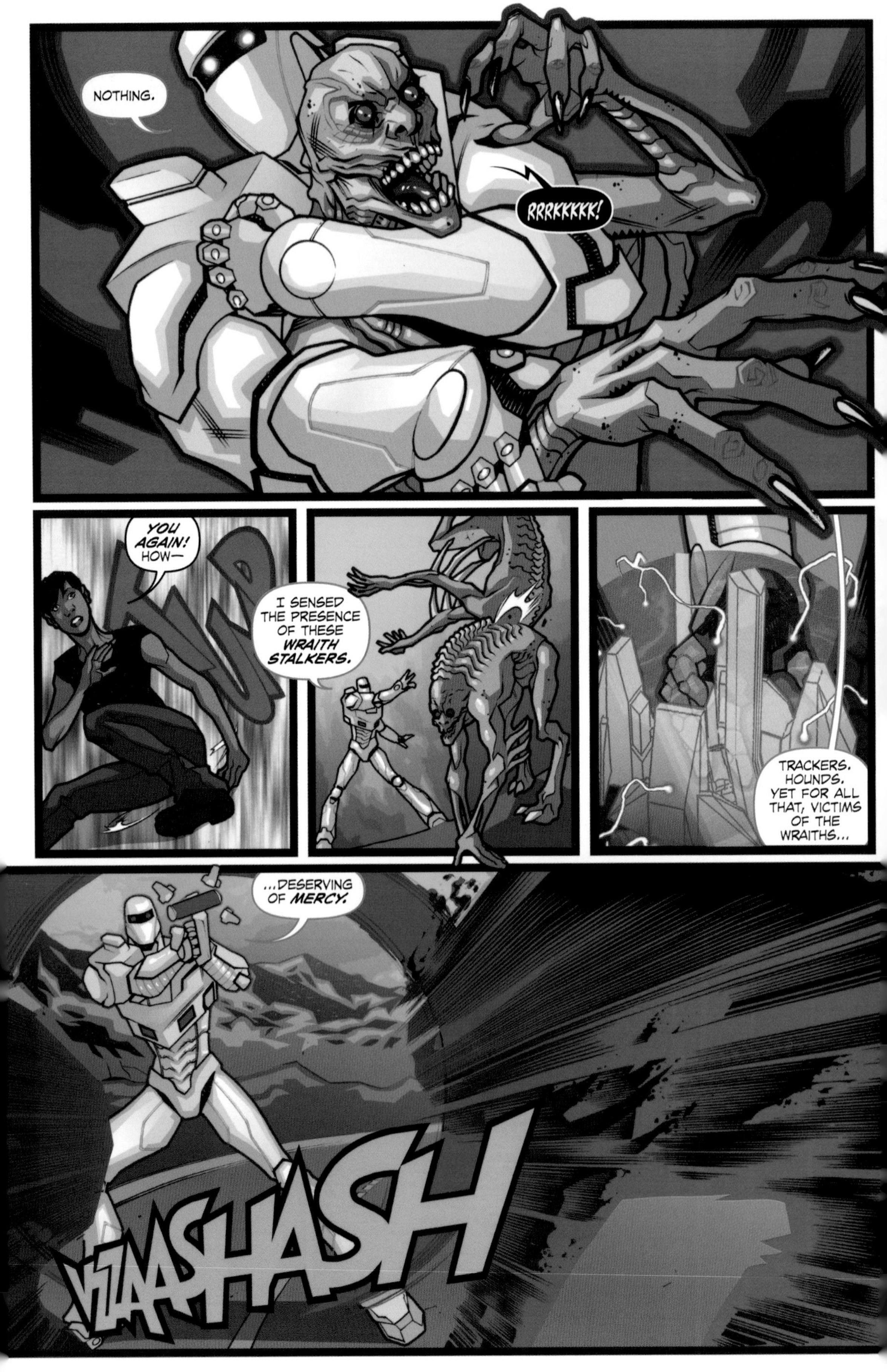
NOTHING.
RRRKKKKK!
YOU AGAIN! HOW—
I SENSED THE PRESENCE OF THESE WRAITH STALKERS.
TRACKERS. HOUNDS. YET FOR ALL THAT, VICTIMS OF THE WRAITHS...
...DESERVING OF MERCY.
VZAASHASH

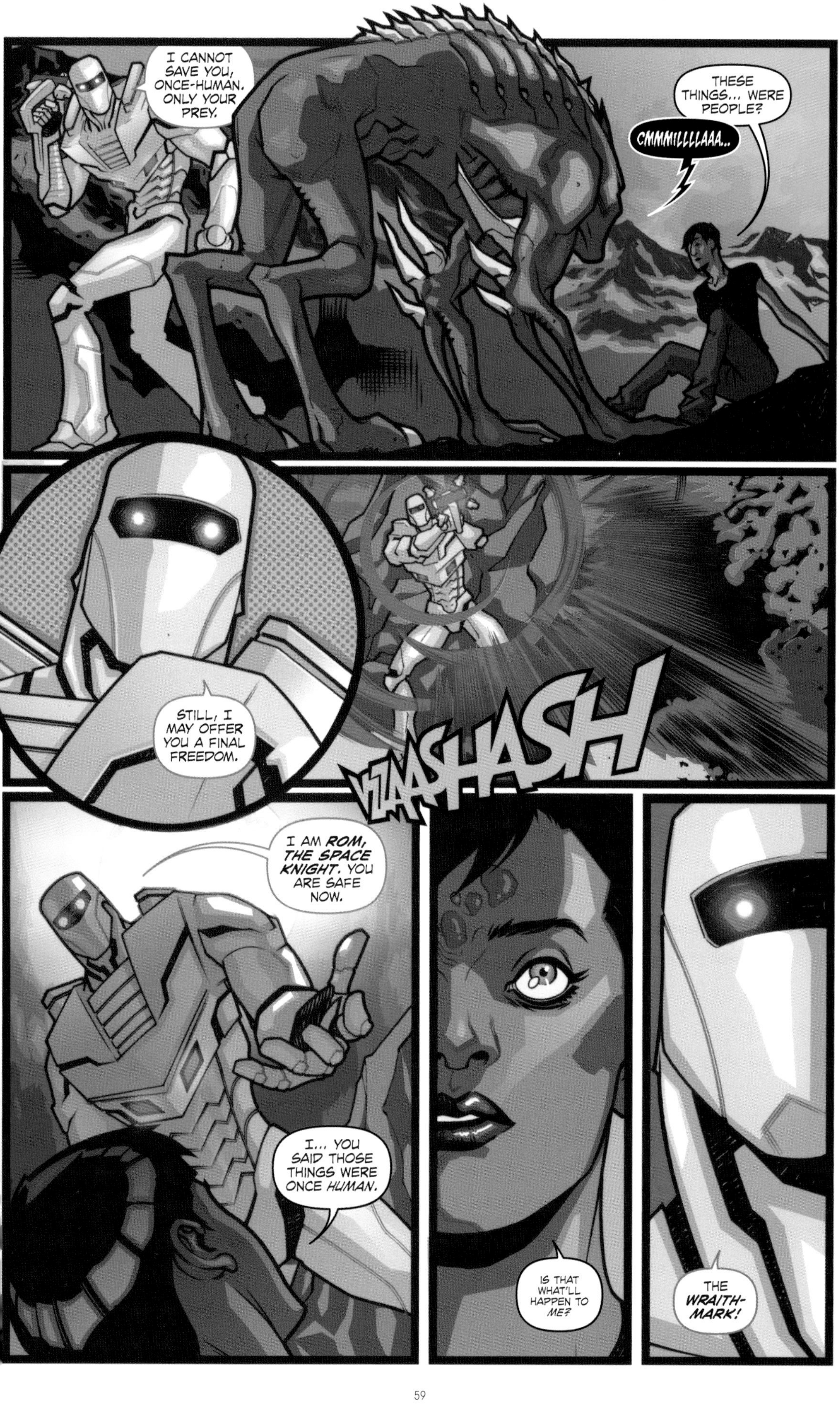
I CANNOT SAVE YOU, ONCE-HUMAN. ONLY YOUR PREY.
THESE THINGS... WERE PEOPLE?
CMMMILLLLAAA...
STILL, I MAY OFFER YOU A FINAL FREEDOM.
VZAASHASH
I AM ROM, THE SPACE KNIGHT. YOU ARE SAFE NOW.
I... YOU SAID THOSE THINGS WERE ONCE HUMAN.
IS THAT WHAT'LL HAPPEN TO ME?
THE WRAITH-MARK!

I... AM SORRY. THE INFECTION IS WITHIN YOU.
BUT I WILL NOT ALLOW IT TO TAKE HOLD.
WAIT!
STEP AWAY FROM THE WOMAN. NOW!
SOLDIERS... OR WRAITHS WEARING THEIR SHAPE.
LET MY ANALYZER SHOW THE TRUTH.
HUMANS. I MUST NOT SLAY THEM. BUT THEY HAVE NO SUCH—
GUHH-H!
BOOM

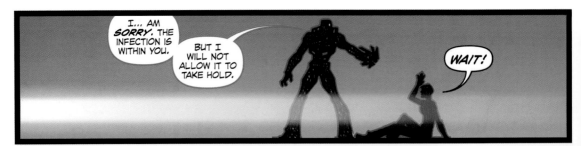

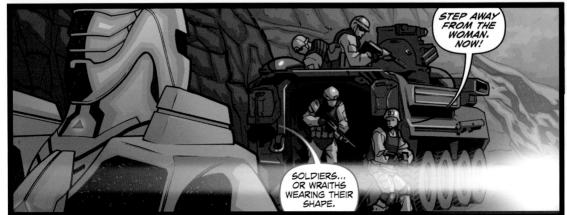

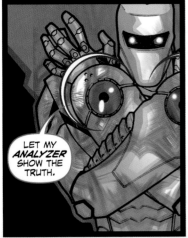

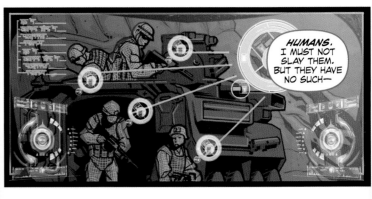

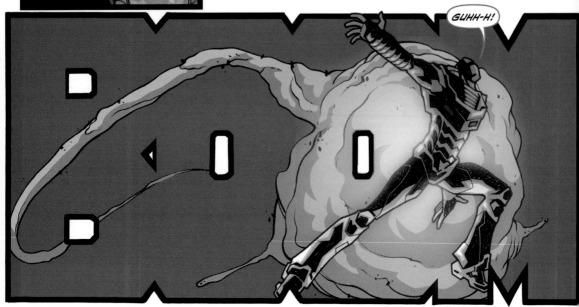

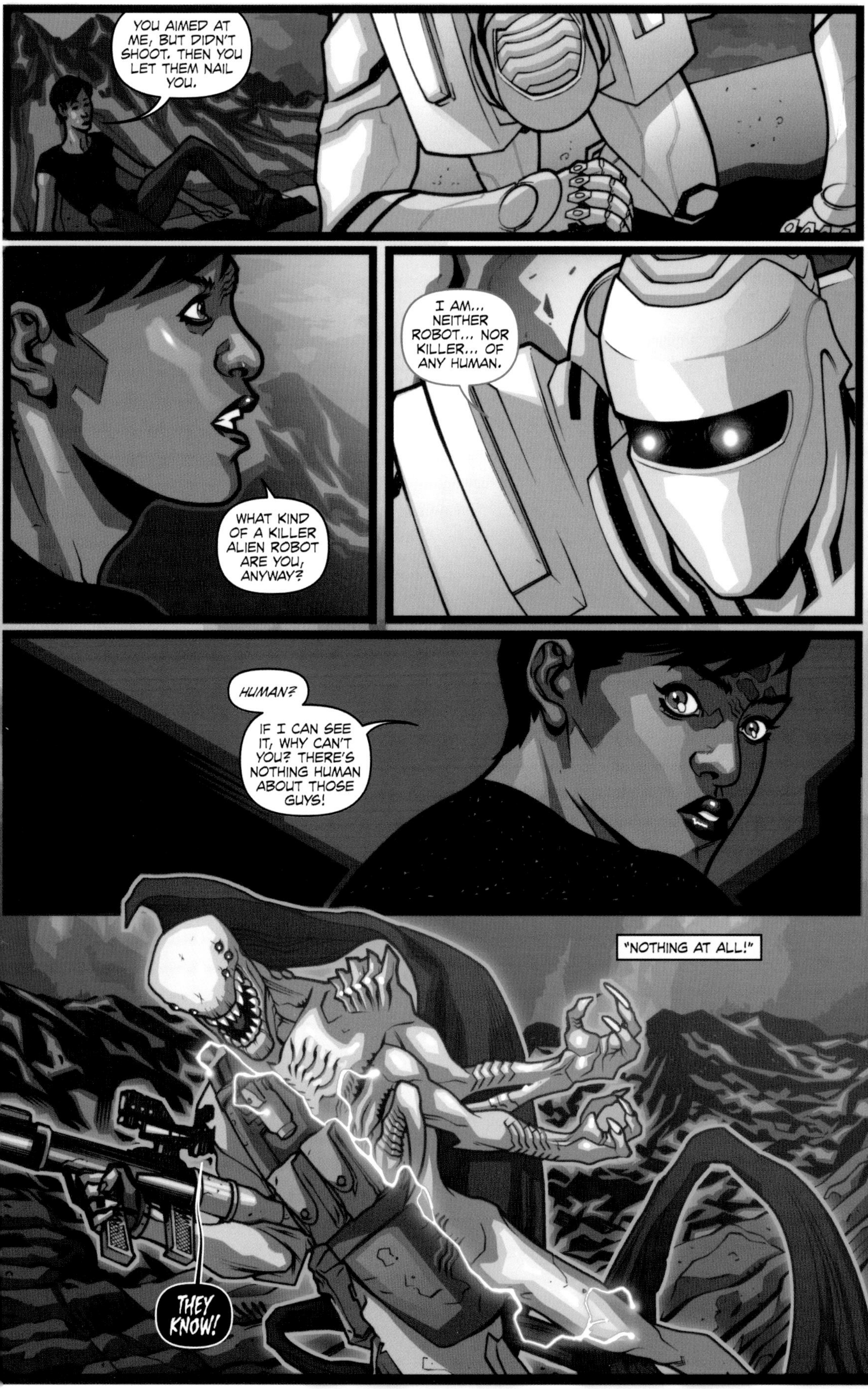
YOU AIMED AT ME, BUT DIDN'T SHOOT. THEN YOU LET THEM NAIL YOU.
WHAT KIND OF A KILLER ALIEN ROBOT ARE YOU, ANYWAY?
I AM... NEITHER ROBOT... NOR KILLER... OF ANY HUMAN.
HUMAN?
IF I CAN SEE IT, WHY CAN'T YOU? THERE'S NOTHING HUMAN ABOUT THOSE GUYS!
"NOTHING AT ALL!"
THEY KNOW!

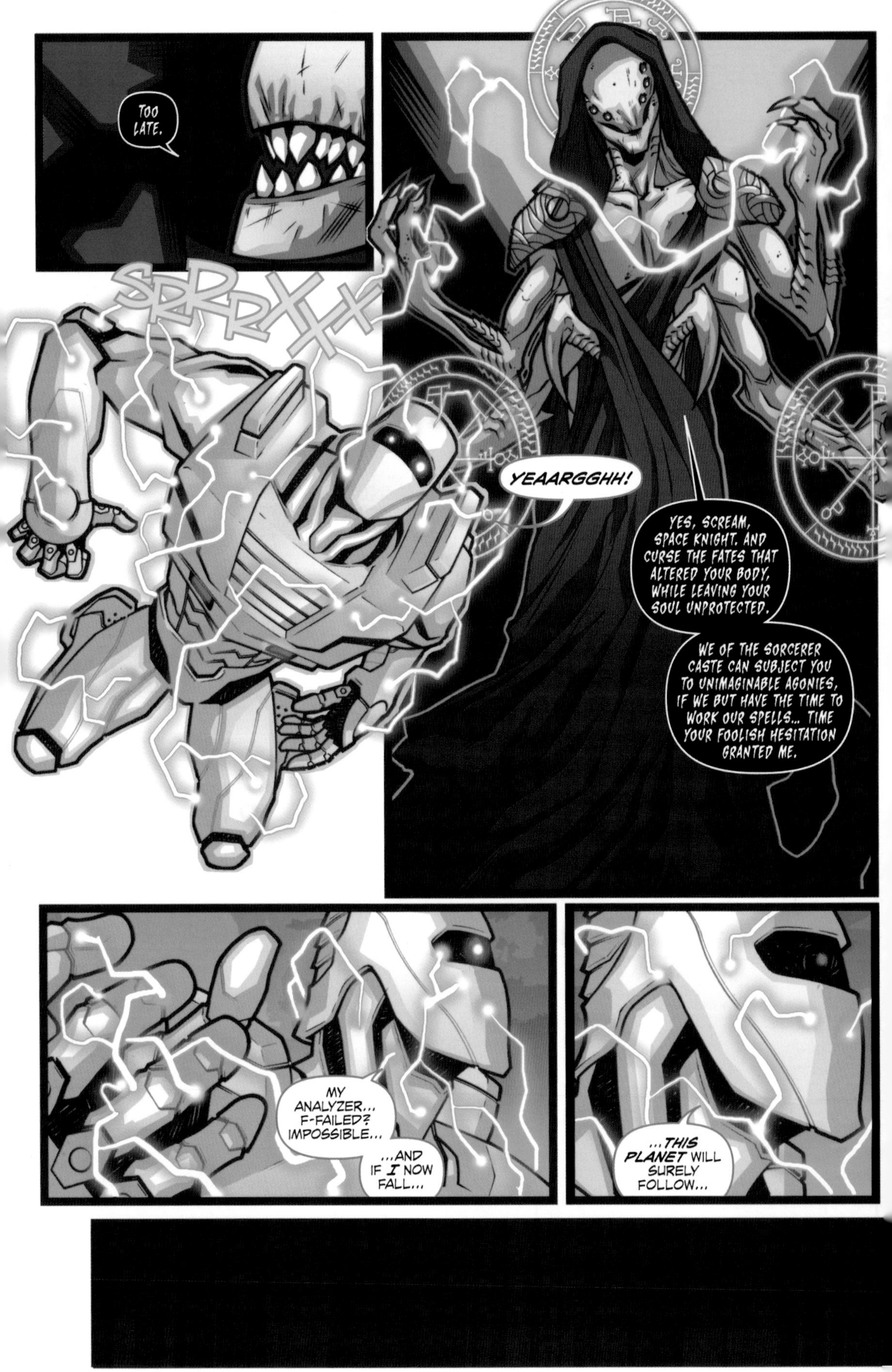
TOO LATE.
SRRRXXX
YEAARGGHH!
YES, SCREAM, SPACE KNIGHT. AND CURSE THE FATES THAT ALTERED YOUR BODY, WHILE LEAVING YOUR SOUL UNPROTECTED.
WE OF THE SORCERER CASTE CAN SUBJECT YOU TO UNIMAGINABLE AGONIES, IF WE BUT HAVE THE TIME TO WORK OUR SPELLS... TIME YOUR FOOLISH HESITATION GRANTED ME.
MY ANALYZER... F-FAILED? IMPOSSIBLE...
...AND IF I NOW FALL...
...THIS PLANET WILL SURELY FOLLOW...

ART BY **MIKE ALLRED**, COLORS BY **LAURA ALLRED**

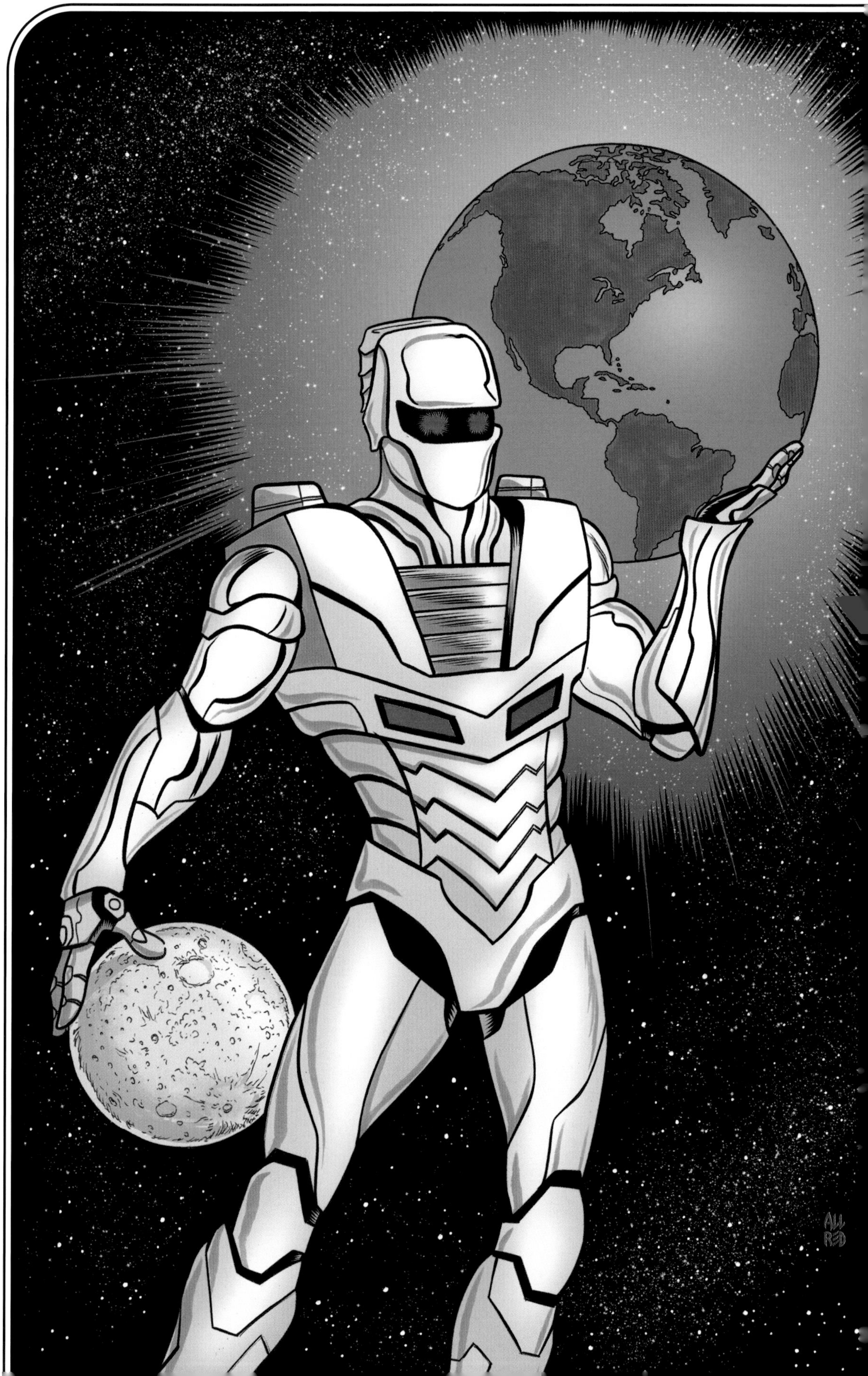

ALL
RED

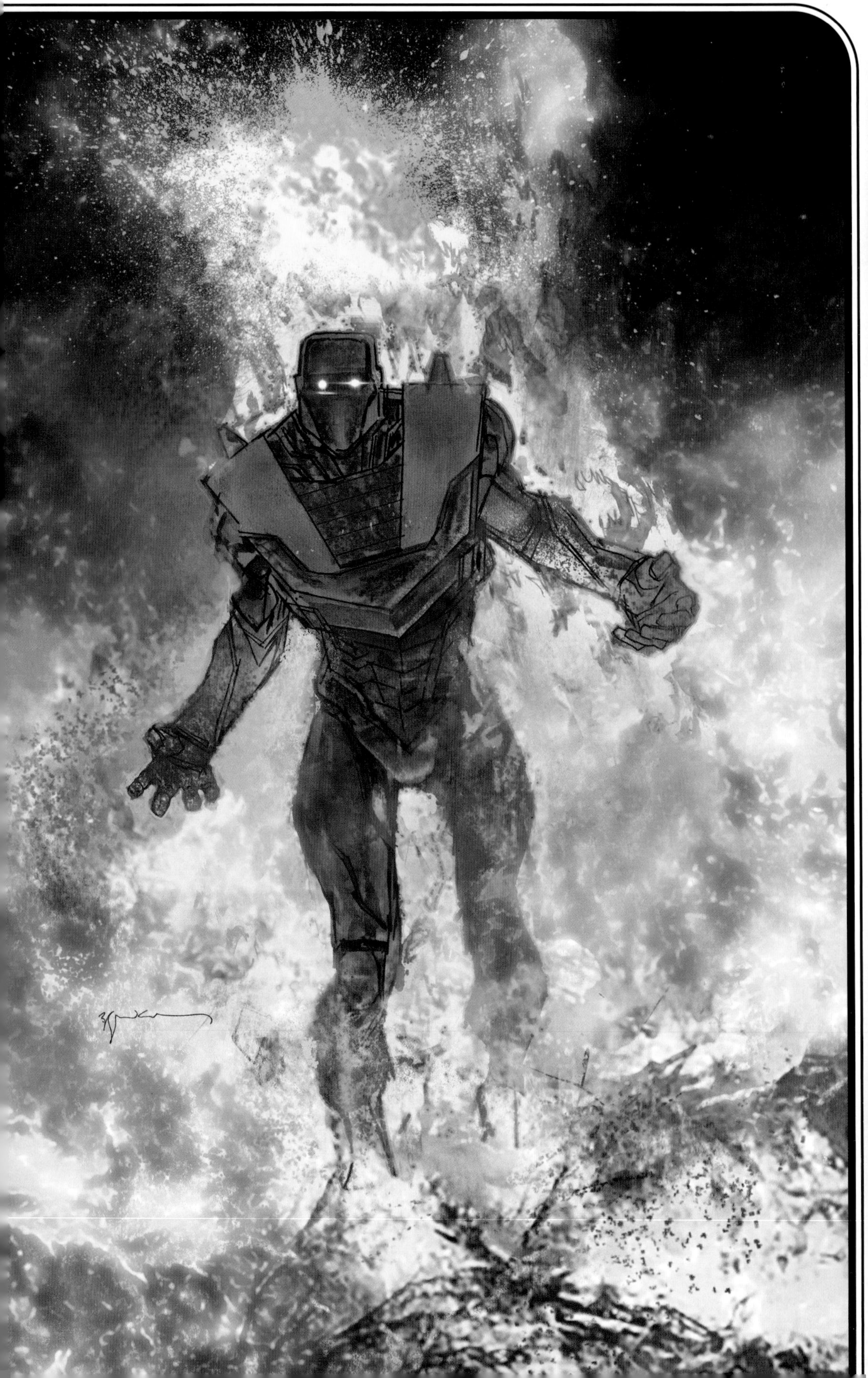

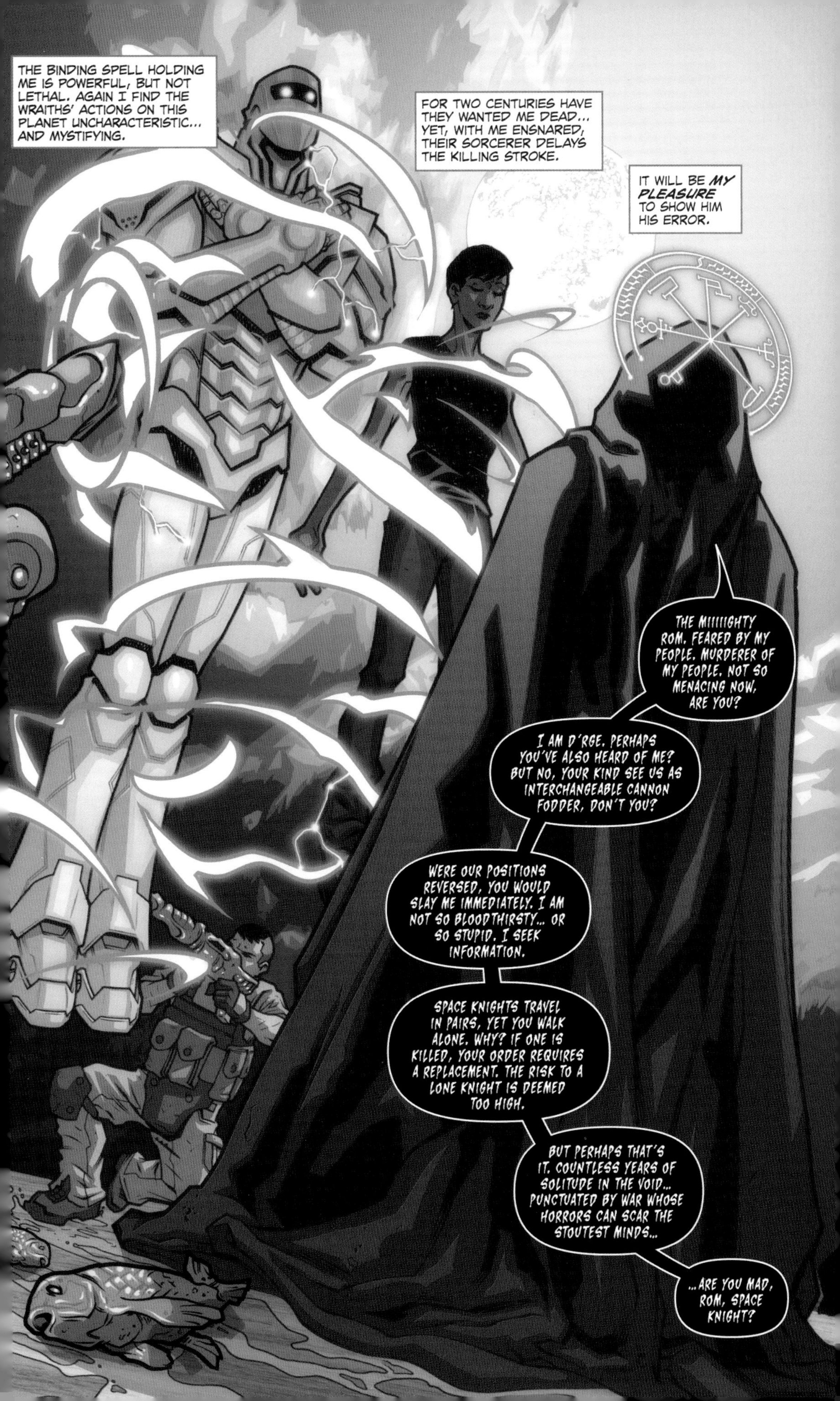
THE BINDING SPELL HOLDING ME IS POWERFUL, BUT NOT LETHAL. AGAIN I FIND THE WRAITHS' ACTIONS ON THIS PLANET UNCHARACTERISTIC... AND MYSTIFYING.
FOR TWO CENTURIES HAVE THEY WANTED ME DEAD... YET, WITH ME ENSNARED, THEIR SORCERER DELAYS THE KILLING STROKE.
IT WILL BE MY PLEASURE TO SHOW HIM HIS ERROR.
THE MIIIIIGHTY ROM. FEARED BY MY PEOPLE. MURDERER OF MY PEOPLE. NOT SO MENACING NOW, ARE YOU?
I AM D'RGE. PERHAPS YOU'VE ALSO HEARD OF ME? BUT NO, YOUR KIND SEE US AS INTERCHANGEABLE CANNON FODDER, DON'T YOU?
WERE OUR POSITIONS REVERSED, YOU WOULD SLAY ME IMMEDIATELY. I AM NOT SO BLOODTHIRSTY... OR SO STUPID. I SEEK INFORMATION.
SPACE KNIGHTS TRAVEL IN PAIRS, YET YOU WALK ALONE. WHY? IF ONE IS KILLED, YOUR ORDER REQUIRES A REPLACEMENT. THE RISK TO A LONE KNIGHT IS DEEMED TOO HIGH.
BUT PERHAPS THAT'S IT. COUNTLESS YEARS OF SOLITUDE IN THE VOID... PUNCTUATED BY WAR WHOSE HORRORS CAN SCAR THE STOUTEST MINDS...
...ARE YOU MAD, ROM, SPACE KNIGHT?

YOUR HOLINESS, WE MUST KILL HIM NOW. WE CAN'T RISK—

WE CANNOT RISK FAILURE, ISN'T THAT WHAT YOU MEANT, WORM?

AND THE GOAL OF ANY ENCOUNTER WITH A SPACE KNIGHT...

...IS TO MAKE THEIR POWER OUR OWN.

WE HAVE SLAIN KNIGHTS. WE KNOW THEIR ARMOR DIES WITH THEM. PERHAPS THAT CAN BE PREVENTED...

...IF I STRIP IT FROM HIS LIVING FLESH.

NNNG...

GODS OF ELONIA, HELP ME... I CANNOT ALLOW THIS. AND YET THE WRAITH'S ELDRITCH ENERGY TEARS AT ME, BODY AND SOUL...

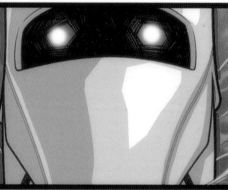

D'RGE WAS RIGHT. MY SOLITUDE WILL BE MY UNDOING. FOR IN MY HOUR OF NEED, THERE IS NO ONE TO HELP—

LEAVE HIM ALONE, YOU MONSTER!

"MONSTER?" THEN WHAT ARE YOU, CHILD? AND WHY DID I FEEL YOUR RAGE ECHO IN MY MIND?

LET ME SEE WHAT LURKS IN YOURS... CAMILLA BYERS.

S-STOP...

AHH, I SEE ALL NOW. YOU BLAME US FOR THE DEATH OF YOUR PARTNER. FOR THE... EVOLUTION OF YOUR FACE.

THE WRAITHMARK IS A SIGN OF BEAUTY, HUMAN. IT REPELS YOU NOW.

BUT SOON... YOU WILL SEE THINGS QUITE DIFFERENTLY.

I'LL FIGHT YOU. EVERYONE ON THIS PLANET WILL FIGHT YOU BEFORE WE LET YOU TAKE IT FROM US!

TAKE IT? MY DEAR, WE INTEND NO SUCH THING. WE ARE HERE TO SAVE IT.

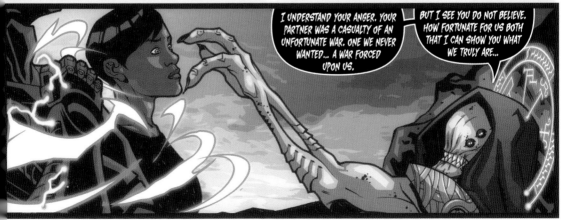

I UNDERSTAND YOUR ANGER. YOUR PARTNER WAS A CASUALTY OF AN UNFORTUNATE WAR. ONE WE NEVER WANTED... A WAR FORCED UPON US.

BUT I SEE YOU DO NOT BELIEVE. HOW FORTUNATE FOR US BOTH THAT I CAN SHOW YOU WHAT WE TRULY ARE...

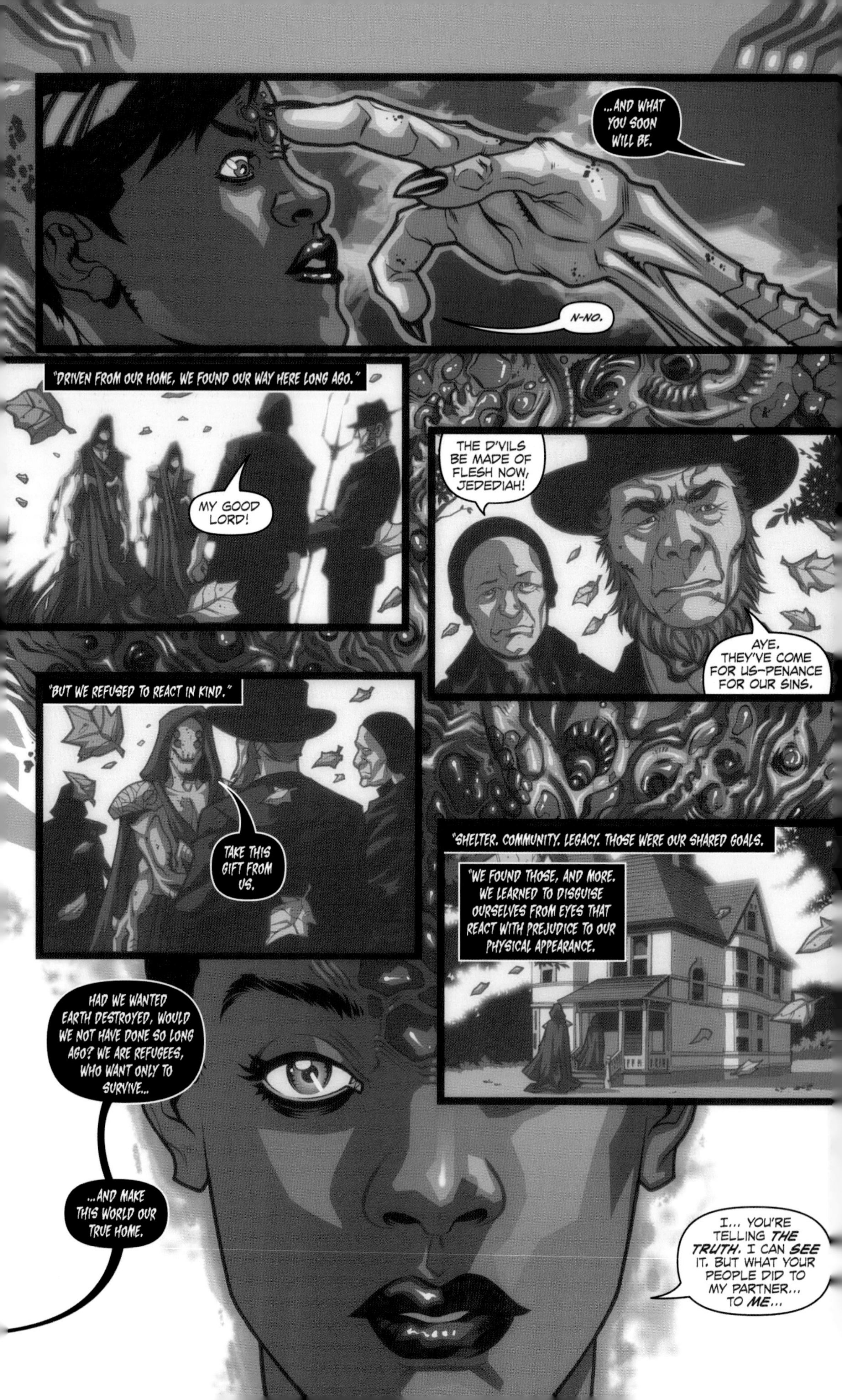
...AND WHAT YOU SOON WILL BE.
N-NO.
"DRIVEN FROM OUR HOME, WE FOUND OUR WAY HERE LONG AGO."
MY GOOD LORD!
THE D'VILS BE MADE OF FLESH NOW, JEDEDIAH!
AYE. THEY'VE COME FOR US—PENANCE FOR OUR SINS.
"BUT WE REFUSED TO REACT IN KIND."
TAKE THIS GIFT FROM US.
"SHELTER. COMMUNITY. LEGACY. THOSE WERE OUR SHARED GOALS.
"WE FOUND THOSE, AND MORE. WE LEARNED TO DISGUISE OURSELVES FROM EYES THAT REACT WITH PREJUDICE TO OUR PHYSICAL APPEARANCE.
HAD WE WANTED EARTH DESTROYED, WOULD WE NOT HAVE DONE SO LONG AGO? WE ARE REFUGEES, WHO WANT ONLY TO SURVIVE...
...AND MAKE THIS WORLD OUR TRUE HOME.
I... YOU'RE TELLING *THE TRUTH*. I CAN *SEE* IT. BUT WHAT YOUR PEOPLE DID TO MY PARTNER... TO *ME*...

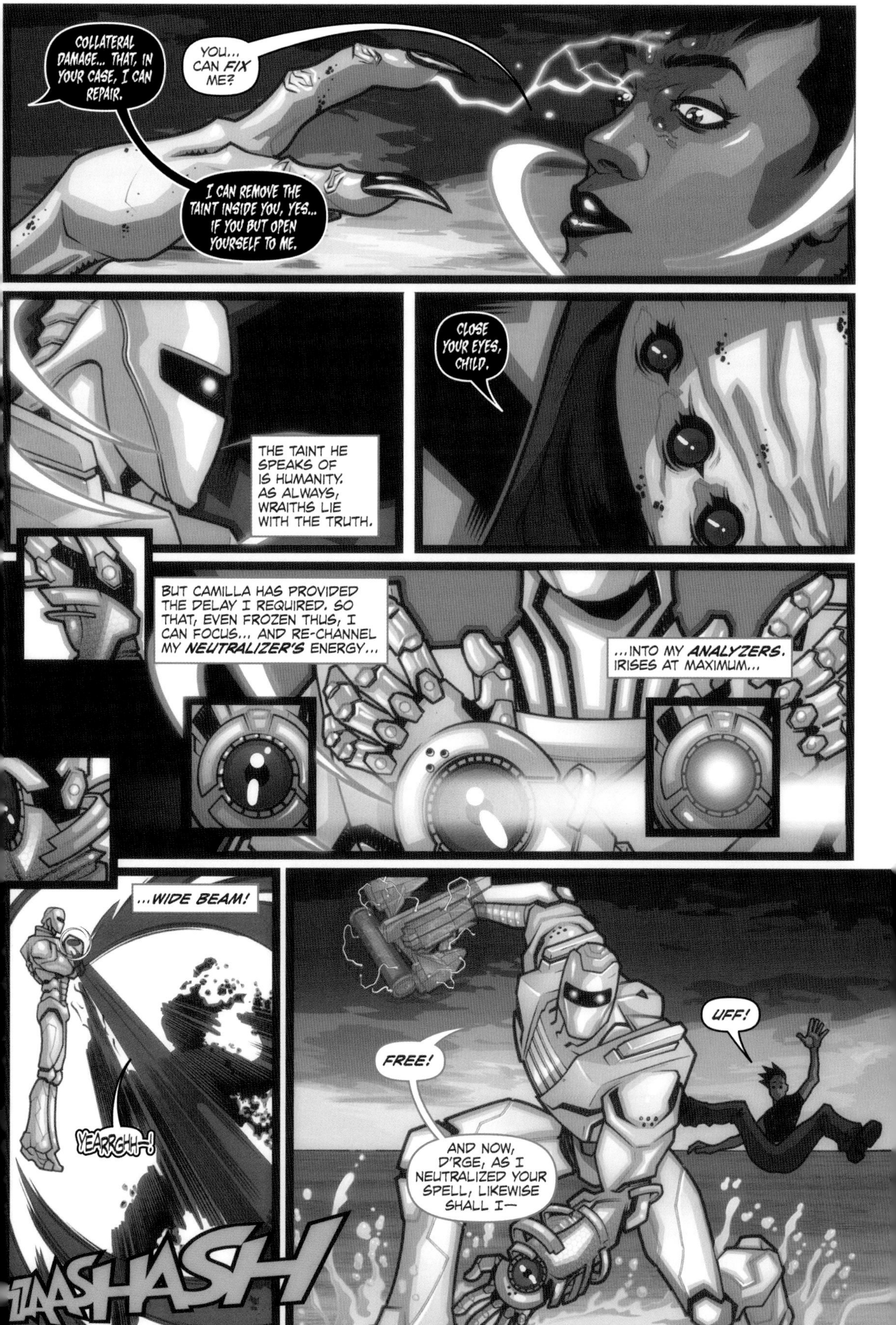

COLLATERAL DAMAGE... THAT, IN YOUR CASE, I CAN REPAIR.
YOU... CAN FIX ME?
I CAN REMOVE THE TAINT INSIDE YOU, YES... IF YOU BUT OPEN YOURSELF TO ME.
THE TAINT HE SPEAKS OF IS HUMANITY. AS ALWAYS, WRAITHS LIE WITH THE TRUTH.
CLOSE YOUR EYES, CHILD.
BUT CAMILLA HAS PROVIDED THE DELAY I REQUIRED. SO THAT, EVEN FROZEN THUS, I CAN FOCUS... AND RE-CHANNEL MY NEUTRALIZER'S ENERGY...
...INTO MY ANALYZERS. IRISES AT MAXIMUM...
...WIDE BEAM!
YEARRGHH-!
ZAASHASH
FREE!
UFF!
AND NOW, D'RGE, AS I NEUTRALIZED YOUR SPELL, LIKEWISE SHALL I—

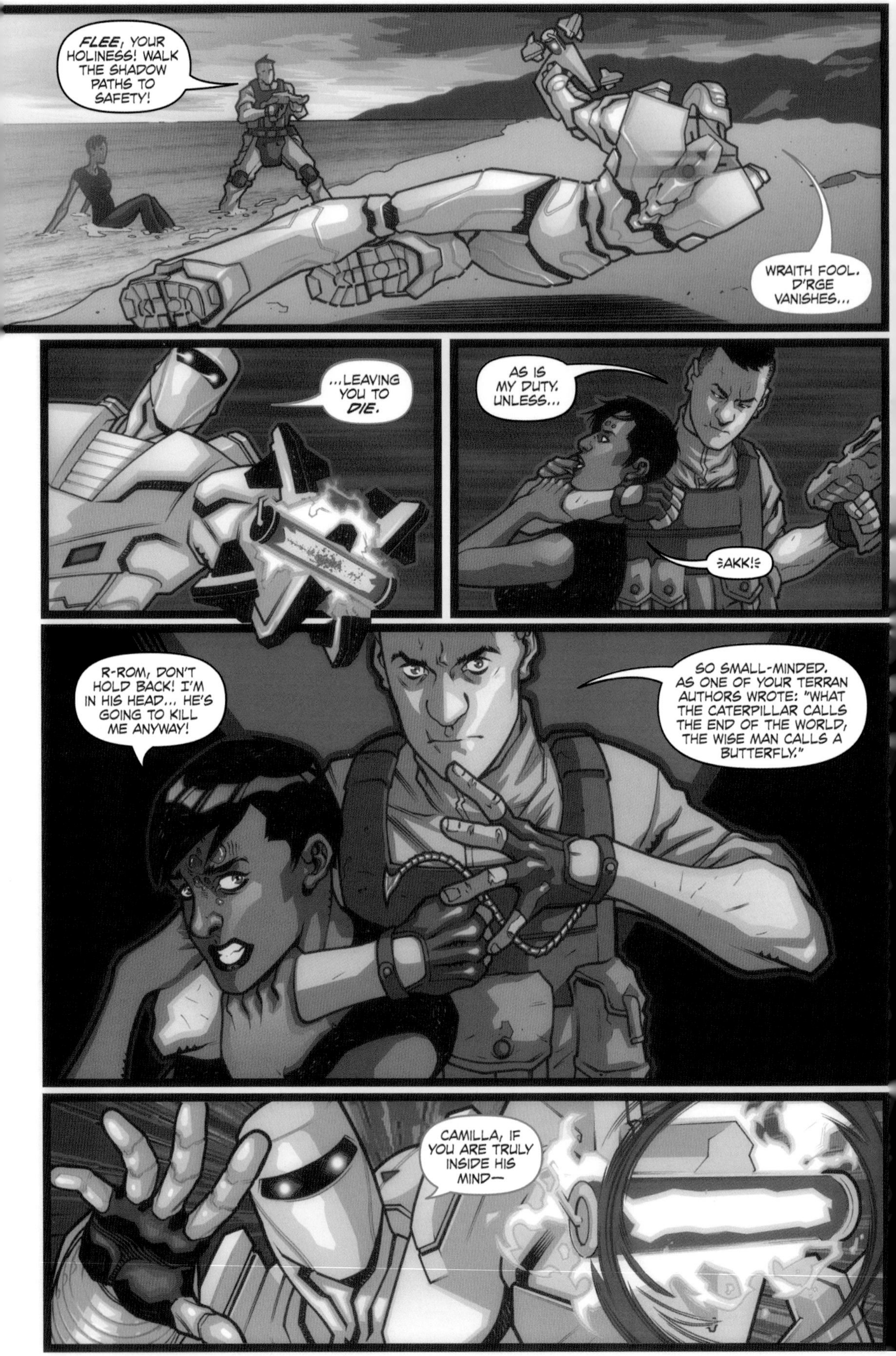
FLEE, YOUR HOLINESS! WALK THE SHADOW PATHS TO SAFETY!
WRAITH FOOL. D'RGE VANISHES...
...LEAVING YOU TO DIE.
AS IS MY DUTY. UNLESS...
AKK!
R-ROM, DON'T HOLD BACK! I'M IN HIS HEAD... HE'S GOING TO KILL ME ANYWAY!
SO SMALL-MINDED. AS ONE OF YOUR TERRAN AUTHORS WROTE: "WHAT THE CATERPILLAR CALLS THE END OF THE WORLD, THE WISE MAN CALLS A BUTTERFLY."
CAMILLA, IF YOU ARE TRULY INSIDE HIS MIND—

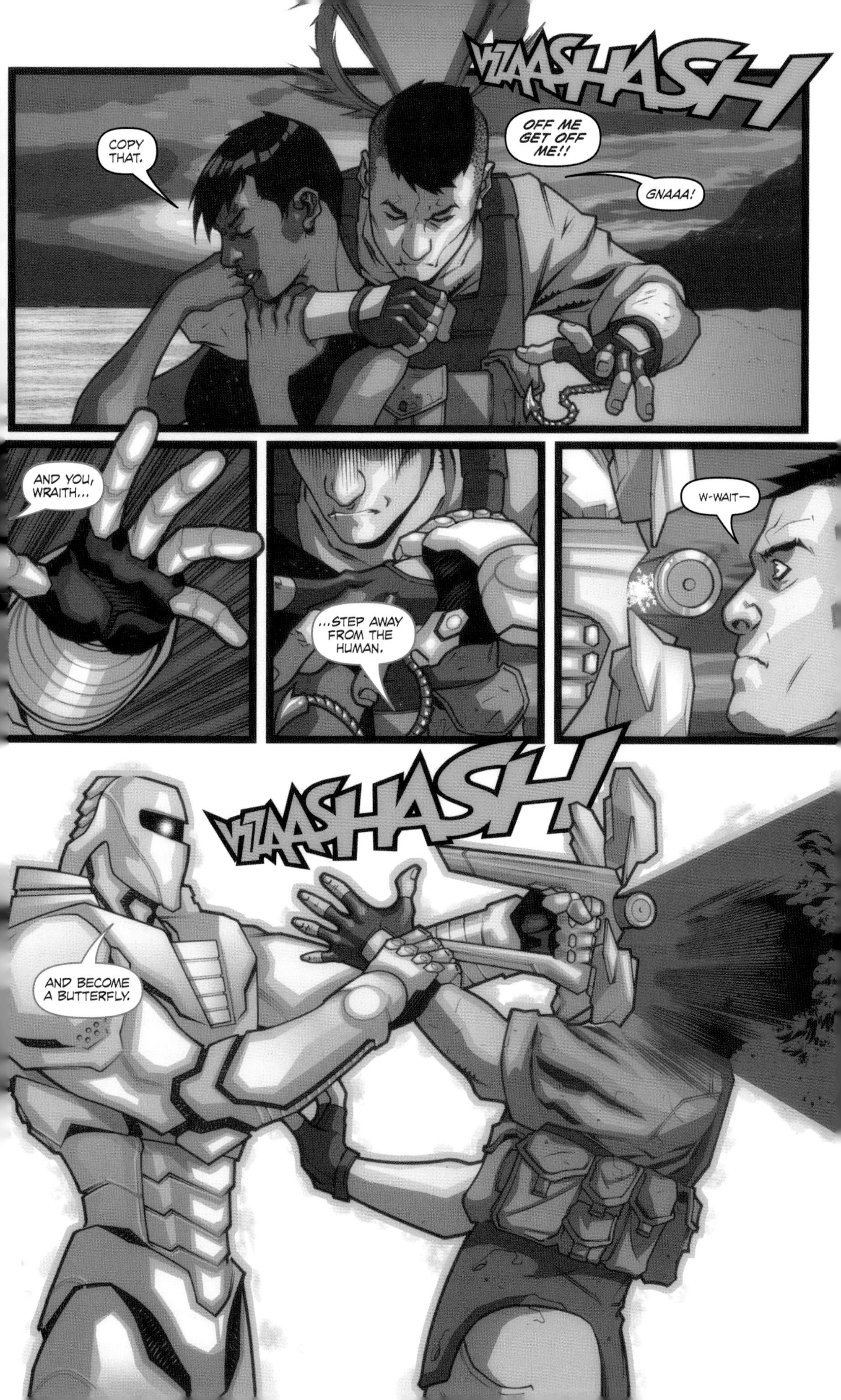

VZAASHASH
COPY THAT.
OFF ME GET OFF ME!!
GNAAA!
AND YOU, WRAITH...
...STEP AWAY FROM THE HUMAN.
W-WAIT—
VZAASHASH
AND BECOME A BUTTERFLY.

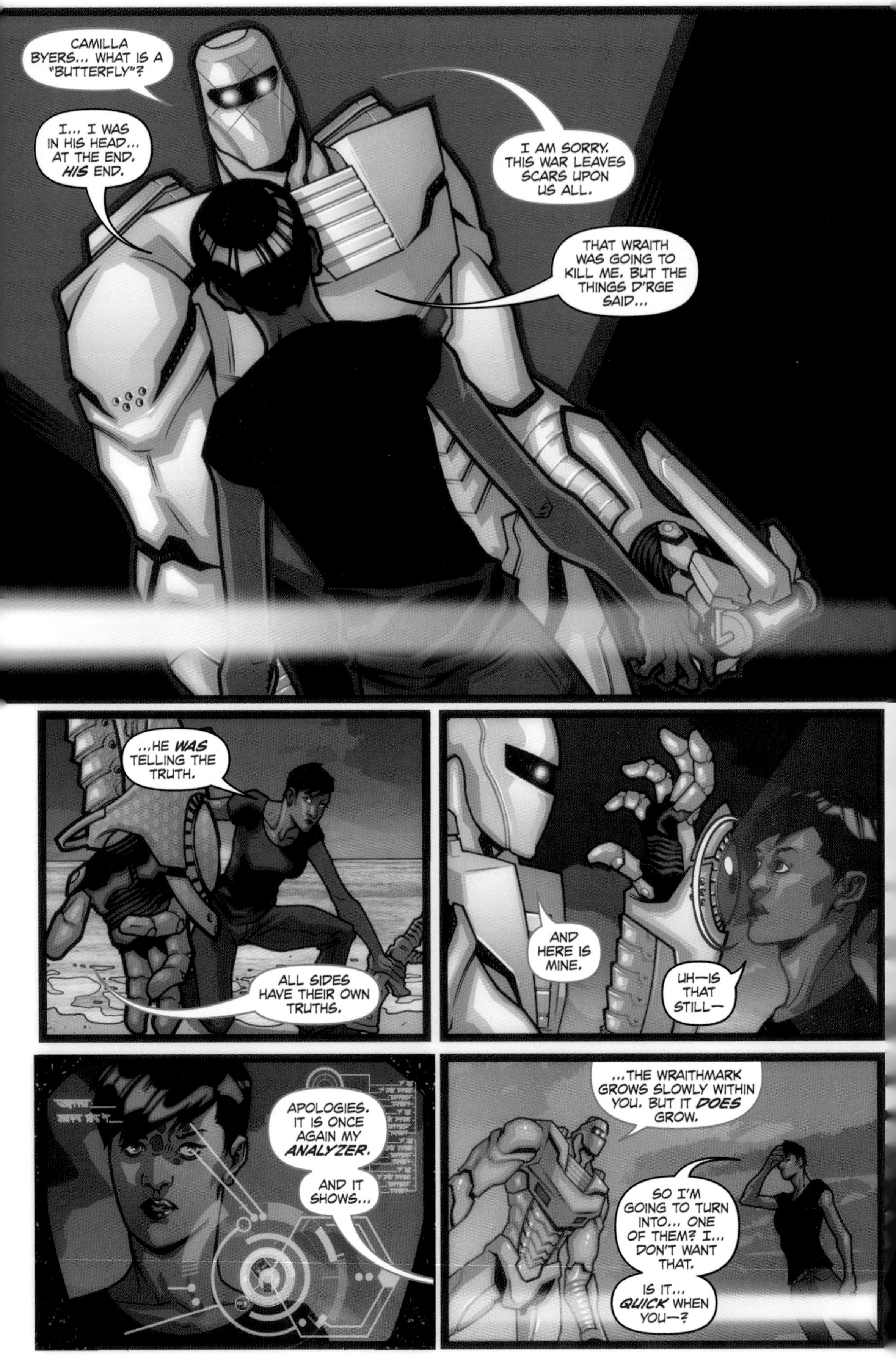
CAMILLA BYERS... WHAT IS A "BUTTERFLY"?
I... I WAS IN HIS HEAD... AT THE END. HIS END.
I AM SORRY. THIS WAR LEAVES SCARS UPON US ALL.
THAT WRAITH WAS GOING TO KILL ME. BUT THE THINGS D'RGE SAID...
...HE WAS TELLING THE TRUTH.
ALL SIDES HAVE THEIR OWN TRUTHS.
AND HERE IS MINE.
UH—IS THAT STILL—
APOLOGIES. IT IS ONCE AGAIN MY ANALYZER.
AND IT SHOWS...
...THE WRAITHMARK GROWS SLOWLY WITHIN YOU. BUT IT DOES GROW.
SO I'M GOING TO TURN INTO... ONE OF THEM? I... DON'T WANT THAT.
IS IT... QUICK WHEN YOU—?

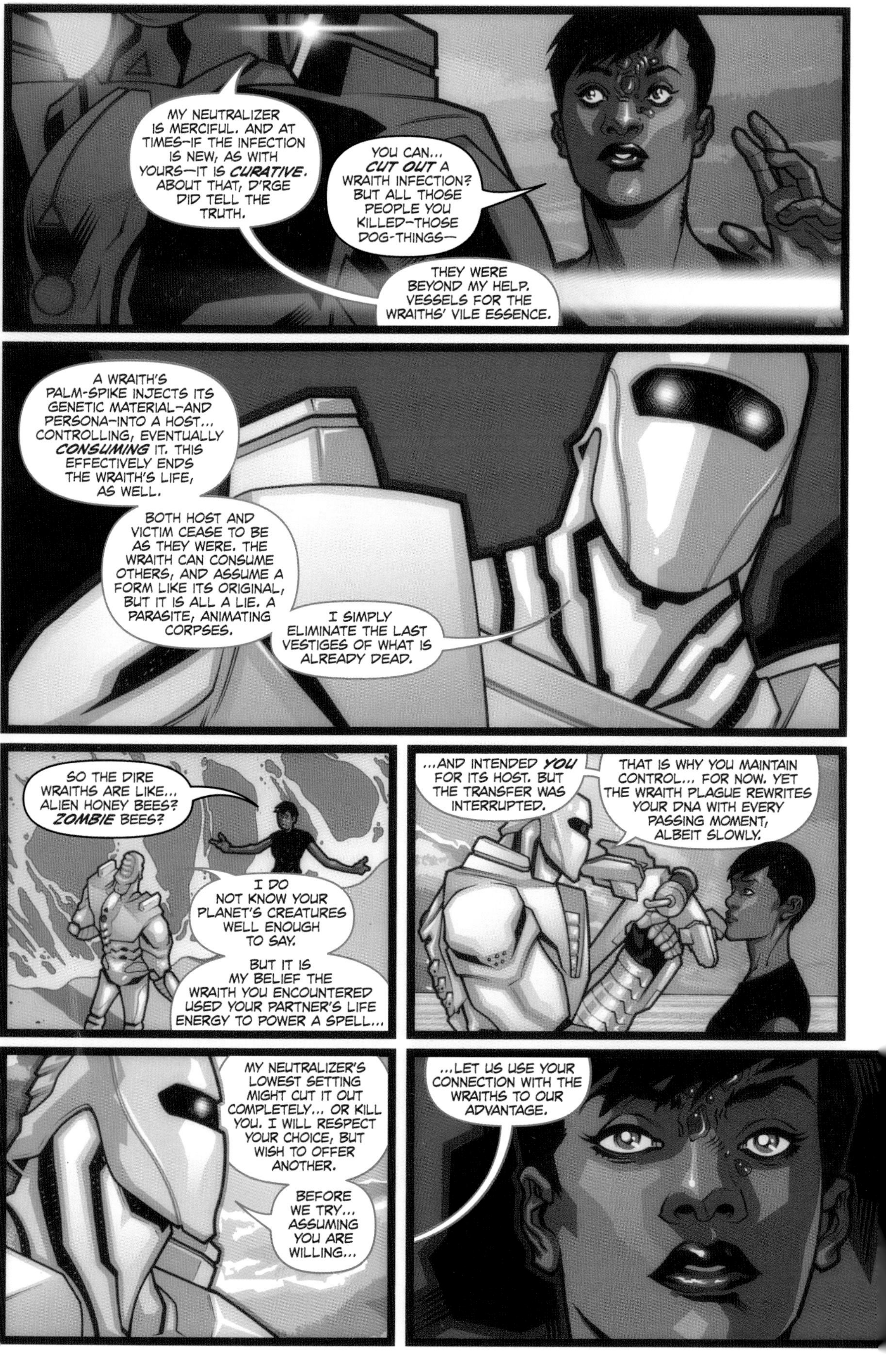
MY NEUTRALIZER IS MERCIFUL. AND AT TIMES—IF THE INFECTION IS NEW, AS WITH YOURS—IT IS CURATIVE. ABOUT THAT, D'RGE DID TELL THE TRUTH.
YOU CAN... CUT OUT A WRAITH INFECTION? BUT ALL THOSE PEOPLE YOU KILLED—THOSE DOG-THINGS—
THEY WERE BEYOND MY HELP. VESSELS FOR THE WRAITHS' VILE ESSENCE.
A WRAITH'S PALM-SPIKE INJECTS ITS GENETIC MATERIAL—AND PERSONA—INTO A HOST... CONTROLLING, EVENTUALLY CONSUMING IT. THIS EFFECTIVELY ENDS THE WRAITH'S LIFE, AS WELL.
BOTH HOST AND VICTIM CEASE TO BE AS THEY WERE. THE WRAITH CAN CONSUME OTHERS, AND ASSUME A FORM LIKE ITS ORIGINAL, BUT IT IS ALL A LIE. A PARASITE, ANIMATING CORPSES.
I SIMPLY ELIMINATE THE LAST VESTIGES OF WHAT IS ALREADY DEAD.
SO THE DIRE WRAITHS ARE LIKE... ALIEN HONEY BEES? ZOMBIE BEES?
I DO NOT KNOW YOUR PLANET'S CREATURES WELL ENOUGH TO SAY.
BUT IT IS MY BELIEF THE WRAITH YOU ENCOUNTERED USED YOUR PARTNER'S LIFE ENERGY TO POWER A SPELL...
...AND INTENDED YOU FOR ITS HOST. BUT THE TRANSFER WAS INTERRUPTED.
THAT IS WHY YOU MAINTAIN CONTROL... FOR NOW. YET THE WRAITH PLAGUE REWRITES YOUR DNA WITH EVERY PASSING MOMENT, ALBEIT SLOWLY.
MY NEUTRALIZER'S LOWEST SETTING MIGHT CUT IT OUT COMPLETELY... OR KILL YOU. I WILL RESPECT YOUR CHOICE, BUT WISH TO OFFER ANOTHER.
BEFORE WE TRY... ASSUMING YOU ARE WILLING...
...LET US USE YOUR CONNECTION WITH THE WRAITHS TO OUR ADVANTAGE.

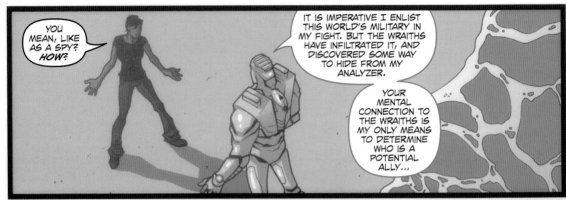

YOU MEAN, LIKE AS A SPY? *HOW?*

IT IS IMPERATIVE I ENLIST THIS WORLD'S MILITARY IN MY FIGHT. BUT THE WRAITHS HAVE INFILTRATED IT, AND DISCOVERED SOME WAY TO HIDE FROM MY ANALYZER.

YOUR MENTAL CONNECTION TO THE WRAITHS IS MY ONLY MEANS TO DETERMINE WHO IS A POTENTIAL ALLY...

"...AND WHO IS THE ENEMY."

DARBY, DOES THE FRESH AIR HELP?

IT DOES, DR. SHEN, THANK YOU FOR UNDERSTANDING. WITH EVERYTHING I'VE EXPERIENCED LATELY, I COULDN'T STAND THE FEELING OF MORE WALLS CLOSING IN.

VANDENBERG AIR FORCE BASE

CAN WE STAY FOCUSED ON WHAT YOU KNOW ABOUT THIS KILLER ROBOT, PLEASE?

I TOLD YOU, I THINK THERE'S A MAN IN THERE. OR... *SOMETHING* ALIVE.

THAT'S WORSE. A MASS MURDERER, NOT A MACHINE.

YOU DON'T HAVE TO TELL ME. IT KILLED MY FAMILY...MY ENTIRE HOMETOWN.

AND WE'LL AVENGE THEM. THAT'S A PROMISE FROM YOUR EX-C.O.

BUT TO FIND IT, WE NEED TO UNDERSTAND THIS... BEING. DO YOU KNOW WHY IT SPARED YOU?

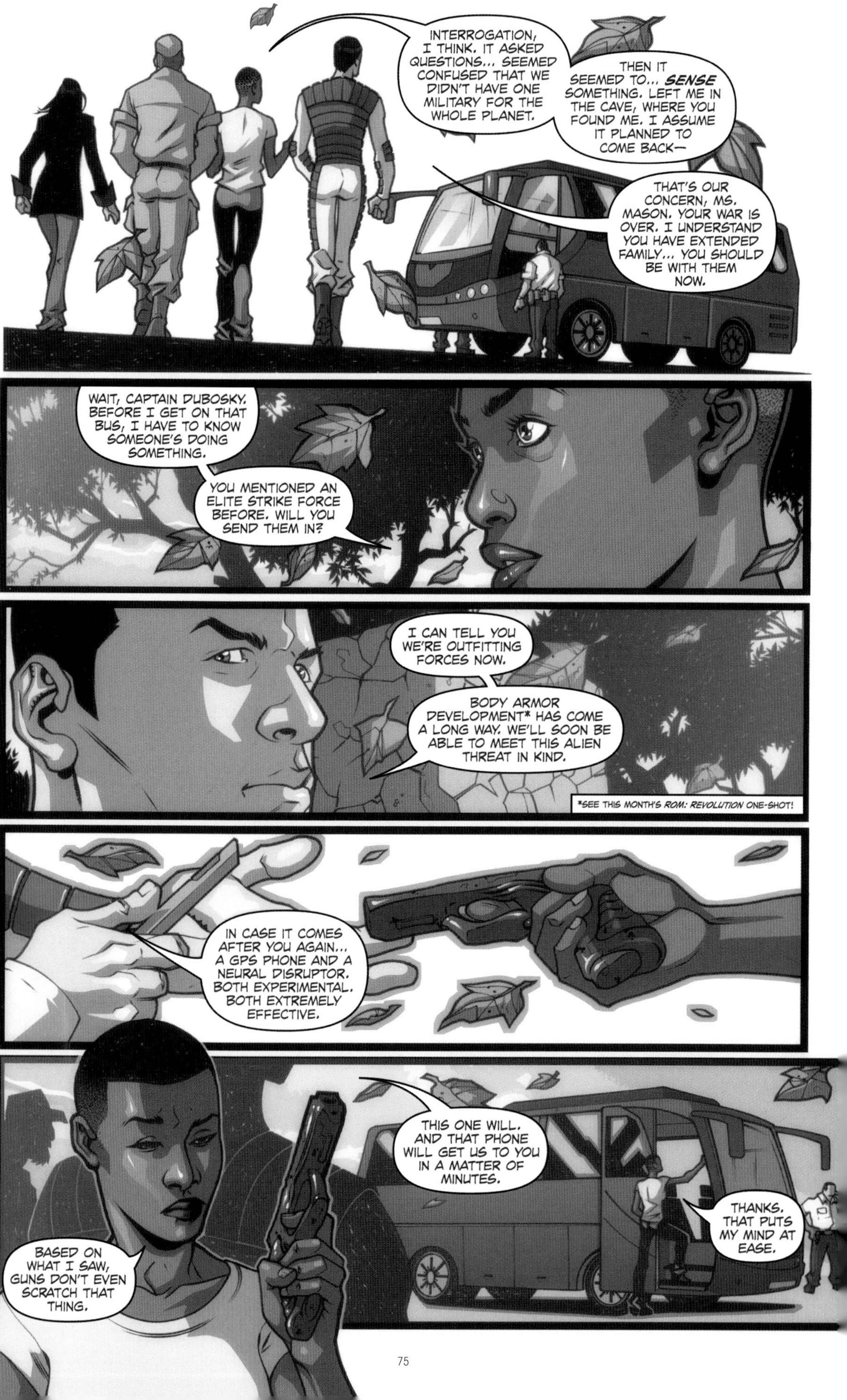
INTERROGATION, I THINK. IT ASKED QUESTIONS... SEEMED CONFUSED THAT WE DIDN'T HAVE ONE MILITARY FOR THE WHOLE PLANET.
THEN IT SEEMED TO... SENSE SOMETHING. LEFT ME IN THE CAVE, WHERE YOU FOUND ME. I ASSUME IT PLANNED TO COME BACK—
THAT'S OUR CONCERN, MS. MASON. YOUR WAR IS OVER. I UNDERSTAND YOU HAVE EXTENDED FAMILY... YOU SHOULD BE WITH THEM NOW.
WAIT, CAPTAIN DUBOSKY. BEFORE I GET ON THAT BUS, I HAVE TO KNOW SOMEONE'S DOING SOMETHING.
YOU MENTIONED AN ELITE STRIKE FORCE BEFORE. WILL YOU SEND THEM IN?
I CAN TELL YOU WE'RE OUTFITTING FORCES NOW.
BODY ARMOR DEVELOPMENT* HAS COME A LONG WAY. WE'LL SOON BE ABLE TO MEET THIS ALIEN THREAT IN KIND.
*SEE THIS MONTH'S ROM: REVOLUTION ONE-SHOT!
IN CASE IT COMES AFTER YOU AGAIN... A GPS PHONE AND A NEURAL DISRUPTOR. BOTH EXPERIMENTAL. BOTH EXTREMELY EFFECTIVE.
BASED ON WHAT I SAW, GUNS DON'T EVEN SCRATCH THAT THING.
THIS ONE WILL. AND THAT PHONE WILL GET US TO YOU IN A MATTER OF MINUTES.
THANKS. THAT PUTS MY MIND AT EASE.

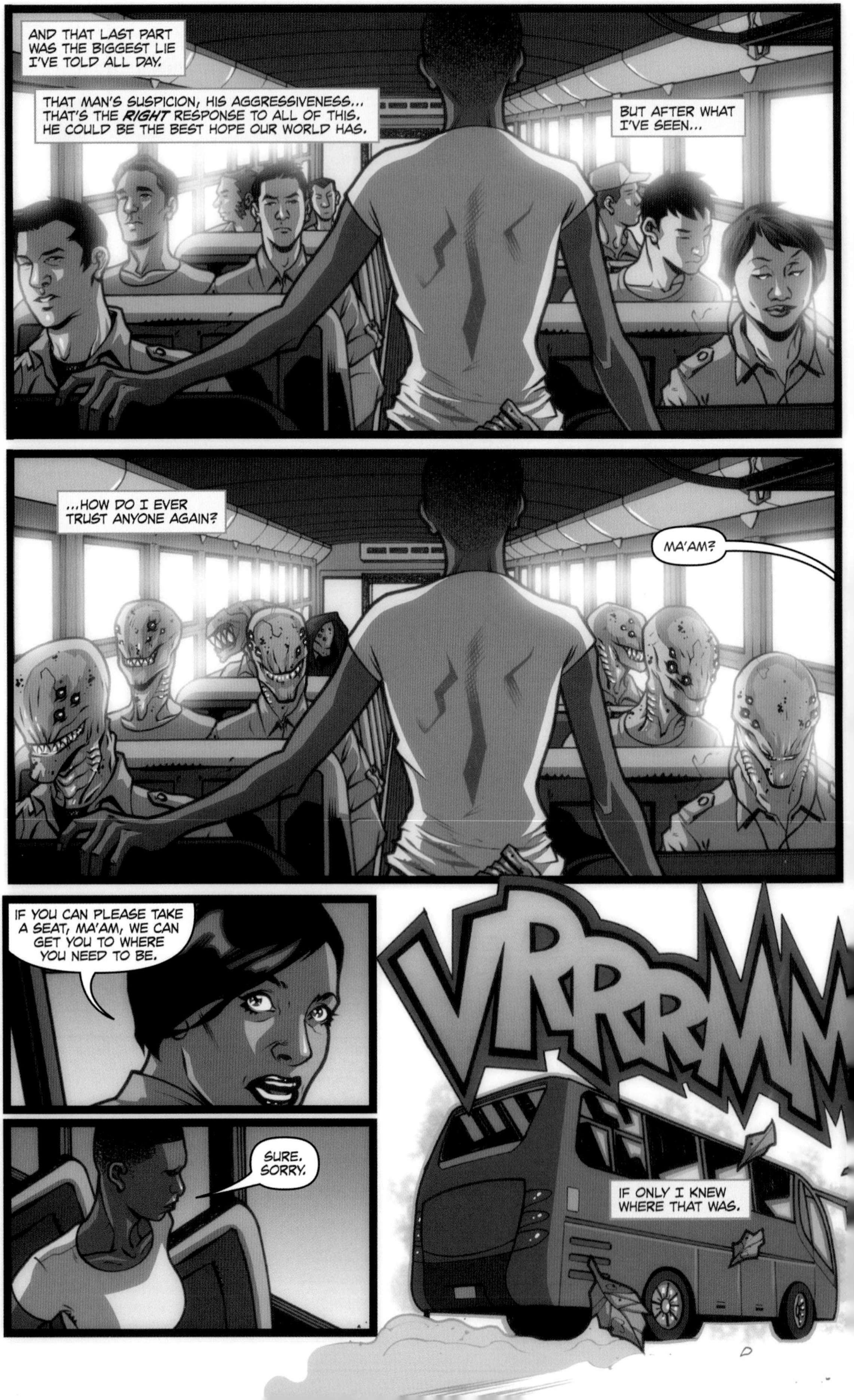
AND THAT LAST PART WAS THE BIGGEST LIE I'VE TOLD ALL DAY.
THAT MAN'S SUSPICION, HIS AGGRESSIVENESS... THAT'S THE *RIGHT* RESPONSE TO ALL OF THIS. HE COULD BE THE BEST HOPE OUR WORLD HAS.
BUT AFTER WHAT I'VE SEEN...
...HOW DO I EVER TRUST ANYONE AGAIN?
MA'AM?
IF YOU CAN PLEASE TAKE A SEAT, MA'AM, WE CAN GET YOU TO WHERE YOU NEED TO BE.
SURE. SORRY.
VRRRMM
IF ONLY I KNEW WHERE THAT WAS.

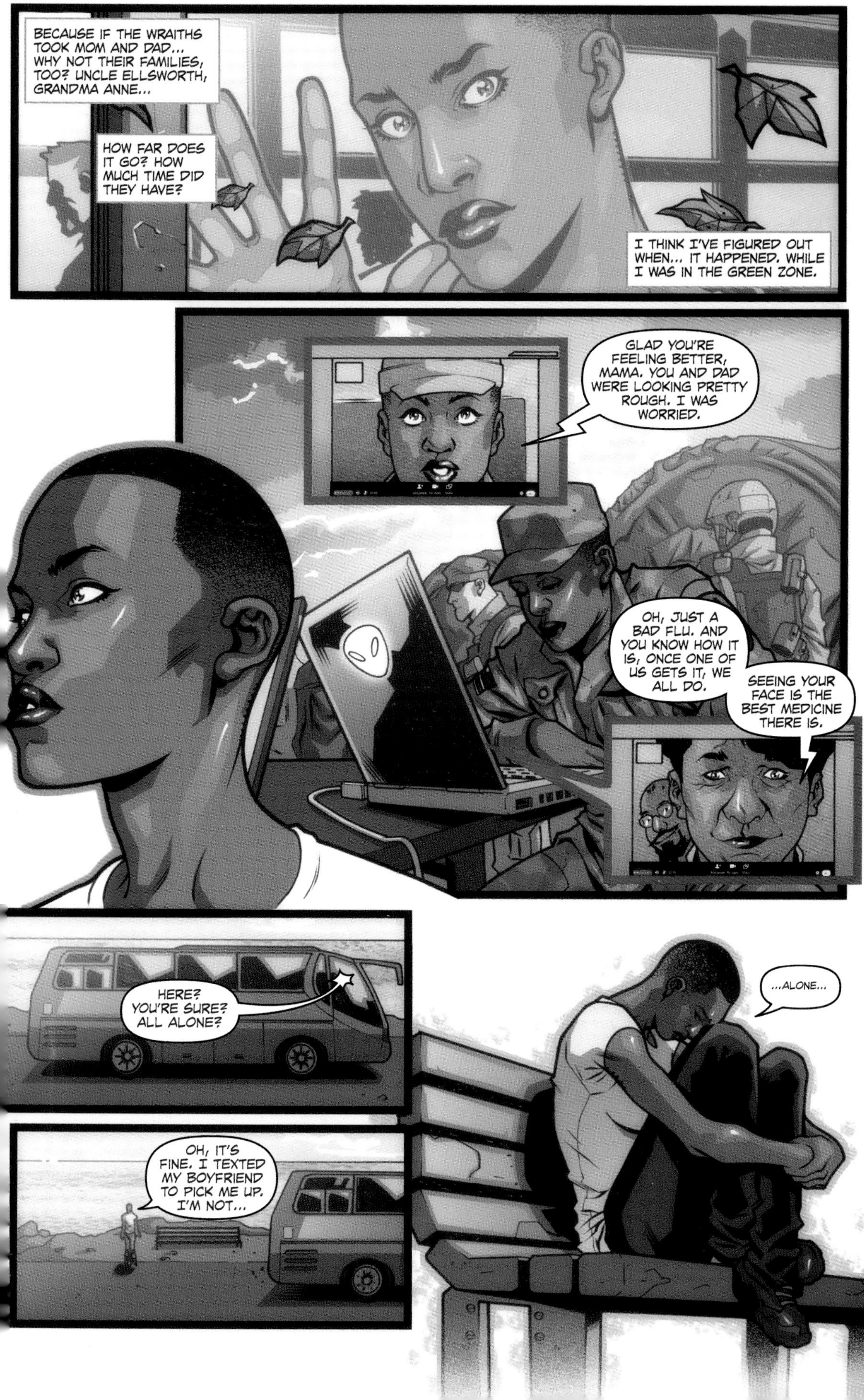

BECAUSE IF THE WRAITHS TOOK MOM AND DAD... WHY NOT THEIR FAMILIES, TOO? UNCLE ELLSWORTH, GRANDMA ANNE...
HOW FAR DOES IT GO? HOW MUCH TIME DID THEY HAVE?
I THINK I'VE FIGURED OUT WHEN... IT HAPPENED. WHILE I WAS IN THE GREEN ZONE.
GLAD YOU'RE FEELING BETTER, MAMA. YOU AND DAD WERE LOOKING PRETTY ROUGH. I WAS WORRIED.
OH, JUST A BAD FLU. AND YOU KNOW HOW IT IS, ONCE ONE OF US GETS IT, WE ALL DO.
SEEING YOUR FACE IS THE BEST MEDICINE THERE IS.
HERE? YOU'RE SURE? ALL ALONE?
...ALONE...
OH, IT'S FINE. I TEXTED MY BOYFRIEND TO PICK ME UP. I'M NOT...

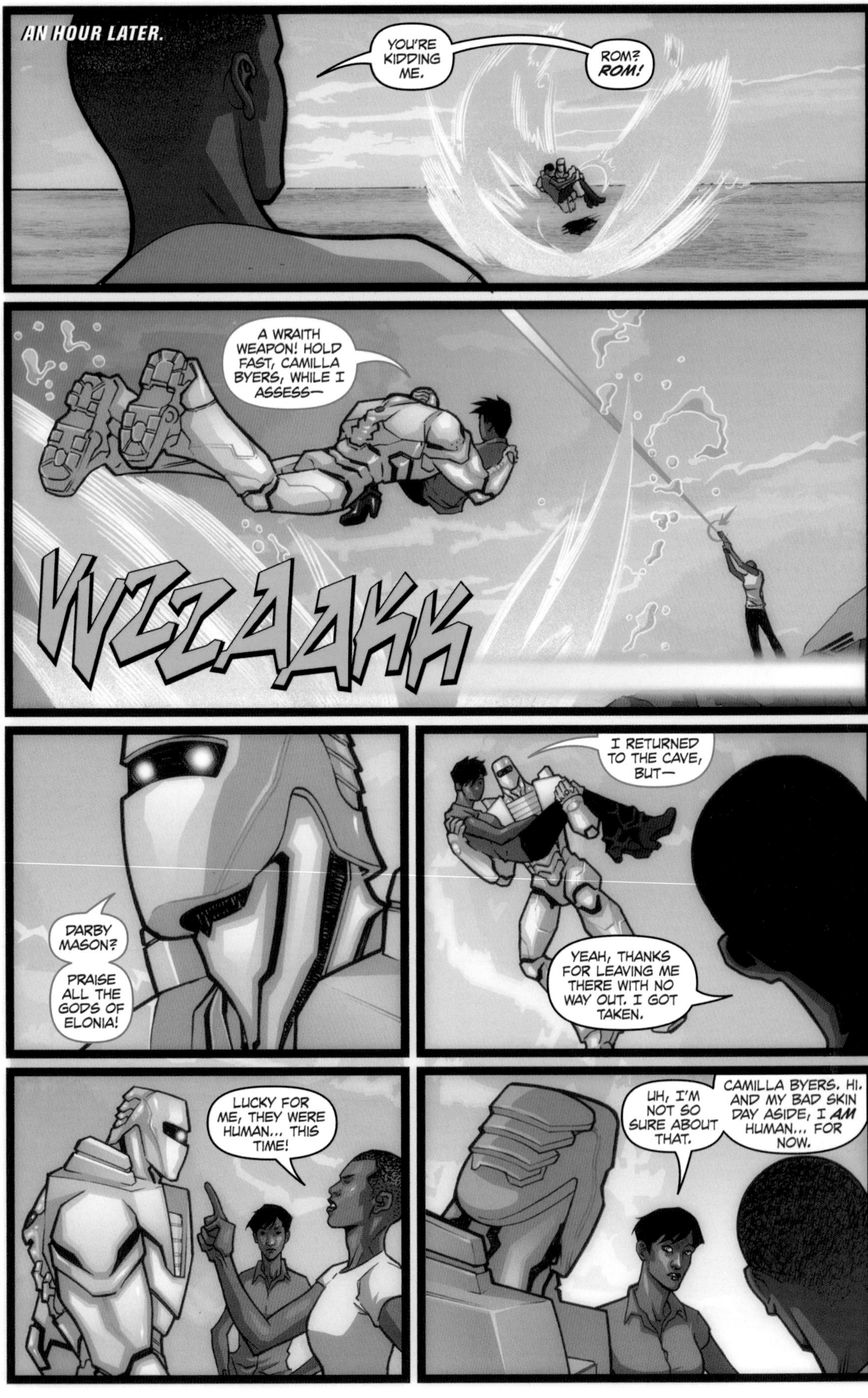
AN HOUR LATER.
YOU'RE KIDDING ME.
ROM? ROM!
A WRAITH WEAPON! HOLD FAST, CAMILLA BYERS, WHILE I ASSESS—
VVZZAAKK
DARBY MASON?
PRAISE ALL THE GODS OF ELONIA!
I RETURNED TO THE CAVE, BUT—
YEAH, THANKS FOR LEAVING ME THERE WITH NO WAY OUT. I GOT TAKEN.
LUCKY FOR ME, THEY WERE HUMAN... THIS TIME!
UH, I'M NOT SO SURE ABOUT THAT.
CAMILLA BYERS. HI. AND MY BAD SKIN DAY ASIDE, I AM HUMAN... FOR NOW.

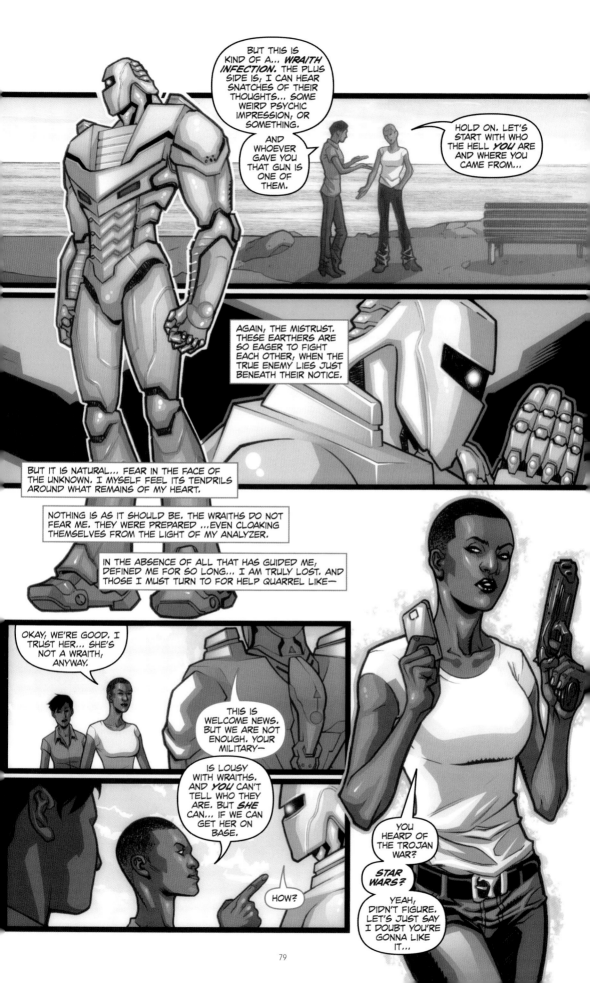

BUT THIS IS KIND OF A... *WRAITH INFECTION.* THE PLUS SIDE IS, I CAN HEAR SNATCHES OF THEIR THOUGHTS... SOME WEIRD PSYCHIC IMPRESSION, OR SOMETHING.

AND WHOEVER GAVE YOU THAT GUN IS ONE OF THEM.

HOLD ON. LET'S START WITH WHO THE HELL *YOU* ARE AND WHERE YOU CAME FROM...

AGAIN, THE MISTRUST. THESE EARTHERS ARE SO EAGER TO FIGHT EACH OTHER, WHEN THE TRUE ENEMY LIES JUST BENEATH THEIR NOTICE.

BUT IT IS NATURAL... FEAR IN THE FACE OF THE UNKNOWN. I MYSELF FEEL ITS TENDRILS AROUND WHAT REMAINS OF MY HEART.

NOTHING IS AS IT SHOULD BE. THE WRAITHS DO NOT FEAR ME. THEY WERE PREPARED ...EVEN CLOAKING THEMSELVES FROM THE LIGHT OF MY ANALYZER.

IN THE ABSENCE OF ALL THAT HAS GUIDED ME, DEFINED ME FOR SO LONG... I AM TRULY LOST. AND THOSE I MUST TURN TO FOR HELP QUARREL LIKE—

OKAY, WE'RE GOOD. I TRUST HER... SHE'S NOT A WRAITH, ANYWAY.

THIS IS WELCOME NEWS. BUT WE ARE NOT ENOUGH. YOUR MILITARY—

IS LOUSY WITH WRAITHS. AND *YOU* CAN'T TELL WHO THEY ARE, BUT *SHE* CAN... IF WE CAN GET HER ON BASE.

HOW?

YOU HEARD OF THE TROJAN WAR?

STAR WARS?

YEAH, DIDN'T FIGURE. LET'S JUST SAY I DOUBT YOU'RE GONNA LIKE IT...

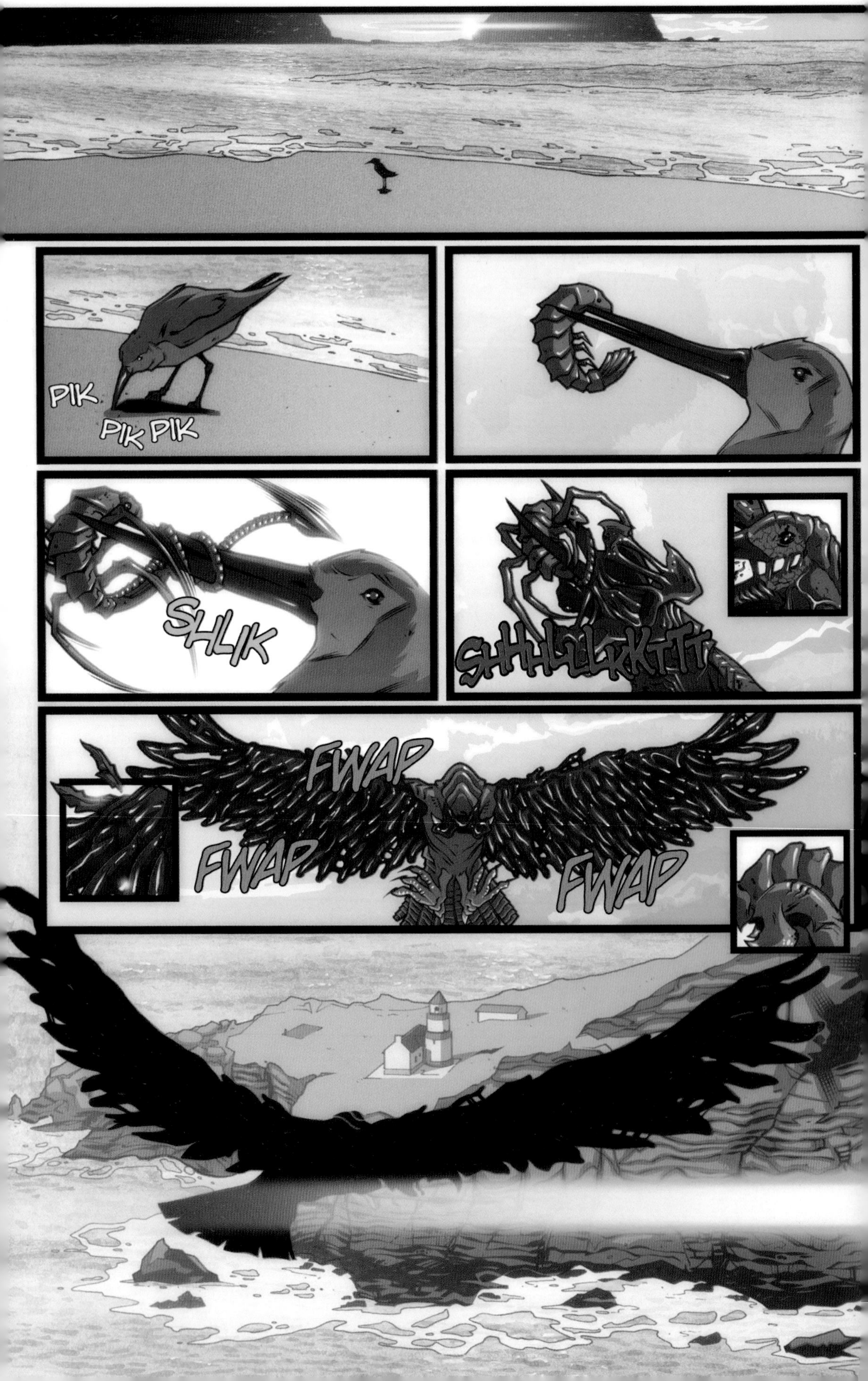
PIK
PIK PIK
SHLIK
SHHHLLLKKTTT
FWAP
FWAP
FWAP

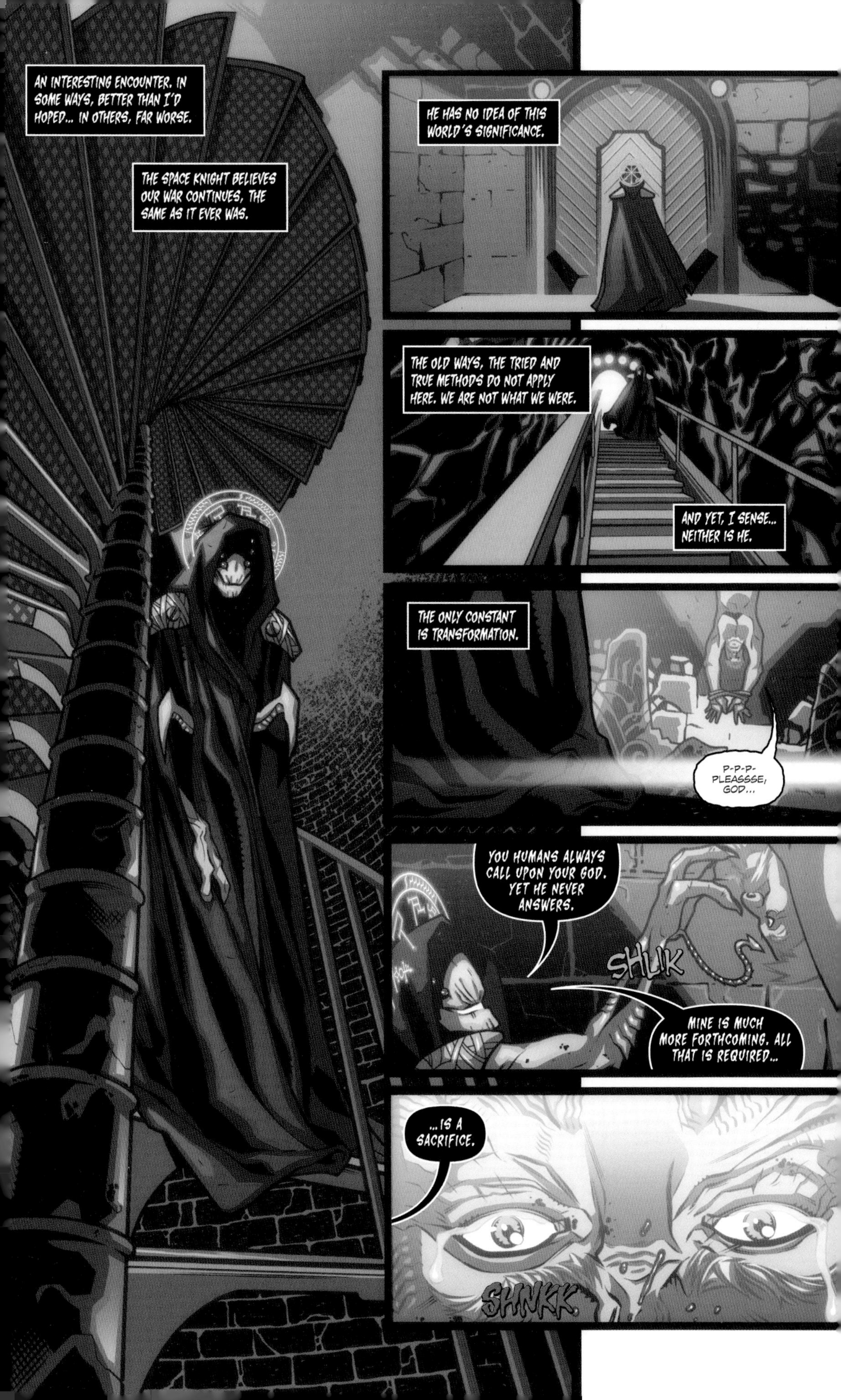
AN INTERESTING ENCOUNTER. IN SOME WAYS, BETTER THAN I'D HOPED... IN OTHERS, FAR WORSE.
THE SPACE KNIGHT BELIEVES OUR WAR CONTINUES, THE SAME AS IT EVER WAS.
HE HAS NO IDEA OF THIS WORLD'S SIGNIFICANCE.
THE OLD WAYS, THE TRIED AND TRUE METHODS DO NOT APPLY HERE. WE ARE NOT WHAT WE WERE.
AND YET, I SENSE... NEITHER IS HE.
THE ONLY CONSTANT IS TRANSFORMATION.
P-P-P-PLEASSSE, GOD...
YOU HUMANS ALWAYS CALL UPON YOUR GOD. YET HE NEVER ANSWERS.
SHLIK
MINE IS MUCH MORE FORTHCOMING. ALL THAT IS REQUIRED...
...IS A SACRIFICE.
SHNKK

LATER.

MY ANALYSIS CONFIRMED IT. THIS IS ROM. NOT ANOTHER SITUATION LIKE THE DEBACLE ON TELLUS-5.

AND THE TESTS WERE POSITIVE. WE SUCCEEDED IN BLOCKING HIS ANALYZER.

BUT BROTHER, I SENSE THE SPACE KNIGHT IS CHANGED FROM HIS LONG CRUSADE. I DO NOT BELIEVE THE SOLSTAR ORDER EVEN KNOWS HE IS HERE.

I KNOW OF OUR PREPARATIONS. OUR YEARS OF PLANNING. BUT WE HAVE AN OPPORTUNITY... I ADVISE THAT WE KILL HIM NOW.

PATIENCE, D'RGE. WE MUST NOT LET ONE OPPORTUNITY MAKE US TURN OUR BACKS ON ANOTHER.

YOU SPEAK OF THE CYBERTRONIANS.

IT FEELS WRONG, BROTHER. FOR SO LONG, WE'VE HAD SUCCESS AVOIDING THEM. OPERATING IN SECRECY. BUILDING A BASE OF POWER.

BUT POWER CANNOT BE BUILT FOREVER. THERE COMES A TIME WHEN IT IS EITHER USED, OR WASTED.

IT IS WORTH THE RISK. YOU SPEAK FROM A PLACE OF FEAR, BROTHER. AND A DIRE WRAITH HAS NO PLACE FOR FEAR...

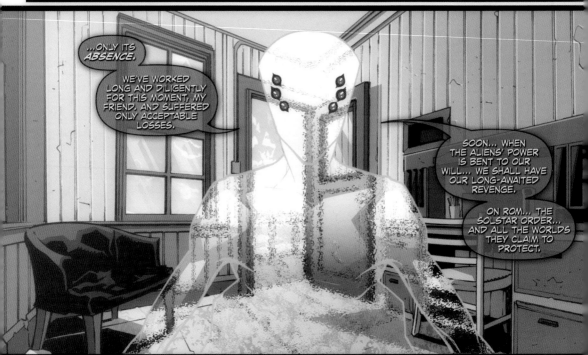

...ONLY ITS ABSENCE.

WE'VE WORKED LONG AND DILIGENTLY FOR THIS MOMENT, MY FRIEND. AND SUFFERED ONLY ACCEPTABLE LOSSES.

SOON... WHEN THE ALIENS' POWER IS BENT TO OUR WILL... WE SHALL HAVE OUR LONG-AWAITED REVENGE.

ON ROM... THE SOLSTAR ORDER... AND ALL THE WORLDS THEY CLAIM TO PROTECT.

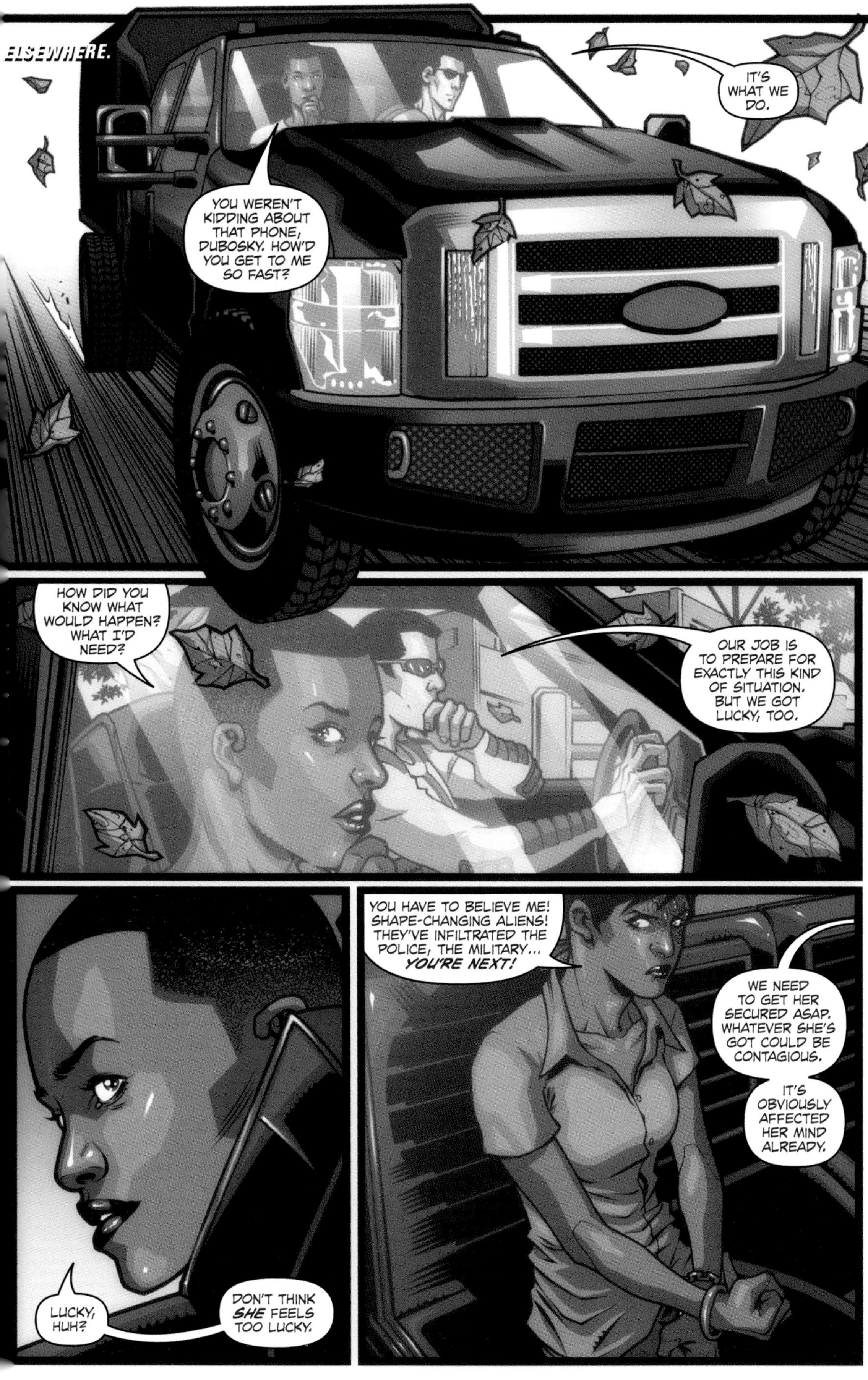

ELSEWHERE.
YOU WEREN'T KIDDING ABOUT THAT PHONE, DUBOSKY. HOW'D YOU GET TO ME SO FAST?
IT'S WHAT WE DO.
HOW DID YOU KNOW WHAT WOULD HAPPEN? WHAT I'D NEED?
OUR JOB IS TO PREPARE FOR EXACTLY THIS KIND OF SITUATION. BUT WE GOT LUCKY, TOO.
LUCKY, HUH?
DON'T THINK SHE FEELS TOO LUCKY.
YOU HAVE TO BELIEVE ME! SHAPE-CHANGING ALIENS! THEY'VE INFILTRATED THE POLICE, THE MILITARY... YOU'RE NEXT!
WE NEED TO GET HER SECURED ASAP. WHATEVER SHE'S GOT COULD BE CONTAGIOUS.
IT'S OBVIOUSLY AFFECTED HER MIND ALREADY.

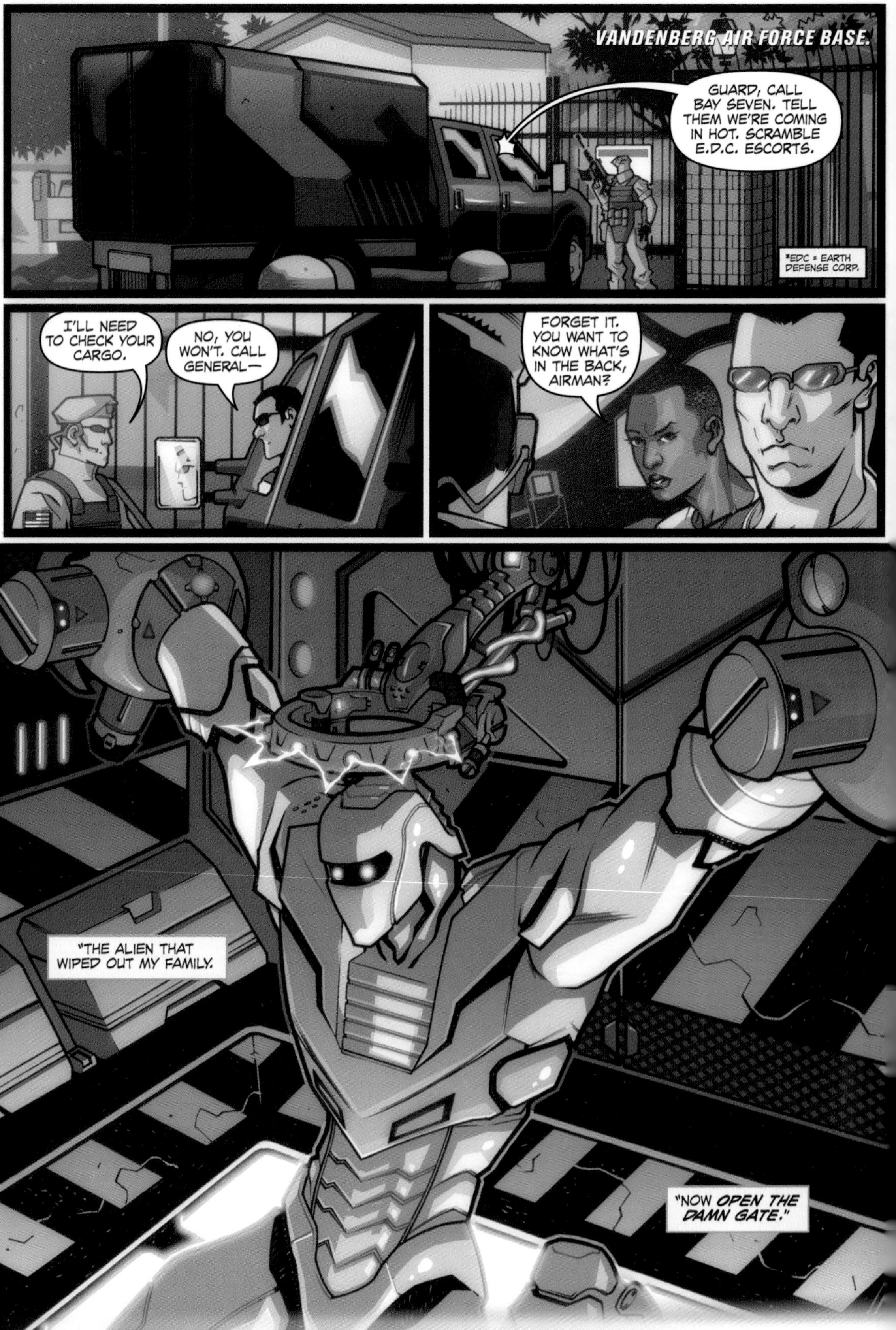

VANDENBERG AIR FORCE BASE.
GUARD, CALL BAY SEVEN. TELL THEM WE'RE COMING IN HOT. SCRAMBLE E.D.C. ESCORTS.
*EDC = EARTH DEFENSE CORP.
I'LL NEED TO CHECK YOUR CARGO.
NO, YOU WON'T. CALL GENERAL—
FORGET IT. YOU WANT TO KNOW WHAT'S IN THE BACK, AIRMAN?
"THE ALIEN THAT WIPED OUT MY FAMILY.
"NOW OPEN THE DAMN GATE."

ART BY **STEVE SCOTT**, COLORS BY **LOVERN KINDZIERSKI**

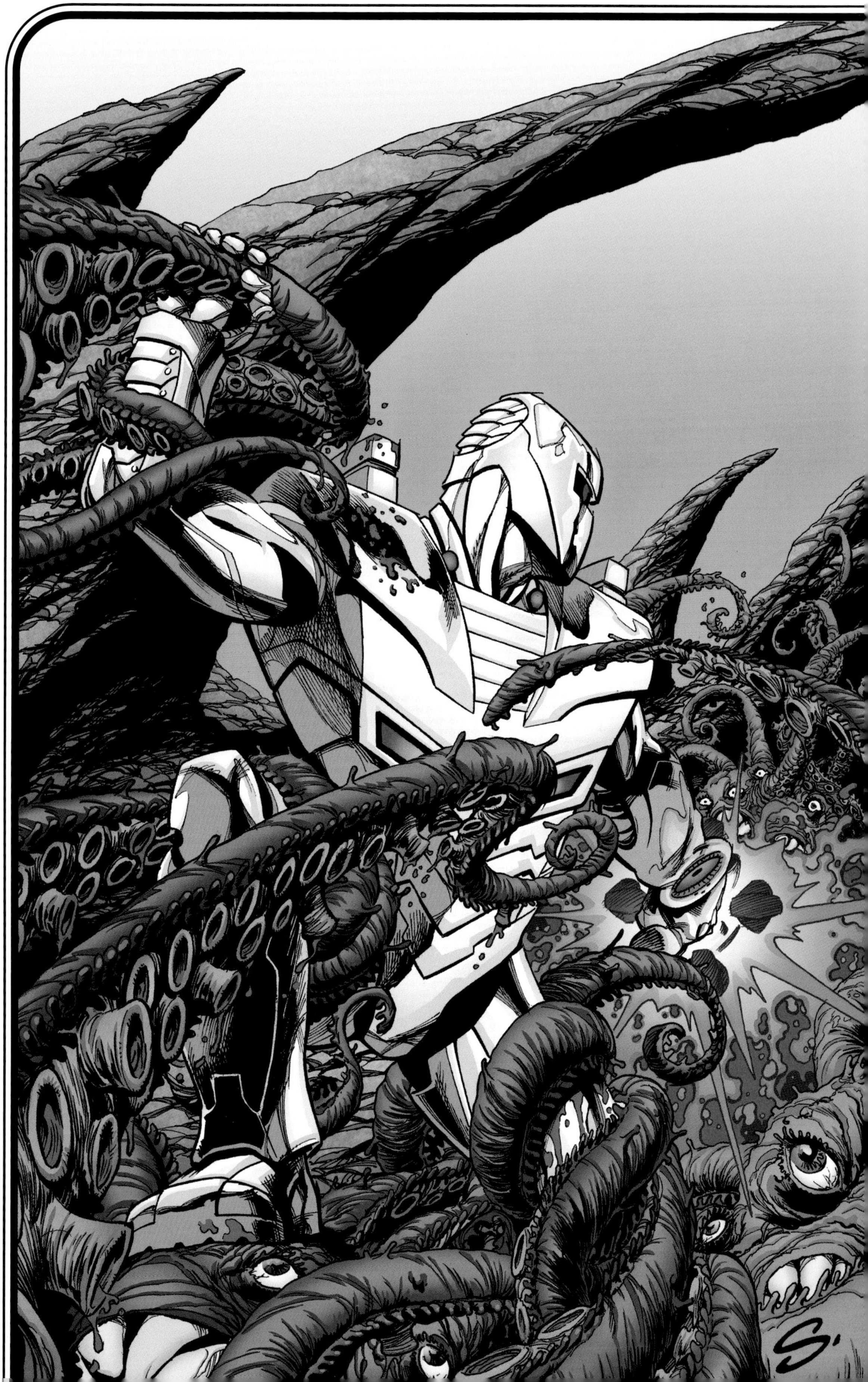

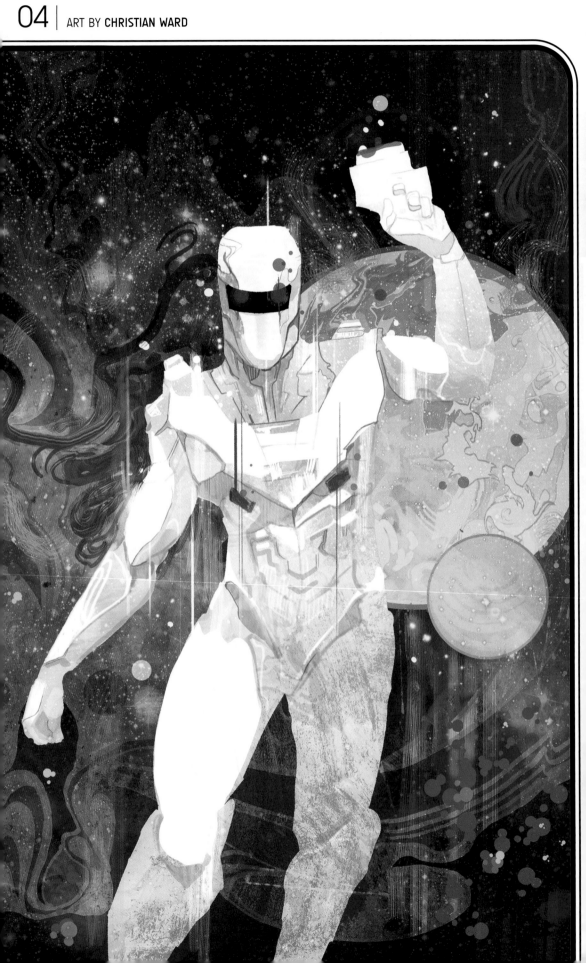

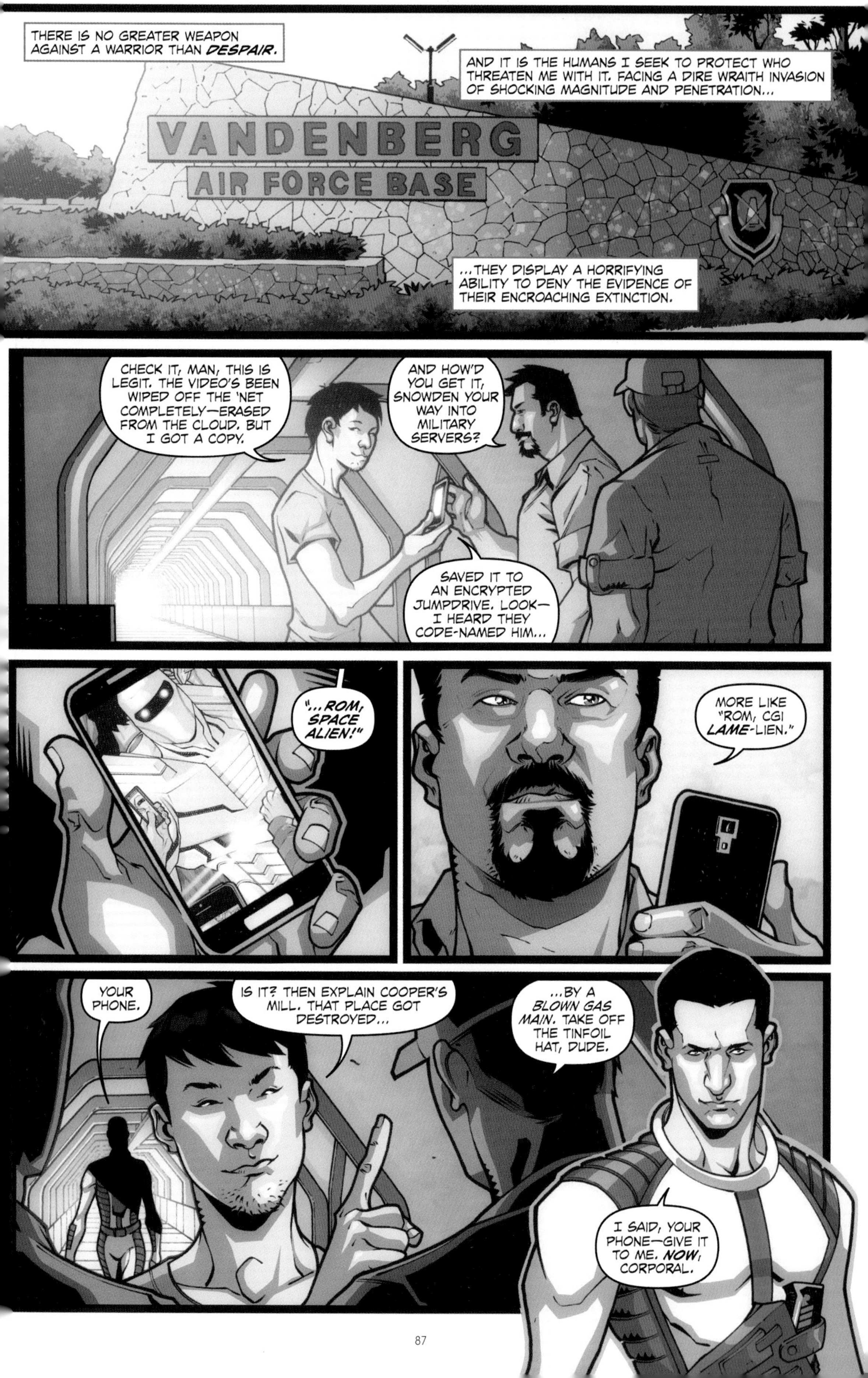
THERE IS NO GREATER WEAPON AGAINST A WARRIOR THAN *DESPAIR*.
AND IT IS THE HUMANS I SEEK TO PROTECT WHO THREATEN ME WITH IT. FACING A DIRE WRAITH INVASION OF SHOCKING MAGNITUDE AND PENETRATION...
VANDENBERG
AIR FORCE BASE
...THEY DISPLAY A HORRIFYING ABILITY TO DENY THE EVIDENCE OF THEIR ENCROACHING EXTINCTION.
CHECK IT, MAN, THIS IS LEGIT. THE VIDEO'S BEEN WIPED OFF THE 'NET COMPLETELY—ERASED FROM THE CLOUD. BUT I GOT A COPY.
AND HOW'D YOU GET IT, SNOWDEN YOUR WAY INTO MILITARY SERVERS?
SAVED IT TO AN ENCRYPTED JUMPDRIVE. LOOK—I HEARD THEY CODE-NAMED HIM...
"...ROM, SPACE ALIEN!"
MORE LIKE "ROM, CGI *LAME*-LIEN."
YOUR PHONE.
IS IT? THEN EXPLAIN COOPER'S MILL. THAT PLACE GOT DESTROYED...
...BY A *BLOWN GAS MAIN*. TAKE OFF THE TINFOIL HAT, DUDE.
I SAID, YOUR PHONE—GIVE IT TO ME. *NOW*, CORPORAL.

DAVID DUBOSKY, E.D.C. I *WON'T* BE RETURNING THIS.

UHH... IS SOMETHING WRONG, SIR?

I NEED THIS DEVICE TO ASCERTAIN THAT. WHAT IS YOUR NAME?

L-LEONARD SONG, SIR.

THIS FOOTAGE, LEONARD SONG—IT'S NOT FOR YOU. NOT FOR ANYONE.

AND YOU TWO—GET LOST.

OKAY, OKAY. JERK.

IT SEEMED *IMPORTANT.* SO I COPIED IT IN A WAY THAT COULDN'T BE WIPED.

HMM. SMART.

DAMN, MAYBE LEN REALLY *IS* THE NEXT SNOWDEN...

WHAT DID YOU HONESTLY MAKE OF THE FOOTAGE?

I THINK IT'S REAL, AND THAT *THING* IS EXTRATERRESTRIAL.

COME WITH ME.

CAME HERE, KILLED AN ENTIRE TOWN AND GOT AWAY WITH IT. YOU ASK ME WHAT I REALLY THINK?

I THINK WE'RE AT WAR.

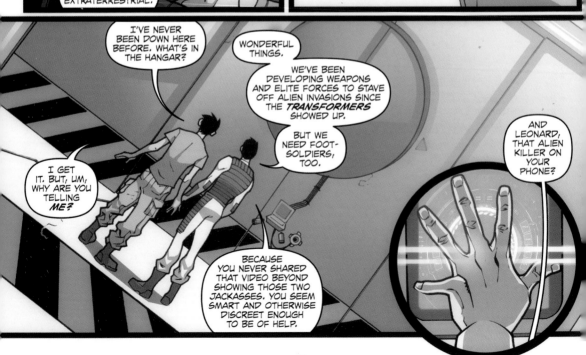

I'VE NEVER BEEN DOWN HERE BEFORE. WHAT'S IN THE HANGAR?

WONDERFUL THINGS.

WE'VE BEEN DEVELOPING WEAPONS AND ELITE FORCES TO STAVE OFF ALIEN INVASIONS SINCE THE *TRANSFORMERS* SHOWED UP.

BUT WE NEED FOOT-SOLDIERS, TOO.

AND LEONARD, THAT ALIEN KILLER ON YOUR PHONE?

I GET IT. BUT, UM, WHY ARE YOU TELLING *ME?*

BECAUSE YOU NEVER SHARED THAT VIDEO BEYOND SHOWING THOSE TWO JACKASSES. YOU SEEM SMART AND OTHERWISE DISCREET ENOUGH TO BE OF HELP.

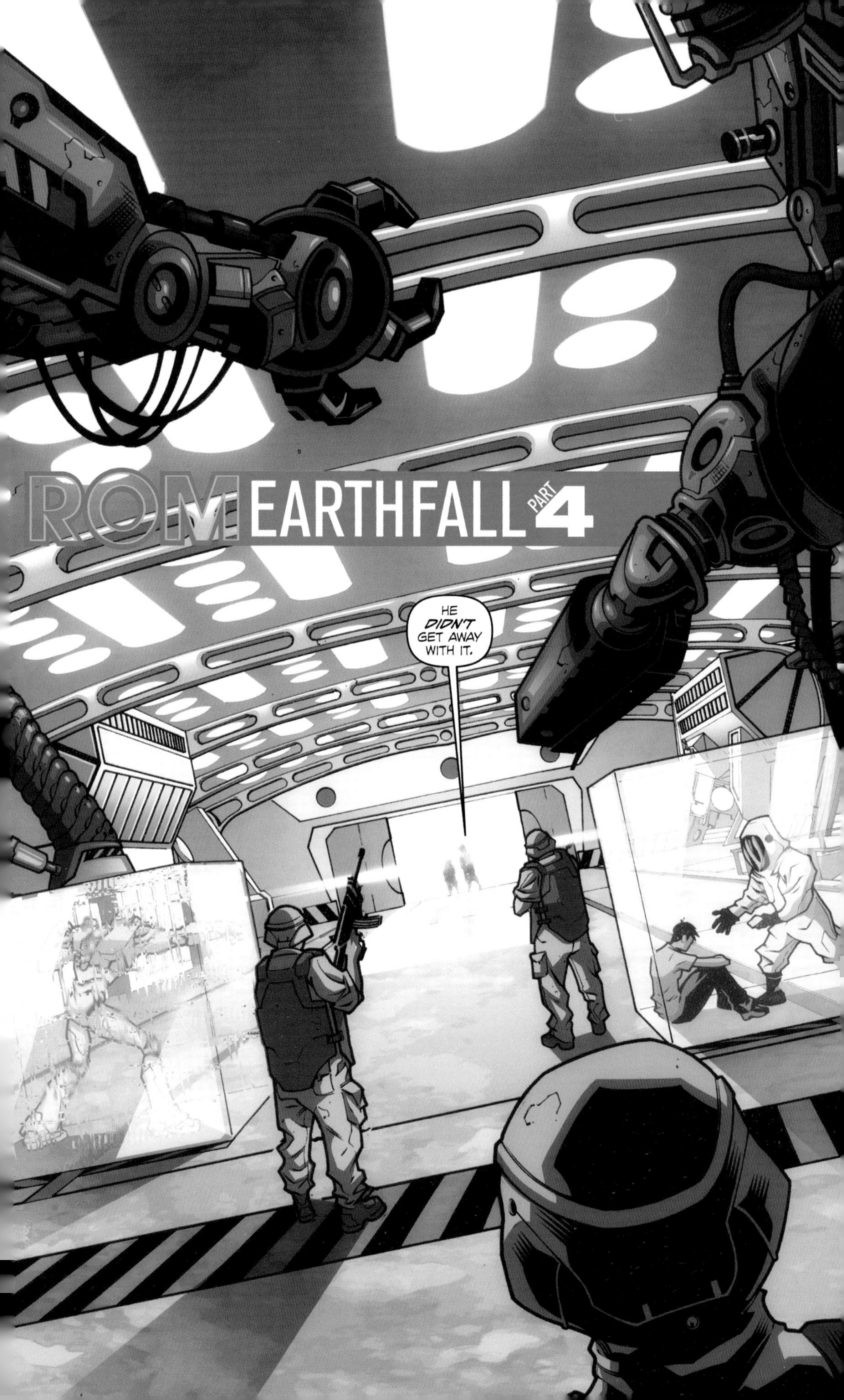
ROM EARTHFALL PART 4
HE DIDN'T GET AWAY WITH IT.

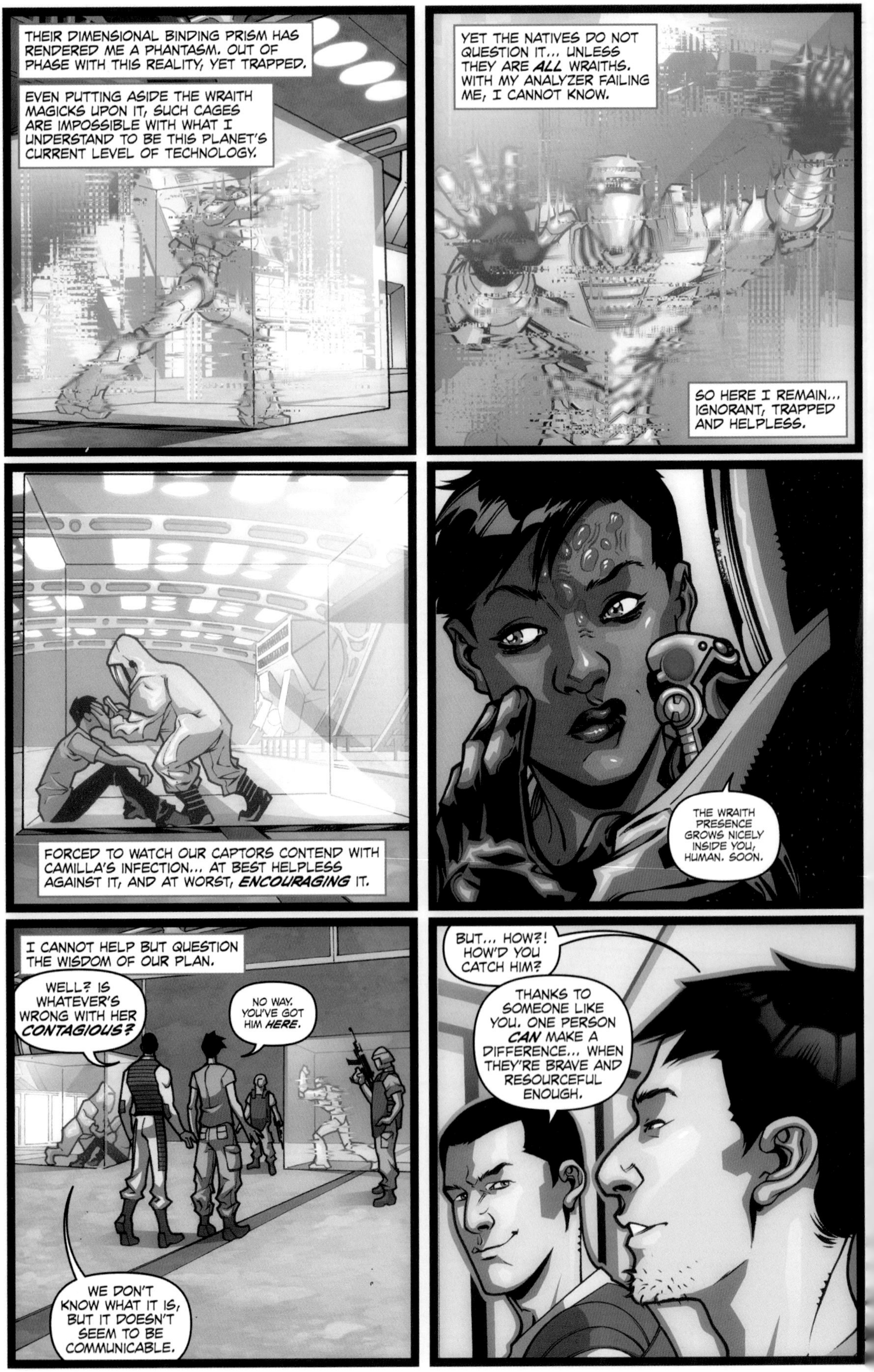
THEIR DIMENSIONAL BINDING PRISM HAS RENDERED ME A PHANTASM. OUT OF PHASE WITH THIS REALITY, YET TRAPPED.
EVEN PUTTING ASIDE THE WRAITH MAGICKS UPON IT, SUCH CAGES ARE IMPOSSIBLE WITH WHAT I UNDERSTAND TO BE THIS PLANET'S CURRENT LEVEL OF TECHNOLOGY.
YET THE NATIVES DO NOT QUESTION IT... UNLESS THEY ARE ALL WRAITHS. WITH MY ANALYZER FAILING ME, I CANNOT KNOW.
SO HERE I REMAIN... IGNORANT, TRAPPED AND HELPLESS.
FORCED TO WATCH OUR CAPTORS CONTEND WITH CAMILLA'S INFECTION... AT BEST HELPLESS AGAINST IT, AND AT WORST, ENCOURAGING IT.
THE WRAITH PRESENCE GROWS NICELY INSIDE YOU, HUMAN. SOON.
I CANNOT HELP BUT QUESTION THE WISDOM OF OUR PLAN.
WELL? IS WHATEVER'S WRONG WITH HER CONTAGIOUS?
NO WAY. YOU'VE GOT HIM HERE.
WE DON'T KNOW WHAT IT IS, BUT IT DOESN'T SEEM TO BE COMMUNICABLE.
BUT... HOW?! HOW'D YOU CATCH HIM?
THANKS TO SOMEONE LIKE YOU. ONE PERSON CAN MAKE A DIFFERENCE... WHEN THEY'RE BRAVE AND RESOURCEFUL ENOUGH.

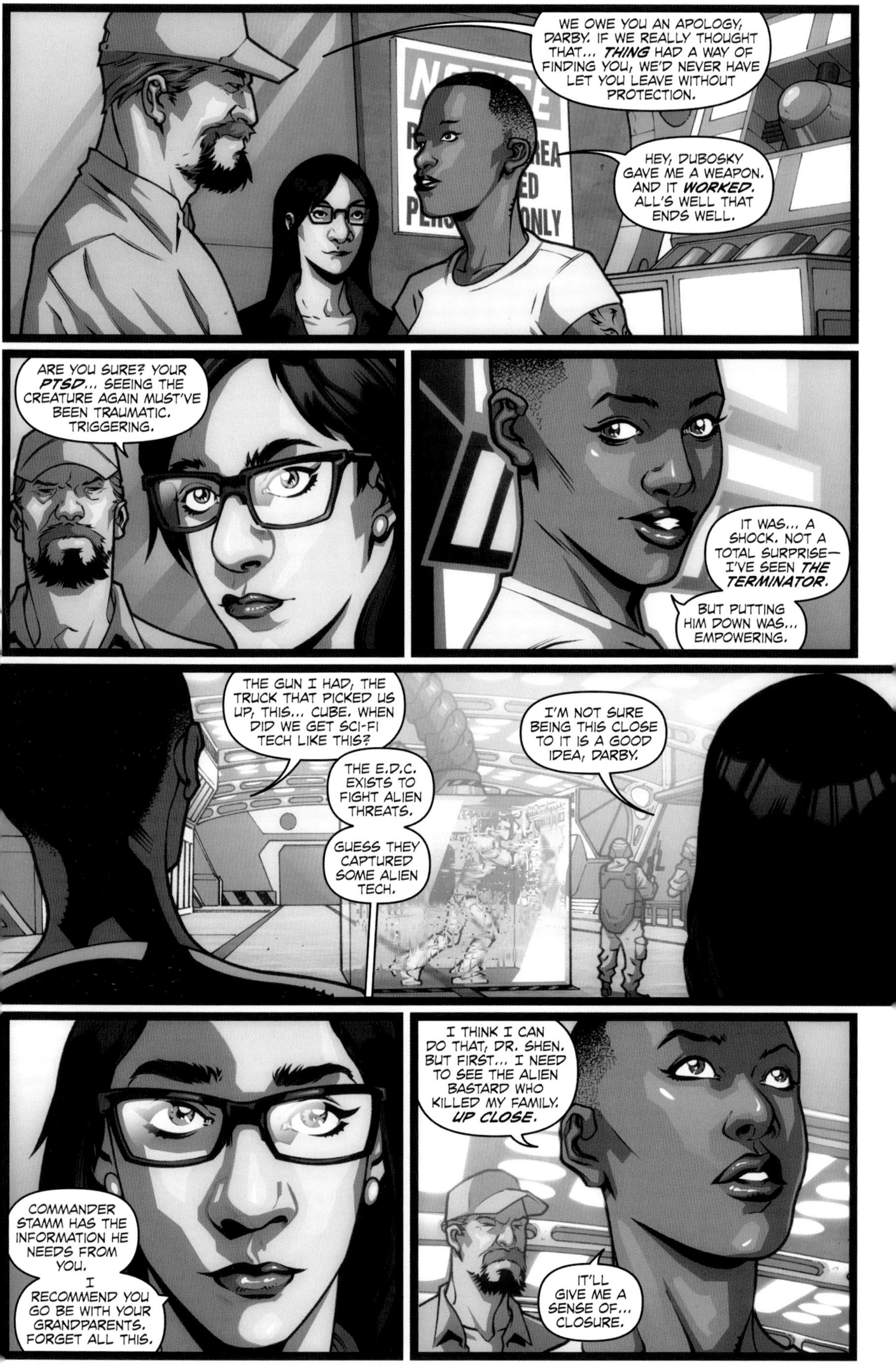

WE OWE YOU AN APOLOGY, DARBY. IF WE REALLY THOUGHT THAT... *THING* HAD A WAY OF FINDING YOU, WE'D NEVER HAVE LET YOU LEAVE WITHOUT PROTECTION.
HEY, DUBOSKY GAVE ME A WEAPON. AND IT *WORKED*. ALL'S WELL THAT ENDS WELL.
ARE YOU SURE? YOUR *PTSD*... SEEING THE CREATURE AGAIN MUST'VE BEEN TRAUMATIC. TRIGGERING.
IT WAS... A SHOCK. NOT A TOTAL SURPRISE— I'VE SEEN *THE TERMINATOR*.
BUT PUTTING HIM DOWN WAS... EMPOWERING.
THE GUN I HAD, THE TRUCK THAT PICKED US UP, THIS... CUBE. WHEN DID WE GET SCI-FI TECH LIKE THIS?
THE E.D.C. EXISTS TO FIGHT ALIEN THREATS.
GUESS THEY CAPTURED SOME ALIEN TECH.
I'M NOT SURE BEING THIS CLOSE TO IT IS A GOOD IDEA, DARBY.
COMMANDER STAMM HAS THE INFORMATION HE NEEDS FROM YOU.
I RECOMMEND YOU GO BE WITH YOUR GRANDPARENTS. FORGET ALL THIS.
I THINK I CAN DO THAT, DR. SHEN. BUT FIRST... I NEED TO SEE THE ALIEN BASTARD WHO KILLED MY FAMILY. *UP CLOSE*.
IT'LL GIVE ME A SENSE OF... CLOSURE.

IF I DON'T LIKE THE WAY THIS IS GOING, I'M PULLING YOU OUT.

AND DON'T EXPECT HIM TO SHOW ANY REMORSE. HE'S NOT EVEN HUMAN.

I'LL BE FINE. I JUST WANT TO LOOK HIM IN THE EYES— OR WHATEVER THOSE ARE—AND TELL HIM HE'S HERE BECAUSE OF *ME*.

THERE'S MY SURE-SHOT NOW.

SO GLAD THAT WEAPON CAME IN HANDY, CORPORAL MASON.

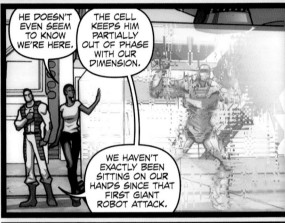

HE DOESN'T EVEN SEEM TO KNOW WE'RE HERE.

THE CELL KEEPS HIM PARTIALLY OUT OF PHASE WITH OUR DIMENSION.

WE HAVEN'T EXACTLY BEEN SITTING ON OUR HANDS SINCE THAT FIRST GIANT ROBOT ATTACK.

GUESS NOT. MY GUN... IT PUT HIM RIGHT DOWN. ALMOST LIKE IT WAS MADE FOR HIM.

SOME KIND OF EMP BLAST, AM I RIGHT?

GOOD EYE. LOCALIZED AND DIRECTED. DISRUPTS ENEMY TECH—OR TECH-BASED ENEMIES—WITHOUT AFFECTING OUR OWN EQUIPMENT.

I'LL BE NEEDING IT BACK NOW THAT HE'S IN CUSTODY. IT'S VERY EXPENSIVE.

WELL... I TRUST YOU'VE GOT THE CLOSURE YOU NEEDED?

SURE. I JUST HAD TO KNOW HE'LL PAY FOR WHAT HE DID TO MY FAMILY... MY TOWN...

...THAT *POOR* WOMAN.

MAKE SURE OF IT.

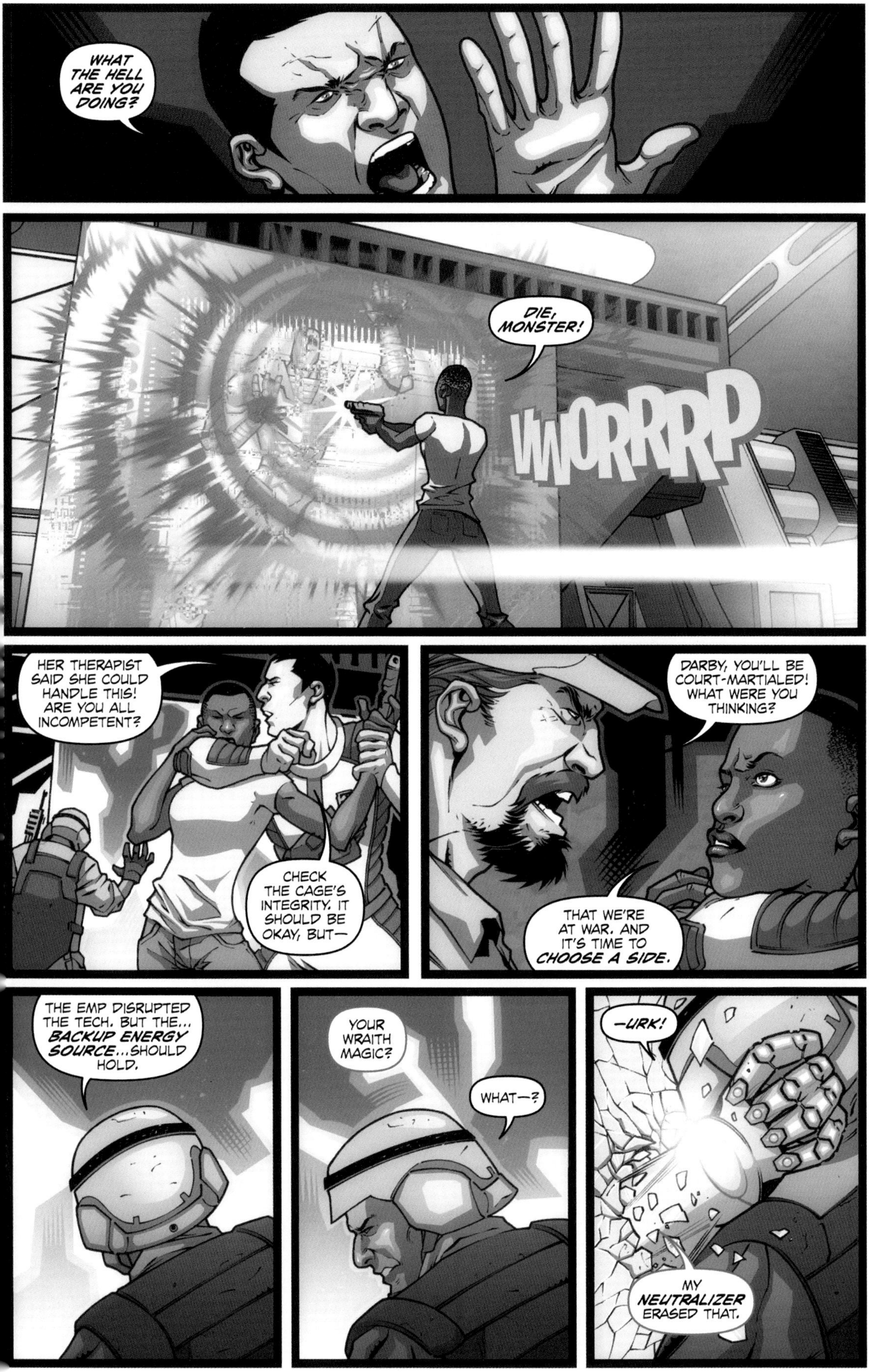
WHAT THE HELL ARE YOU DOING?
DIE, MONSTER!
WWORRRP
HER THERAPIST SAID SHE COULD HANDLE THIS! ARE YOU ALL INCOMPETENT?
CHECK THE CAGE'S INTEGRITY. IT SHOULD BE OKAY, BUT—
DARBY, YOU'LL BE COURT-MARTIALED! WHAT WERE YOU THINKING?
THAT WE'RE AT WAR. AND IT'S TIME TO CHOOSE A SIDE.
THE EMP DISRUPTED THE TECH. BUT THE... BACKUP ENERGY SOURCE...SHOULD HOLD.
YOUR WRAITH MAGIC?
WHAT—?
—URK!
MY NEUTRALIZER ERASED THAT.

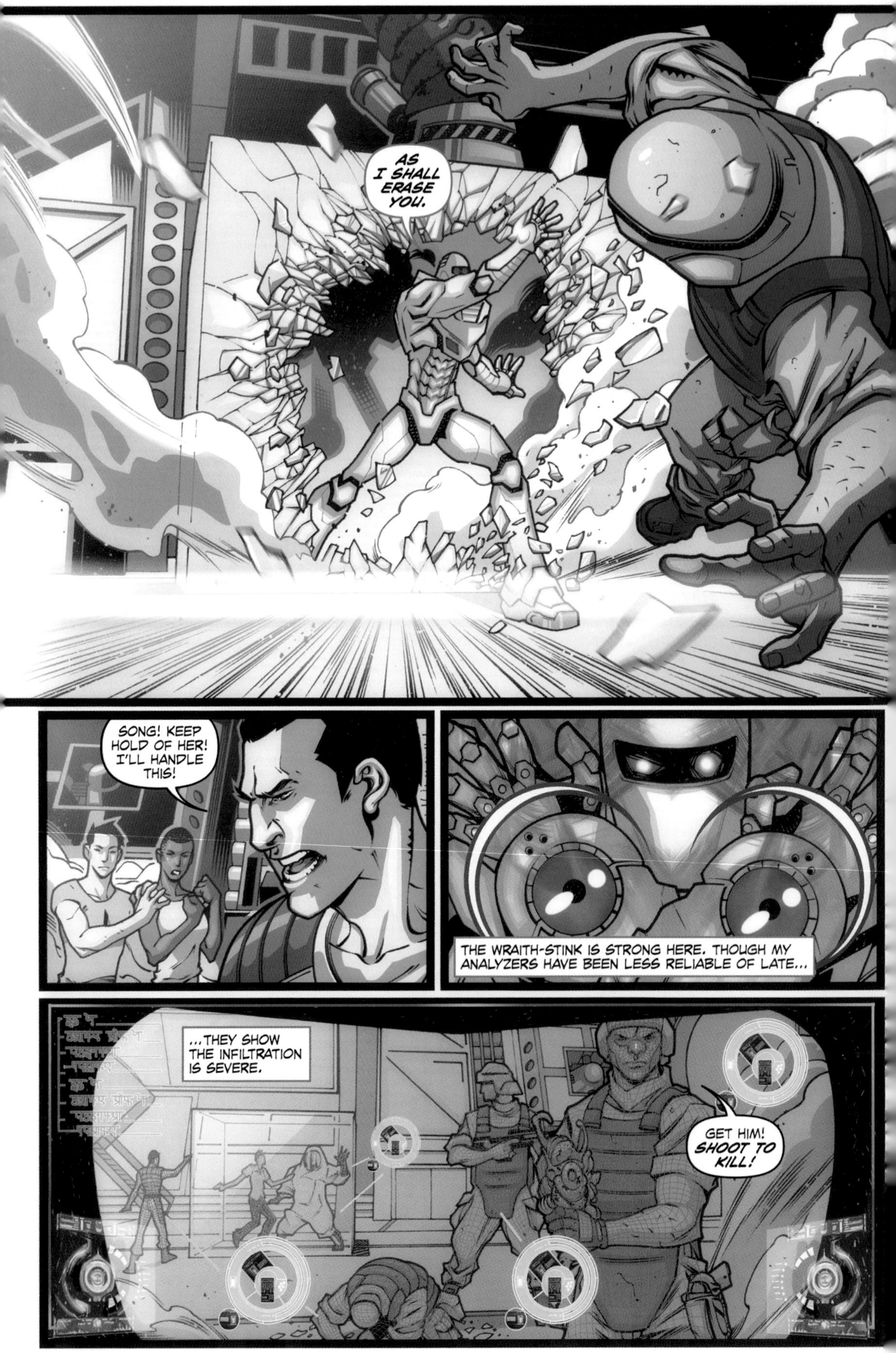
AS I SHALL ERASE YOU.
SONG! KEEP HOLD OF HER! I'LL HANDLE THIS!
THE WRAITH-STINK IS STRONG HERE. THOUGH MY ANALYZERS HAVE BEEN LESS RELIABLE OF LATE...
...THEY SHOW THE INFILTRATION IS SEVERE.
GET HIM! SHOOT TO KILL!

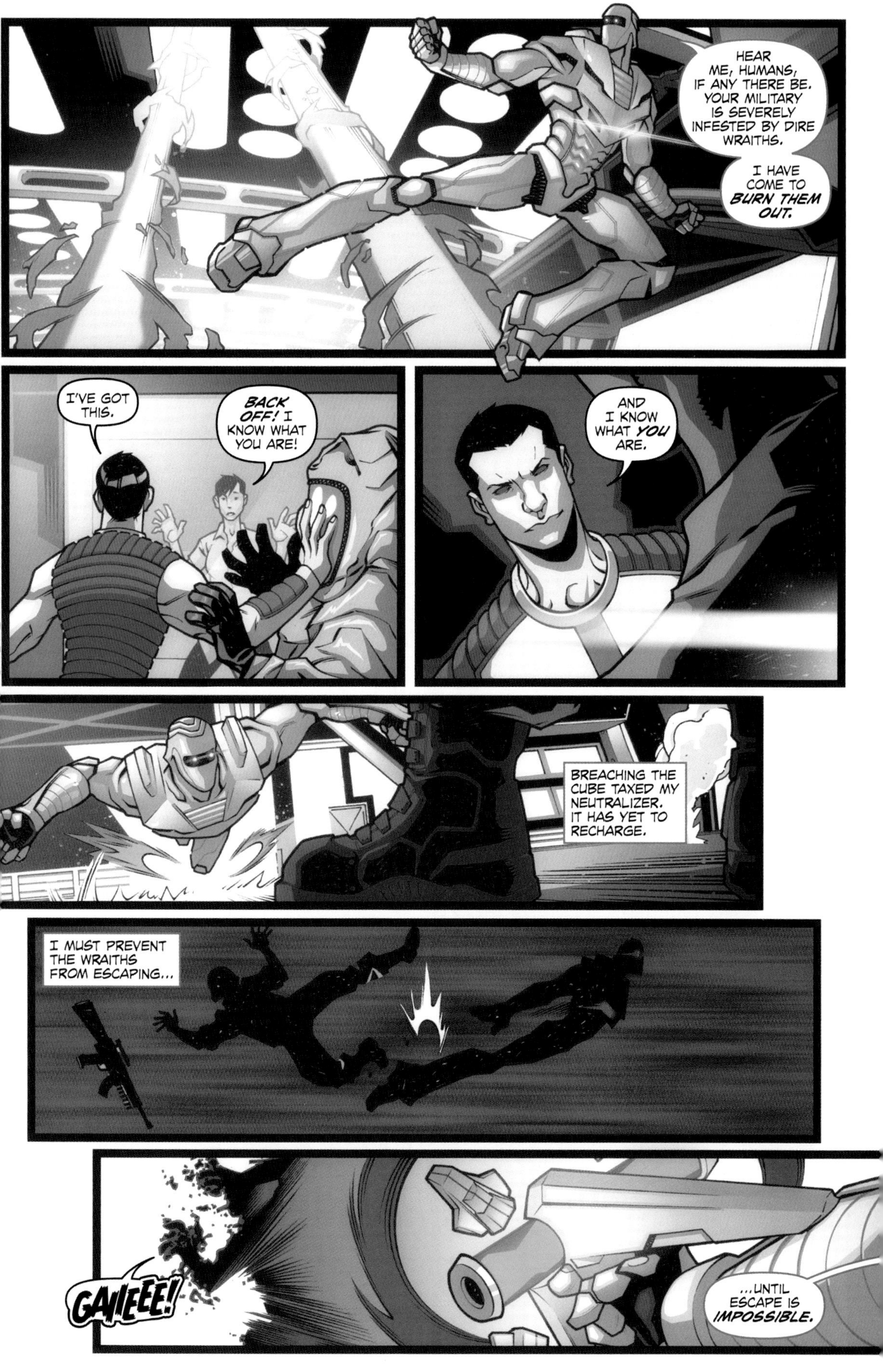
HEAR ME, HUMANS, IF ANY THERE BE. YOUR MILITARY IS SEVERELY INFESTED BY DIRE WRAITHS.
I HAVE COME TO BURN THEM OUT.
I'VE GOT THIS.
BACK OFF! I KNOW WHAT YOU ARE!
AND I KNOW WHAT YOU ARE.
BREACHING THE CUBE TAXED MY NEUTRALIZER. IT HAS YET TO RECHARGE.
I MUST PREVENT THE WRAITHS FROM ESCAPING...
GAIIEEE!
...UNTIL ESCAPE IS IMPOSSIBLE.

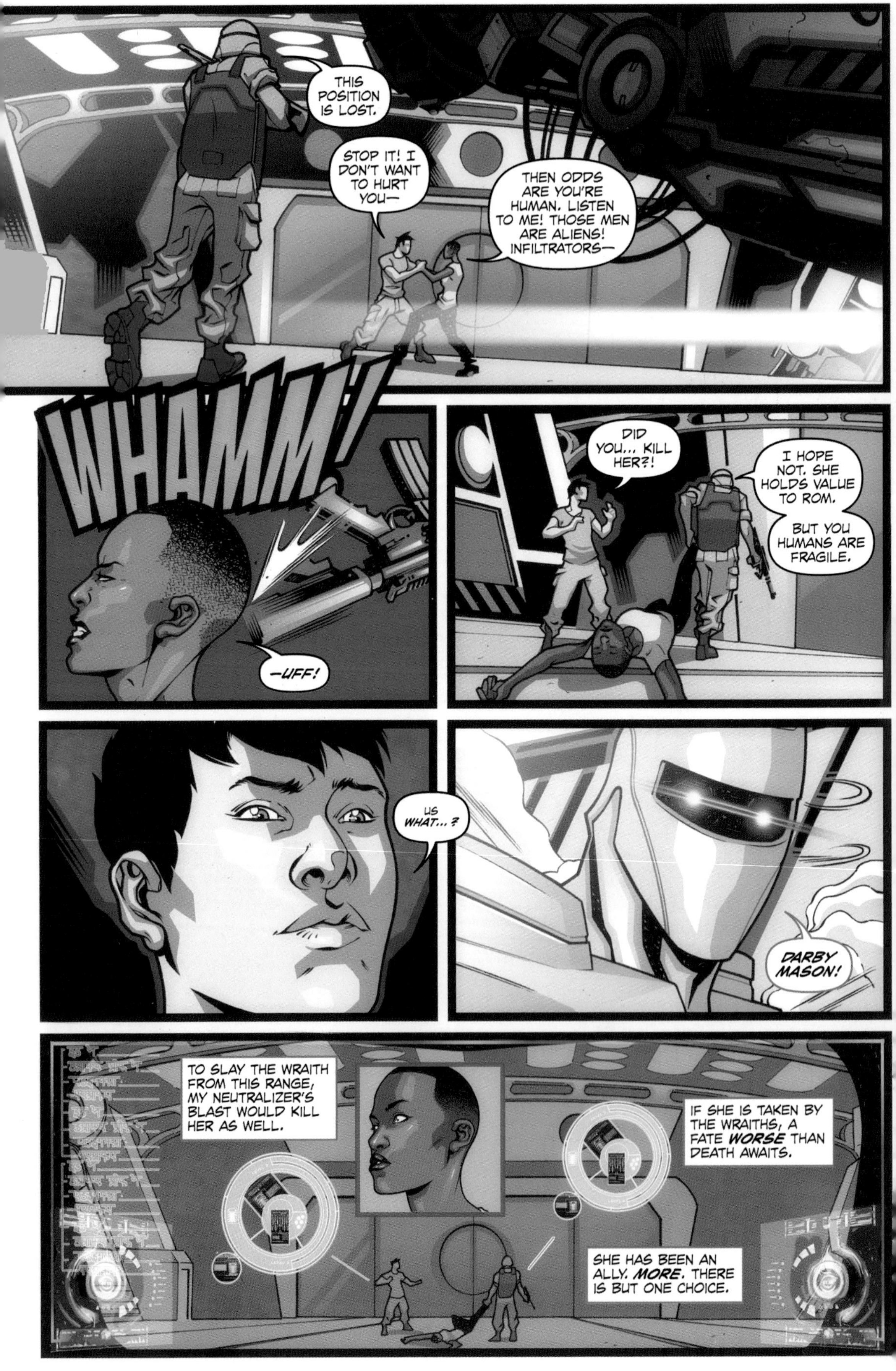

THIS POSITION IS LOST.
STOP IT! I DON'T WANT TO HURT YOU—
THEN ODDS ARE YOU'RE HUMAN. LISTEN TO ME! THOSE MEN ARE ALIENS! INFILTRATORS—
WHAMM!
—UFF!
DID YOU... KILL HER?!
I HOPE NOT. SHE HOLDS VALUE TO ROM.
BUT YOU HUMANS ARE FRAGILE.
US WHAT...?
DARBY MASON!
TO SLAY THE WRAITH FROM THIS RANGE, MY NEUTRALIZER'S BLAST WOULD KILL HER AS WELL.
IF SHE IS TAKEN BY THE WRAITHS, A FATE WORSE THAN DEATH AWAITS.
SHE HAS BEEN AN ALLY. MORE. THERE IS BUT ONE CHOICE.

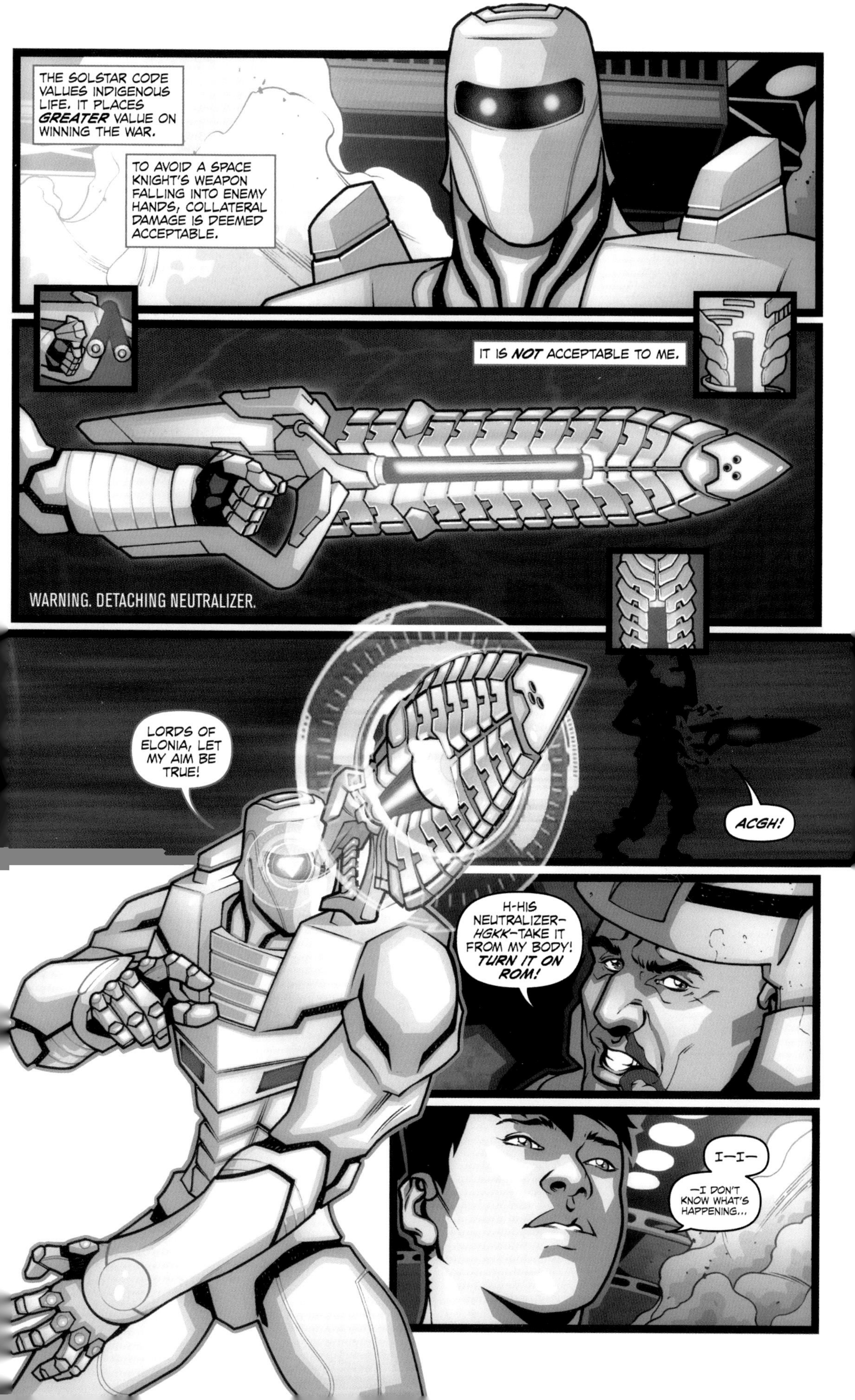
THE SOLSTAR CODE VALUES INDIGENOUS LIFE. IT PLACES GREATER VALUE ON WINNING THE WAR.
TO AVOID A SPACE KNIGHT'S WEAPON FALLING INTO ENEMY HANDS, COLLATERAL DAMAGE IS DEEMED ACCEPTABLE.
IT IS NOT ACCEPTABLE TO ME.
WARNING. DETACHING NEUTRALIZER.
LORDS OF ELONIA, LET MY AIM BE TRUE!
ACGH!
H-HIS NEUTRALIZER—HGKK—TAKE IT FROM MY BODY! TURN IT ON ROM!
I—I—
—I DON'T KNOW WHAT'S HAPPENING...

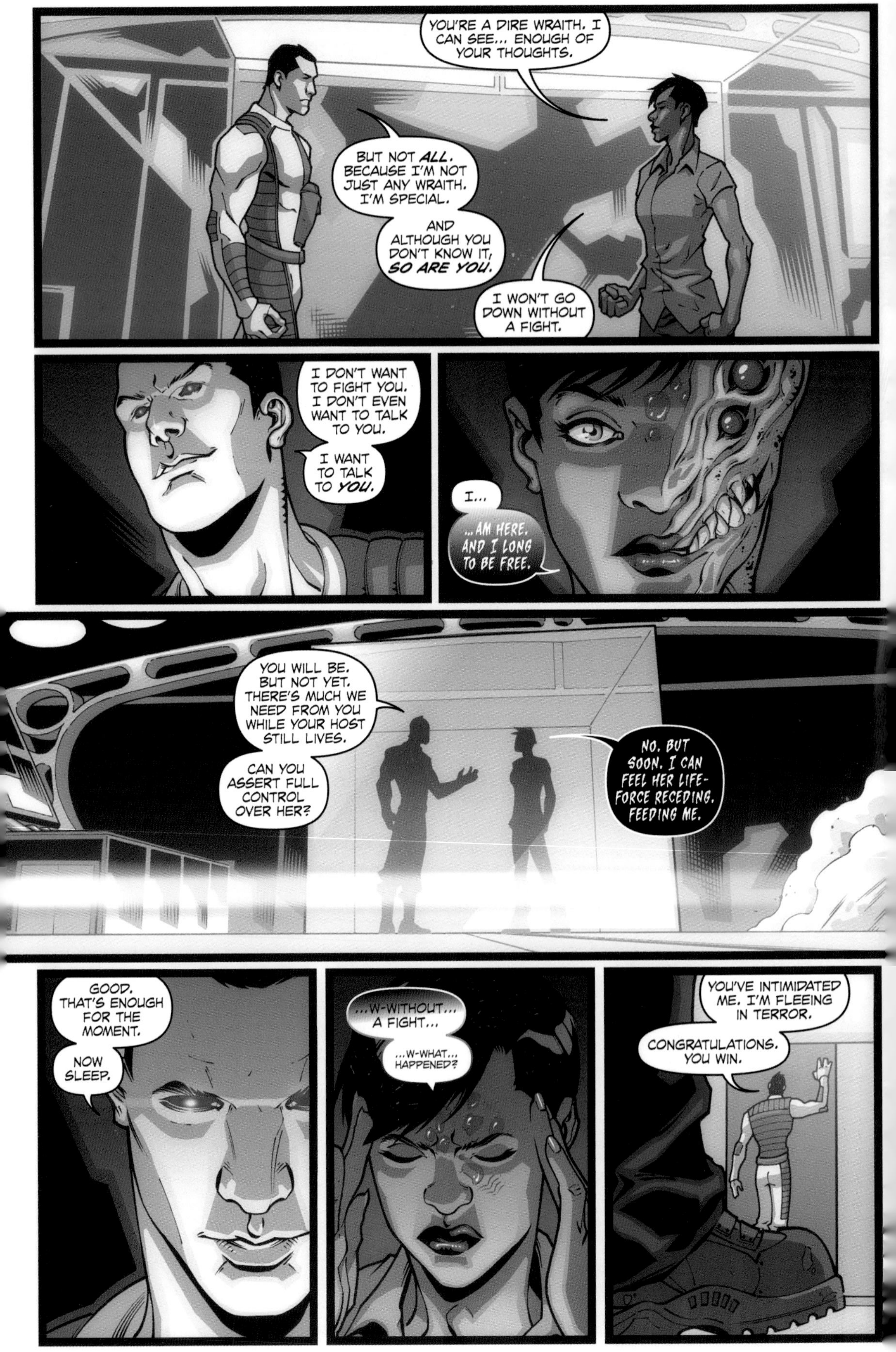
YOU'RE A DIRE WRAITH. I CAN SEE... ENOUGH OF YOUR THOUGHTS.
BUT NOT ALL. BECAUSE I'M NOT JUST ANY WRAITH. I'M SPECIAL.
AND ALTHOUGH YOU DON'T KNOW IT, SO ARE YOU.
I WON'T GO DOWN WITHOUT A FIGHT.
I DON'T WANT TO FIGHT YOU. I DON'T EVEN WANT TO TALK TO YOU.
I WANT TO TALK TO YOU.
I...
...AM HERE. AND I LONG TO BE FREE.
YOU WILL BE. BUT NOT YET. THERE'S MUCH WE NEED FROM YOU WHILE YOUR HOST STILL LIVES.
CAN YOU ASSERT FULL CONTROL OVER HER?
NO. BUT SOON. I CAN FEEL HER LIFE-FORCE RECEDING. FEEDING ME.
GOOD. THAT'S ENOUGH FOR THE MOMENT.
NOW SLEEP.
...W-WITHOUT... A FIGHT...
...W-WHAT... HAPPENED?
YOU'VE INTIMIDATED ME. I'M FLEEING IN TERROR.
CONGRATULATIONS. YOU WIN.

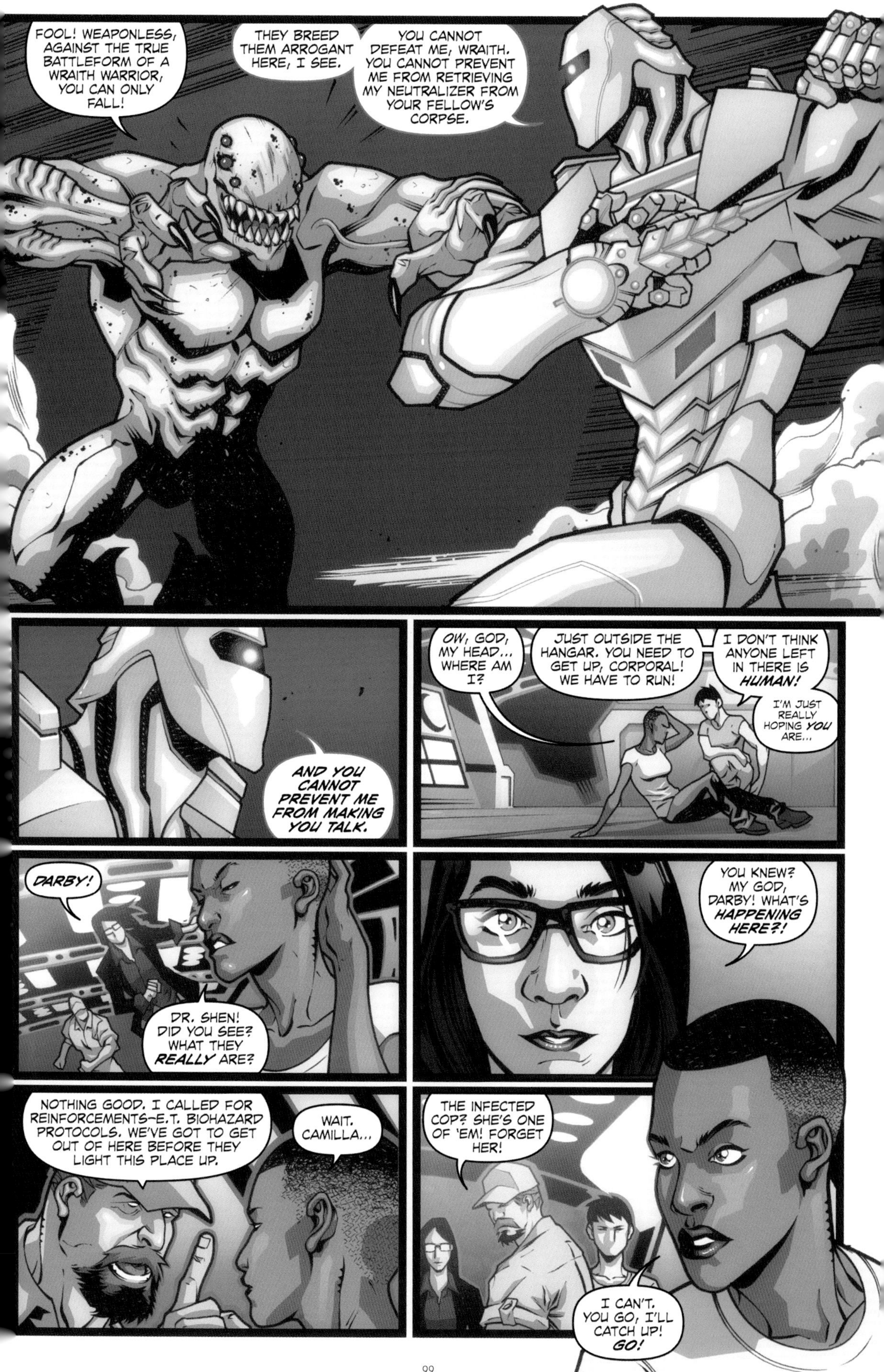

FOOL! WEAPONLESS, AGAINST THE TRUE BATTLEFORM OF A WRAITH WARRIOR, YOU CAN ONLY FALL!
THEY BREED THEM ARROGANT HERE, I SEE.
YOU CANNOT DEFEAT ME, WRAITH. YOU CANNOT PREVENT ME FROM RETRIEVING MY NEUTRALIZER FROM YOUR FELLOW'S CORPSE.
AND YOU CANNOT PREVENT ME FROM MAKING YOU TALK.
OW, GOD, MY HEAD... WHERE AM I?
JUST OUTSIDE THE HANGAR. YOU NEED TO GET UP, CORPORAL! WE HAVE TO RUN!
I DON'T THINK ANYONE LEFT IN THERE IS HUMAN!
I'M JUST REALLY HOPING YOU ARE...
DARBY!
DR. SHEN! DID YOU SEE? WHAT THEY REALLY ARE?
YOU KNEW? MY GOD, DARBY! WHAT'S HAPPENING HERE?!
NOTHING GOOD. I CALLED FOR REINFORCEMENTS--E.T. BIOHAZARD PROTOCOLS. WE'VE GOT TO GET OUT OF HERE BEFORE THEY LIGHT THIS PLACE UP.
WAIT. CAMILLA...
THE INFECTED COP? SHE'S ONE OF 'EM! FORGET HER!
I CAN'T. YOU GO, I'LL CATCH UP! GO!

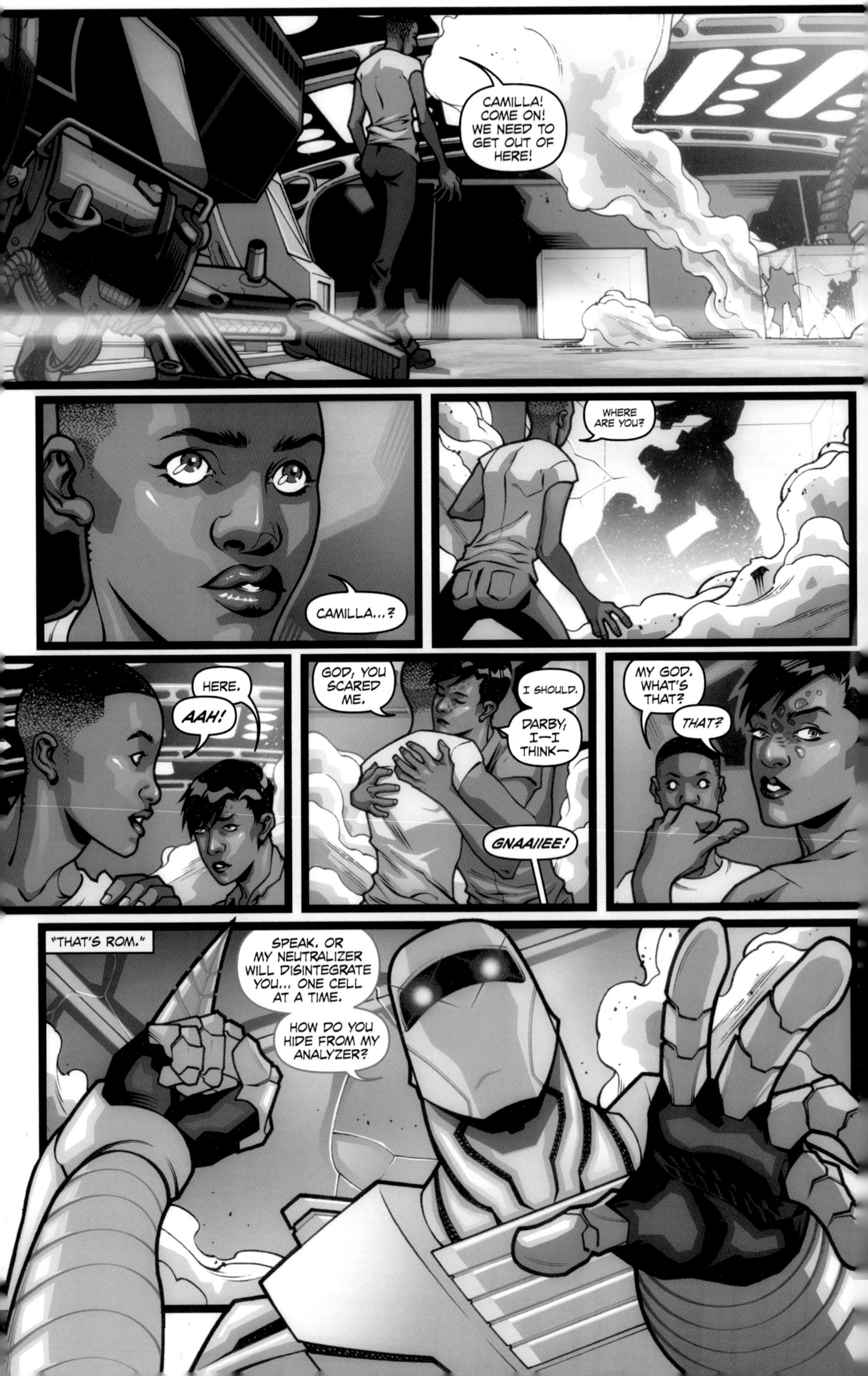
CAMILLA! COME ON! WE NEED TO GET OUT OF HERE!
CAMILLA...?
WHERE ARE YOU?
HERE.
AAH!
GOD, YOU SCARED ME.
I SHOULD.
DARBY, I—I THINK—
GNAAIIEE!
MY GOD. WHAT'S THAT?
THAT?
"THAT'S ROM."
SPEAK. OR MY NEUTRALIZER WILL DISINTEGRATE YOU... ONE CELL AT A TIME.
HOW DO YOU HIDE FROM MY ANALYZER?

AAH! MERCY! I KNOW NOTHING, I'M JUST A SOLDIER!
ONE PLACED AMONG THE HUMANS' SOLDIERS. YOU KNOW SOMETHING. AND YOU WILL TELL IT TO ME.
I HAVE BEEN KILLING WRAITHS FOR TWO HUNDRED YEARS. IMAGINE HOW LONG I CAN MAKE YOU SUFFER.
CLOAKING TECHNOLOGY. PROVEN EVEN AGAINST YOUR ANALYZER!
IT'S RARE, BUT OUR LEADERS SEEK TO MAKE MORE!
HOW? WHERE IS IT FROM?
THAT'S ALL I KNOW! I SWEAR TO YOU!
WRAITH LIES. BUT WE WILL SEE—
ROM!
STOP IT!
YOU'RE BETTER THAN THIS!
ONCE, PERHAPS. BUT IT HAS BEEN A LONG WAR. AND I HAVE SEEN THE COST OF LOSING.
I DO AS I MUST, DARBY MASON.

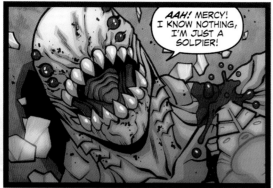

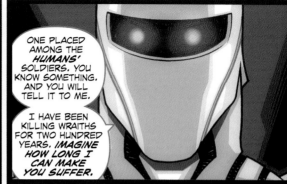

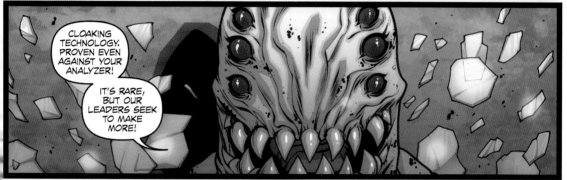

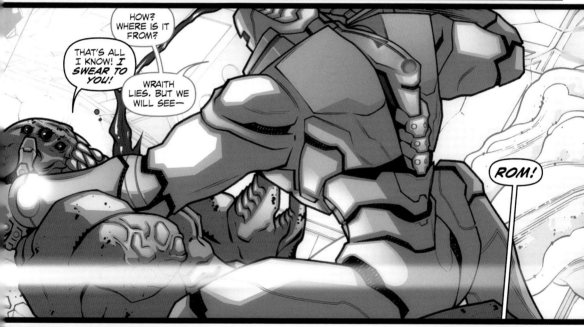

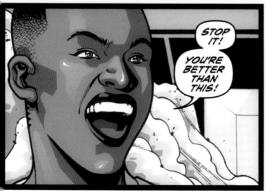

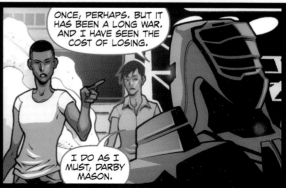

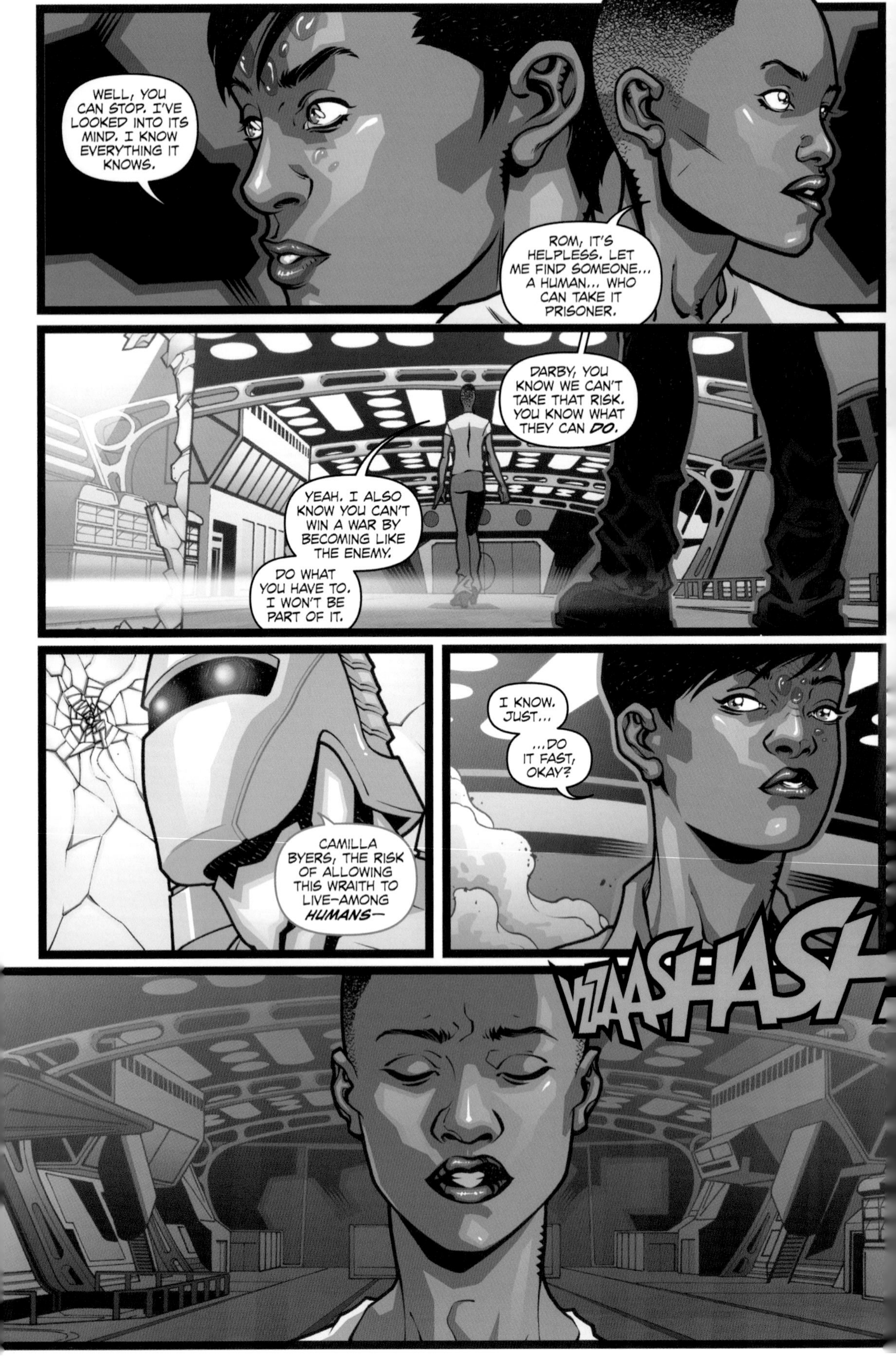

WELL, YOU CAN STOP. I'VE LOOKED INTO ITS MIND. I KNOW EVERYTHING IT KNOWS.
ROM, IT'S HELPLESS. LET ME FIND SOMEONE... A HUMAN... WHO CAN TAKE IT PRISONER.
DARBY, YOU KNOW WE CAN'T TAKE THAT RISK. YOU KNOW WHAT THEY CAN DO.
YEAH. I ALSO KNOW YOU CAN'T WIN A WAR BY BECOMING LIKE THE ENEMY.
DO WHAT YOU HAVE TO. I WON'T BE PART OF IT.
CAMILLA BYERS, THE RISK OF ALLOWING THIS WRAITH TO LIVE–AMONG HUMANS—
I KNOW. JUST...
...DO IT FAST, OKAY?
VZAASHASH

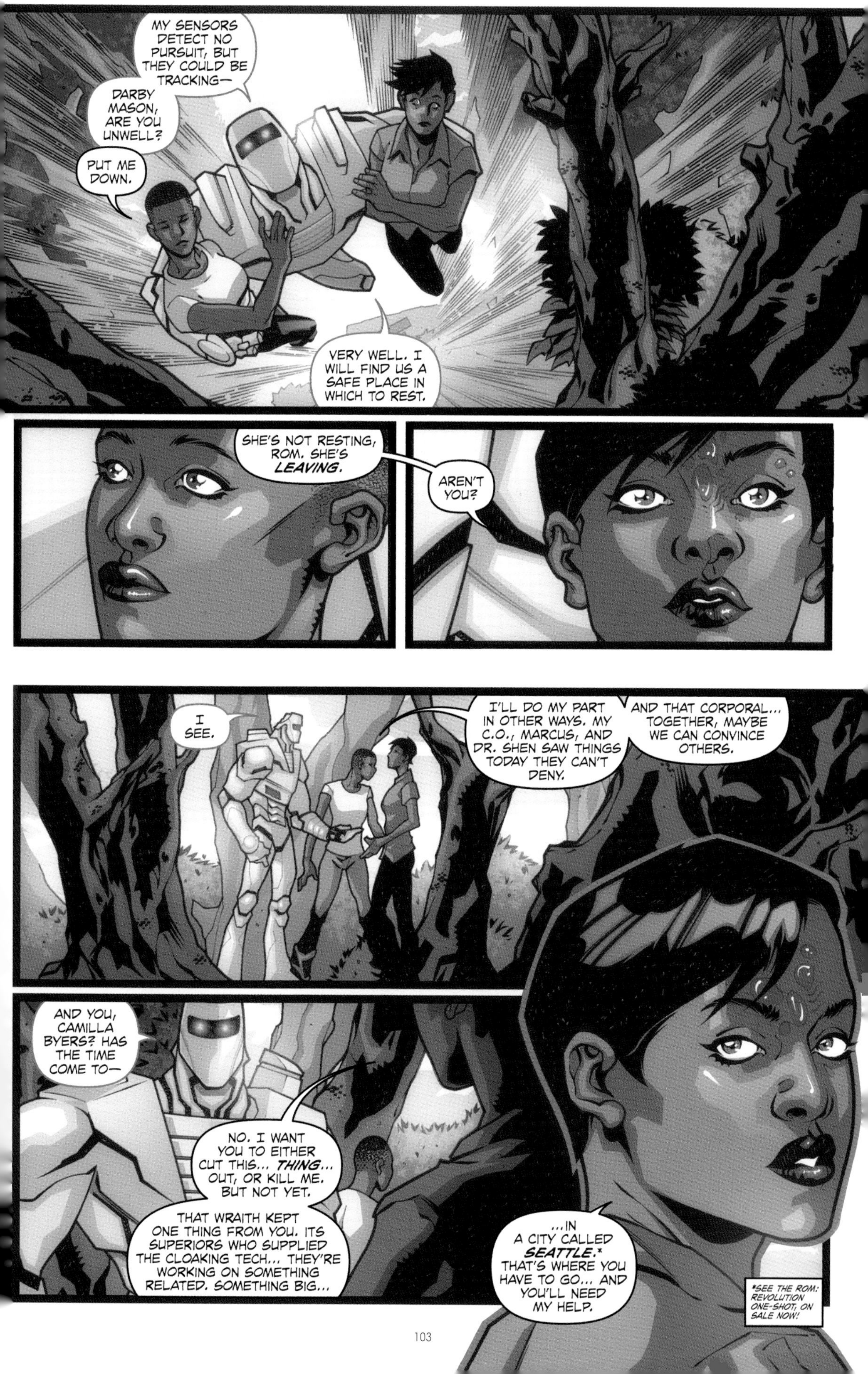
MY SENSORS DETECT NO PURSUIT, BUT THEY COULD BE TRACKING—
DARBY MASON, ARE YOU UNWELL?
PUT ME DOWN.
VERY WELL. I WILL FIND US A SAFE PLACE IN WHICH TO REST.
SHE'S NOT RESTING, ROM. SHE'S LEAVING.
AREN'T YOU?
I SEE.
I'LL DO MY PART IN OTHER WAYS. MY C.O., MARCUS, AND DR. SHEN SAW THINGS TODAY THEY CAN'T DENY.
AND THAT CORPORAL... TOGETHER, MAYBE WE CAN CONVINCE OTHERS.
AND YOU, CAMILLA BYERS? HAS THE TIME COME TO—
NO. I WANT YOU TO EITHER CUT THIS... THING... OUT, OR KILL ME. BUT NOT YET.
THAT WRAITH KEPT ONE THING FROM YOU. ITS SUPERIORS WHO SUPPLIED THE CLOAKING TECH... THEY'RE WORKING ON SOMETHING RELATED. SOMETHING BIG...
...IN A CITY CALLED SEATTLE.* THAT'S WHERE YOU HAVE TO GO... AND YOU'LL NEED MY HELP.
*SEE THE ROM: REVOLUTION ONE-SHOT, ON SALE NOW!

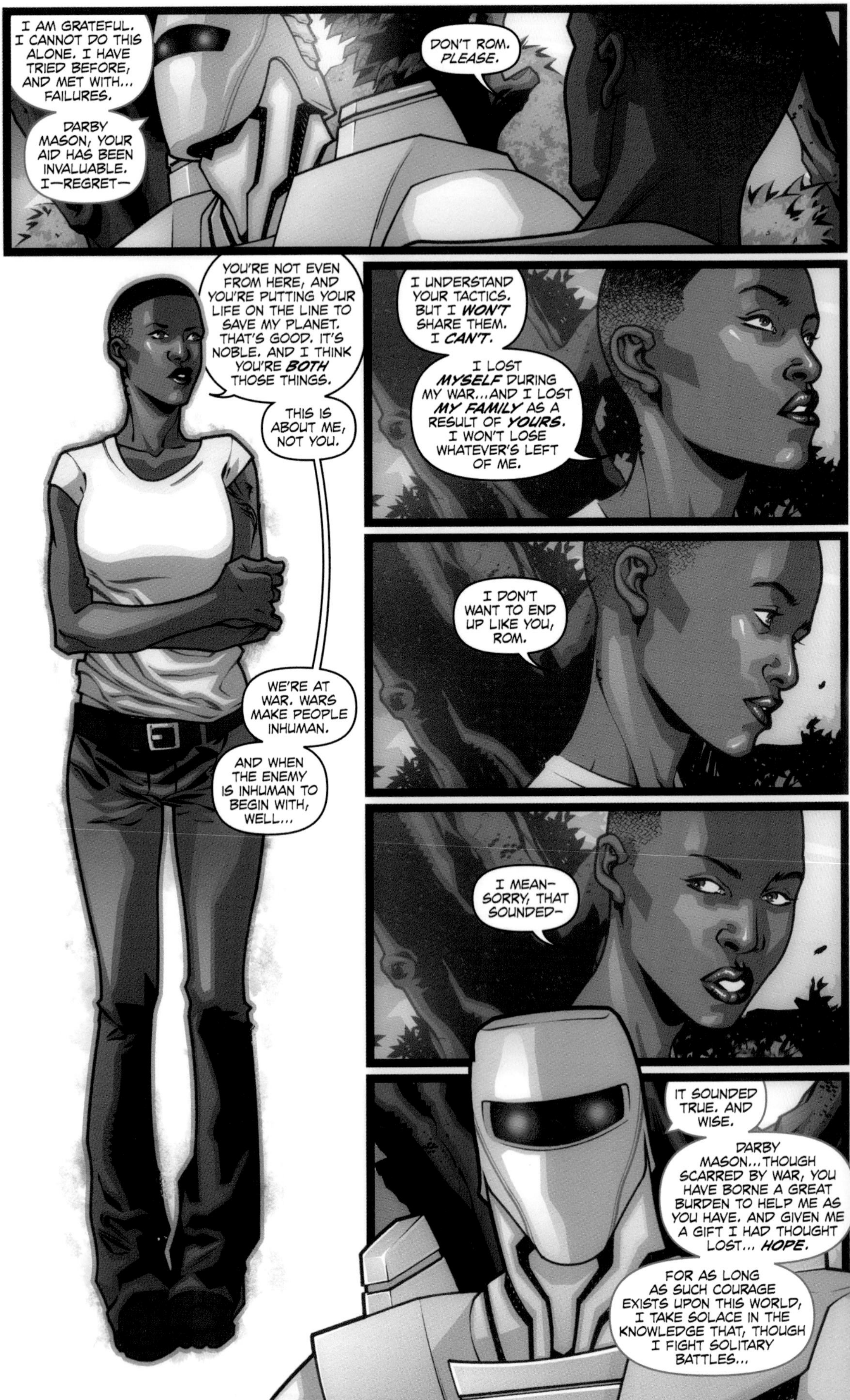
I AM GRATEFUL. I CANNOT DO THIS ALONE. I HAVE TRIED BEFORE, AND MET WITH... FAILURES.
DARBY MASON, YOUR AID HAS BEEN INVALUABLE. I—REGRET—
DON'T ROM. PLEASE.
YOU'RE NOT EVEN FROM HERE, AND YOU'RE PUTTING YOUR LIFE ON THE LINE TO SAVE MY PLANET. THAT'S GOOD. IT'S NOBLE. AND I THINK YOU'RE BOTH THOSE THINGS.
THIS IS ABOUT ME, NOT YOU.
WE'RE AT WAR. WARS MAKE PEOPLE INHUMAN.
AND WHEN THE ENEMY IS INHUMAN TO BEGIN WITH, WELL...
I UNDERSTAND YOUR TACTICS. BUT I WON'T SHARE THEM. I CAN'T.
I LOST MYSELF DURING MY WAR...AND I LOST MY FAMILY AS A RESULT OF YOURS. I WON'T LOSE WHATEVER'S LEFT OF ME.
I DON'T WANT TO END UP LIKE YOU, ROM.
I MEAN- SORRY, THAT SOUNDED-
IT SOUNDED TRUE. AND WISE.
DARBY MASON...THOUGH SCARRED BY WAR, YOU HAVE BORNE A GREAT BURDEN TO HELP ME AS YOU HAVE. AND GIVEN ME A GIFT I HAD THOUGHT LOST... HOPE.
FOR AS LONG AS SUCH COURAGE EXISTS UPON THIS WORLD, I TAKE SOLACE IN THE KNOWLEDGE THAT, THOUGH I FIGHT SOLITARY BATTLES...

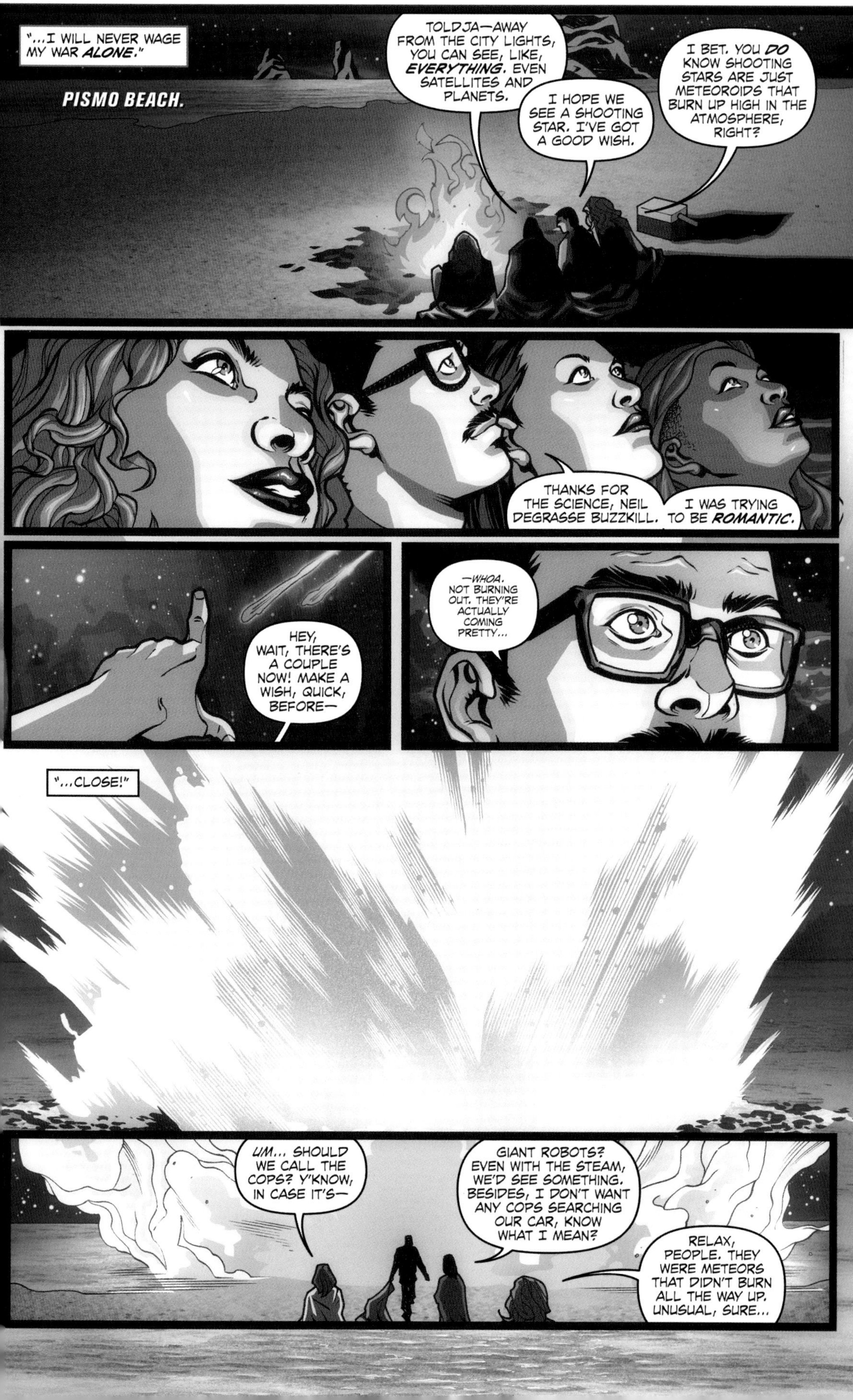
"...I WILL NEVER WAGE MY WAR *ALONE*."
PISMO BEACH.
TOLDJA—AWAY FROM THE CITY LIGHTS, YOU CAN SEE, LIKE, *EVERYTHING*. EVEN SATELLITES AND PLANETS.
I HOPE WE SEE A SHOOTING STAR. I'VE GOT A GOOD WISH.
I BET. YOU *DO* KNOW SHOOTING STARS ARE JUST METEOROIDS THAT BURN UP HIGH IN THE ATMOSPHERE, RIGHT?
THANKS FOR THE SCIENCE, NEIL DEGRASSE BUZZKILL.
I WAS TRYING TO BE *ROMANTIC*.
HEY, WAIT, THERE'S A COUPLE NOW! MAKE A WISH, QUICK, BEFORE—
—WHOA. NOT BURNING OUT. THEY'RE ACTUALLY COMING PRETTY...
"...CLOSE!"
UM... SHOULD WE CALL THE COPS? Y'KNOW, IN CASE IT'S—
GIANT ROBOTS? EVEN WITH THE STEAM, WE'D SEE SOMETHING. BESIDES, I DON'T WANT ANY COPS SEARCHING OUR CAR, KNOW WHAT I MEAN?
RELAX, PEOPLE. THEY WERE METEORS THAT DIDN'T BURN ALL THE WAY UP. UNUSUAL, SURE...

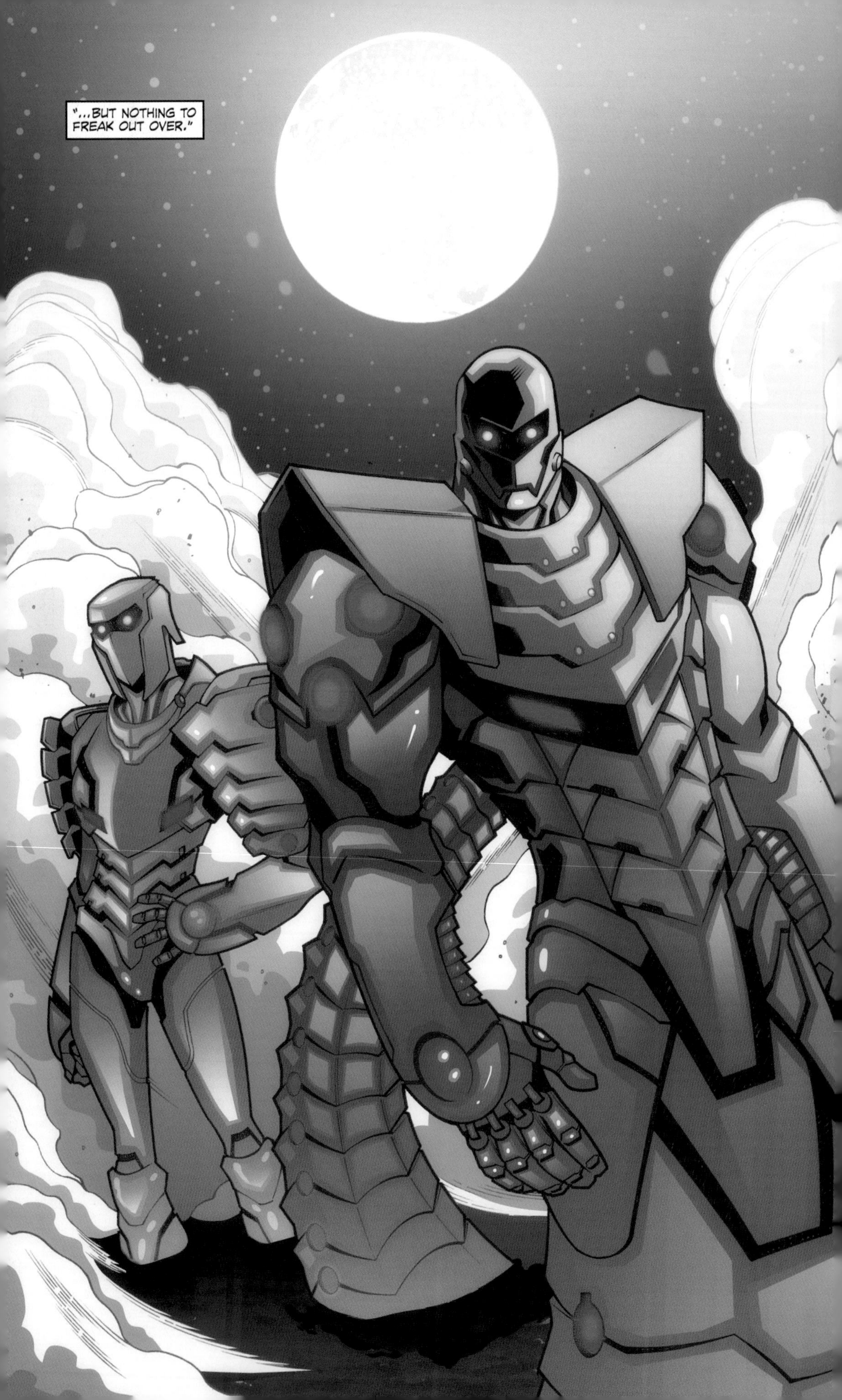
"...BUT NOTHING TO FREAK OUT OVER."

ART BY **AL MILGROM**, COLORS BY **LOVERN KINDZIERSKI**

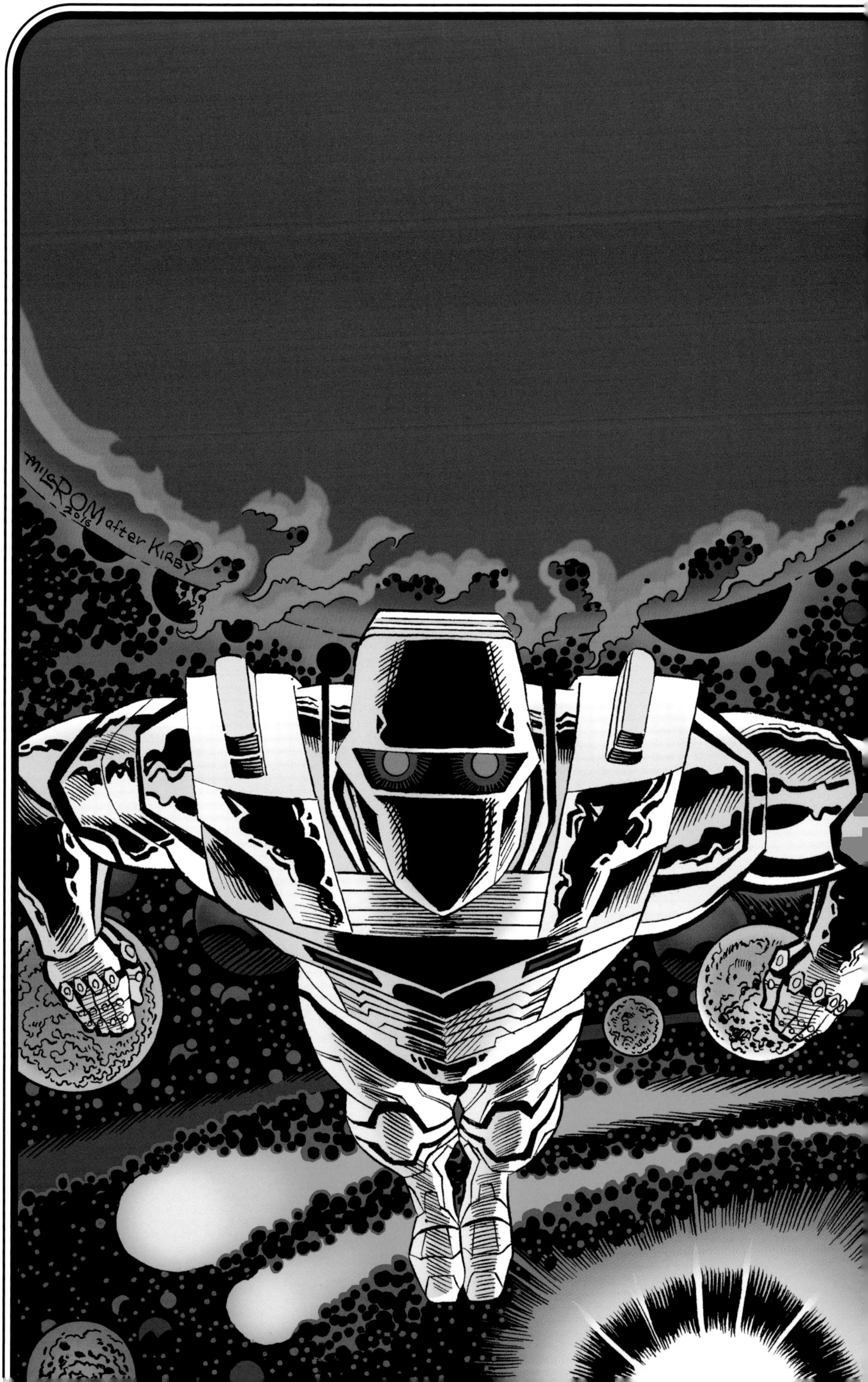
MILGROM 2016 after KIRBY

ART BY **ASHLEY WOOD**

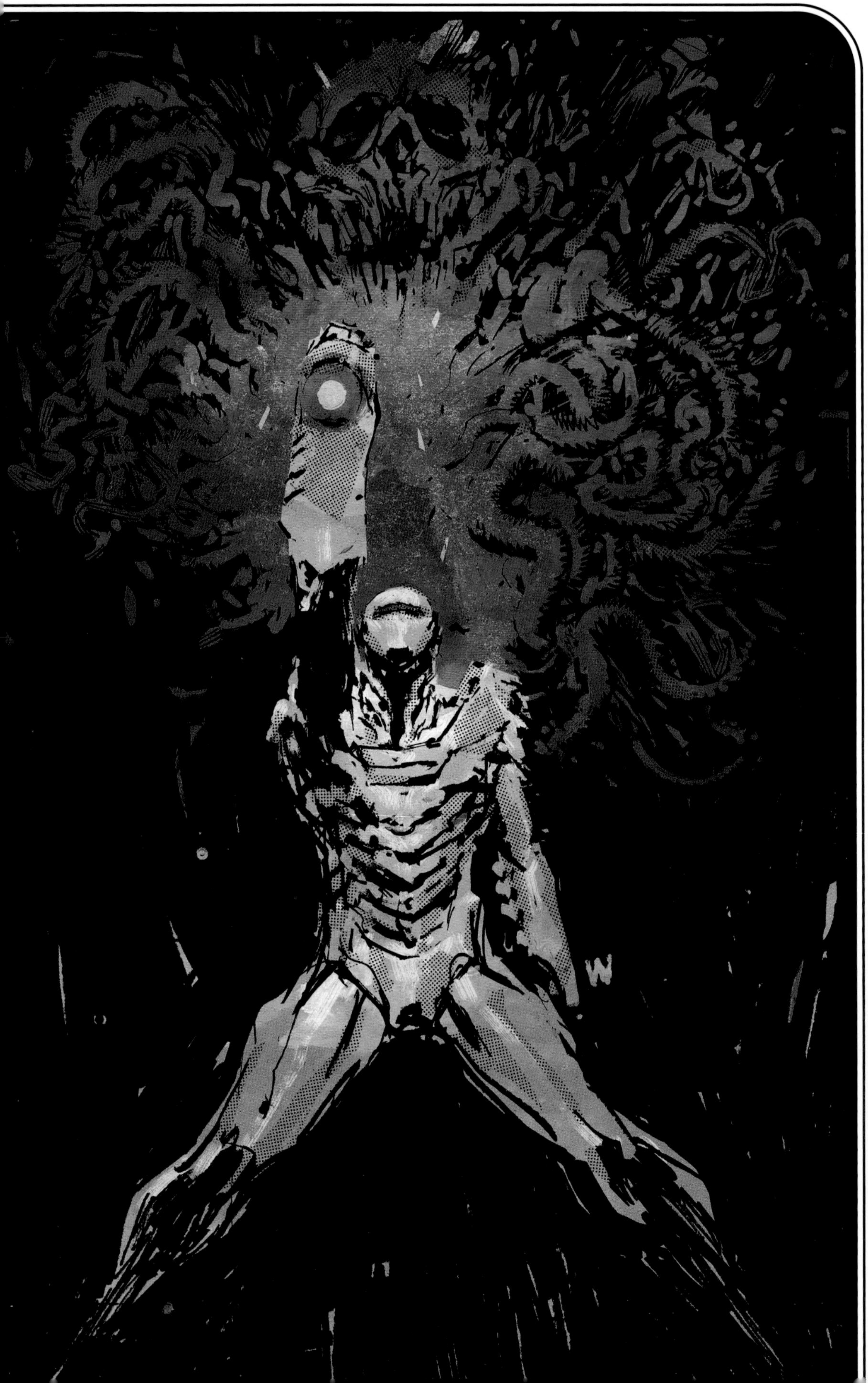

W

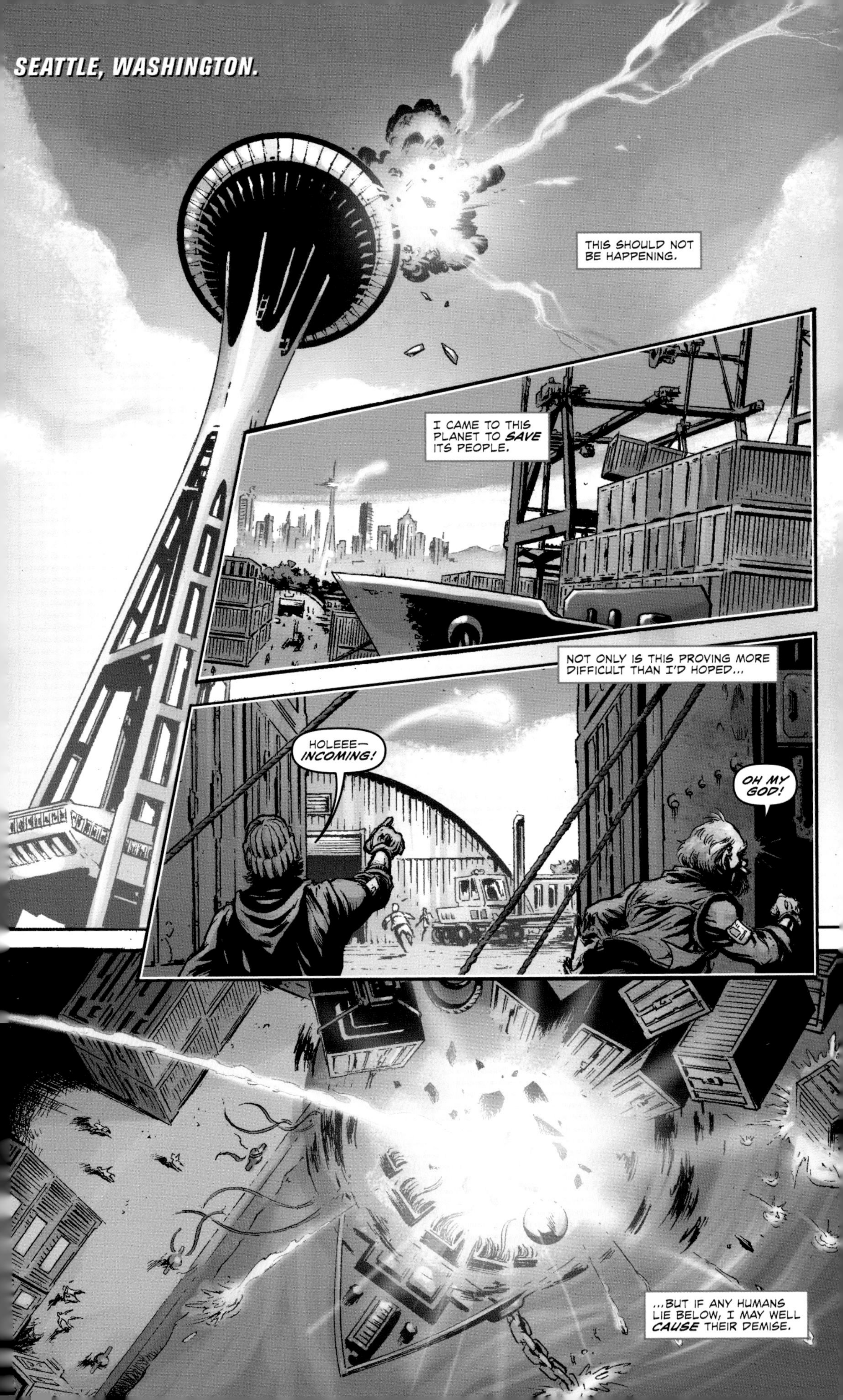
SEATTLE, WASHINGTON.
THIS SHOULD NOT BE HAPPENING.
I CAME TO THIS PLANET TO SAVE ITS PEOPLE.
NOT ONLY IS THIS PROVING MORE DIFFICULT THAN I'D HOPED...
HOLEEE— INCOMING!
OH MY GOD!
...BUT IF ANY HUMANS LIE BELOW, I MAY WELL CAUSE THEIR DEMISE.

A REVOLUTION EVENT

ROM

FIELD TEST

RYALL • GAGE • JOSEPH • FOTOS

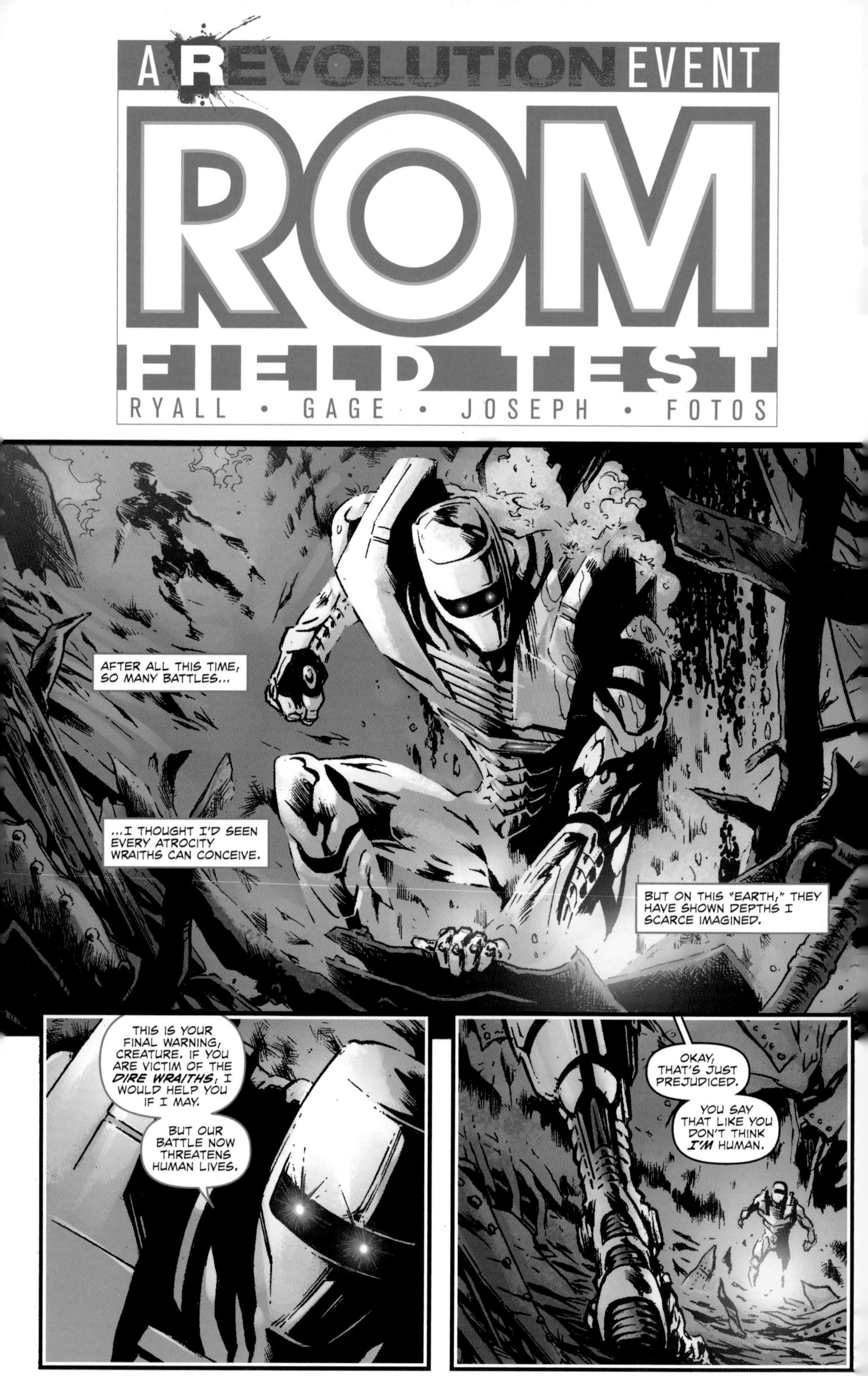

AFTER ALL THIS TIME, SO MANY BATTLES...
...I THOUGHT I'D SEEN EVERY ATROCITY WRAITHS CAN CONCEIVE.
BUT ON THIS "EARTH," THEY HAVE SHOWN DEPTHS I SCARCE IMAGINED.
THIS IS YOUR FINAL WARNING, CREATURE. IF YOU ARE VICTIM OF THE *DIRE WRAITHS*, I WOULD HELP YOU IF I MAY.
BUT OUR BATTLE NOW THREATENS HUMAN LIVES.
OKAY, THAT'S JUST PREJUDICED.
YOU SAY THAT LIKE YOU DON'T THINK *I'M* HUMAN.

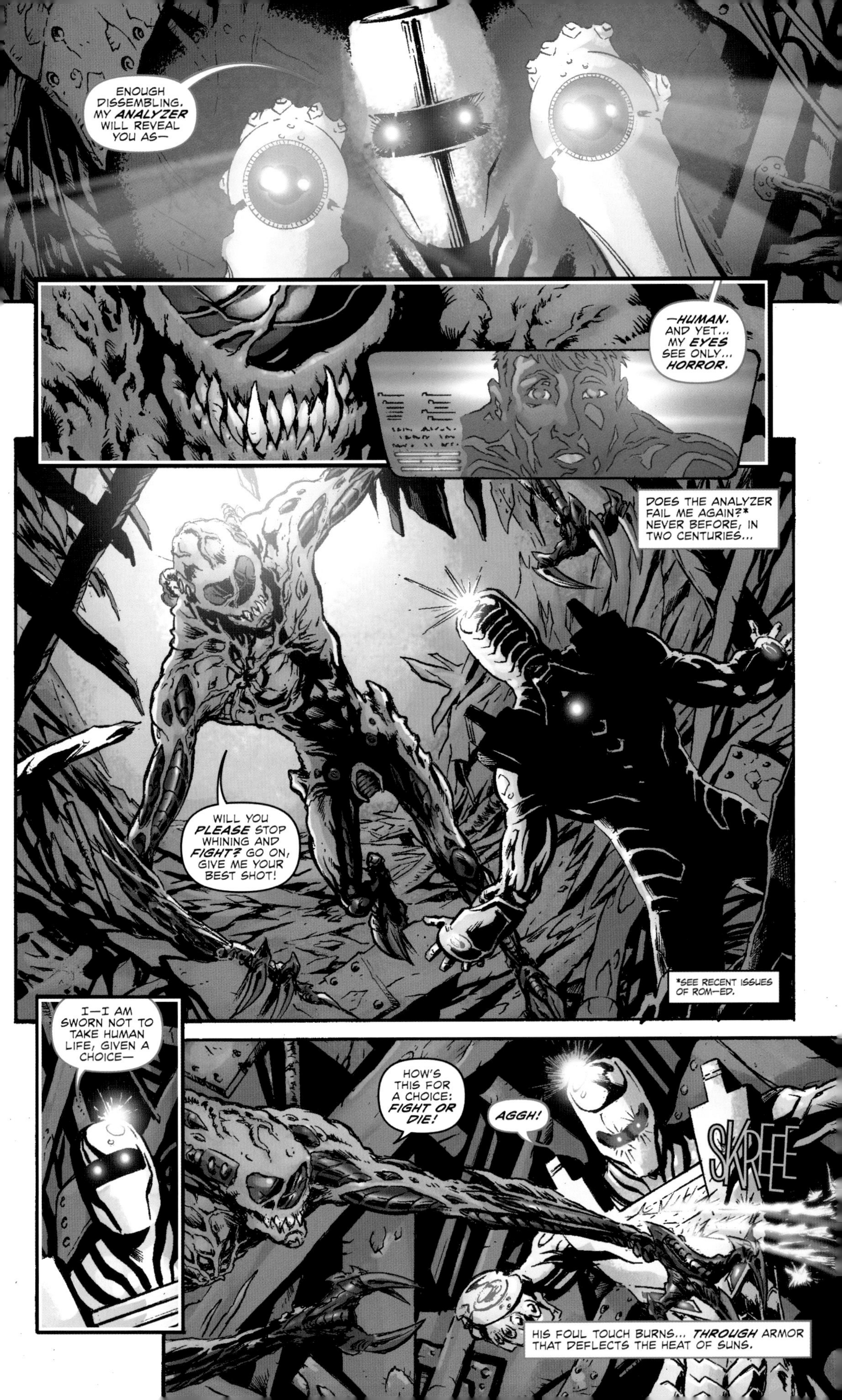
ENOUGH DISSEMBLING. MY ANALYZER WILL REVEAL YOU AS—
—HUMAN. AND YET... MY EYES SEE ONLY... HORROR.
DOES THE ANALYZER FAIL ME AGAIN?* NEVER BEFORE, IN TWO CENTURIES...
WILL YOU PLEASE STOP WHINING AND FIGHT? GO ON, GIVE ME YOUR BEST SHOT!
*SEE RECENT ISSUES OF ROM—ED.
I—I AM SWORN NOT TO TAKE HUMAN LIFE, GIVEN A CHOICE—
HOW'S THIS FOR A CHOICE: FIGHT OR DIE!
AGGH!
SKREEE
HIS FOUL TOUCH BURNS... THROUGH ARMOR THAT DEFLECTS THE HEAT OF SUNS.

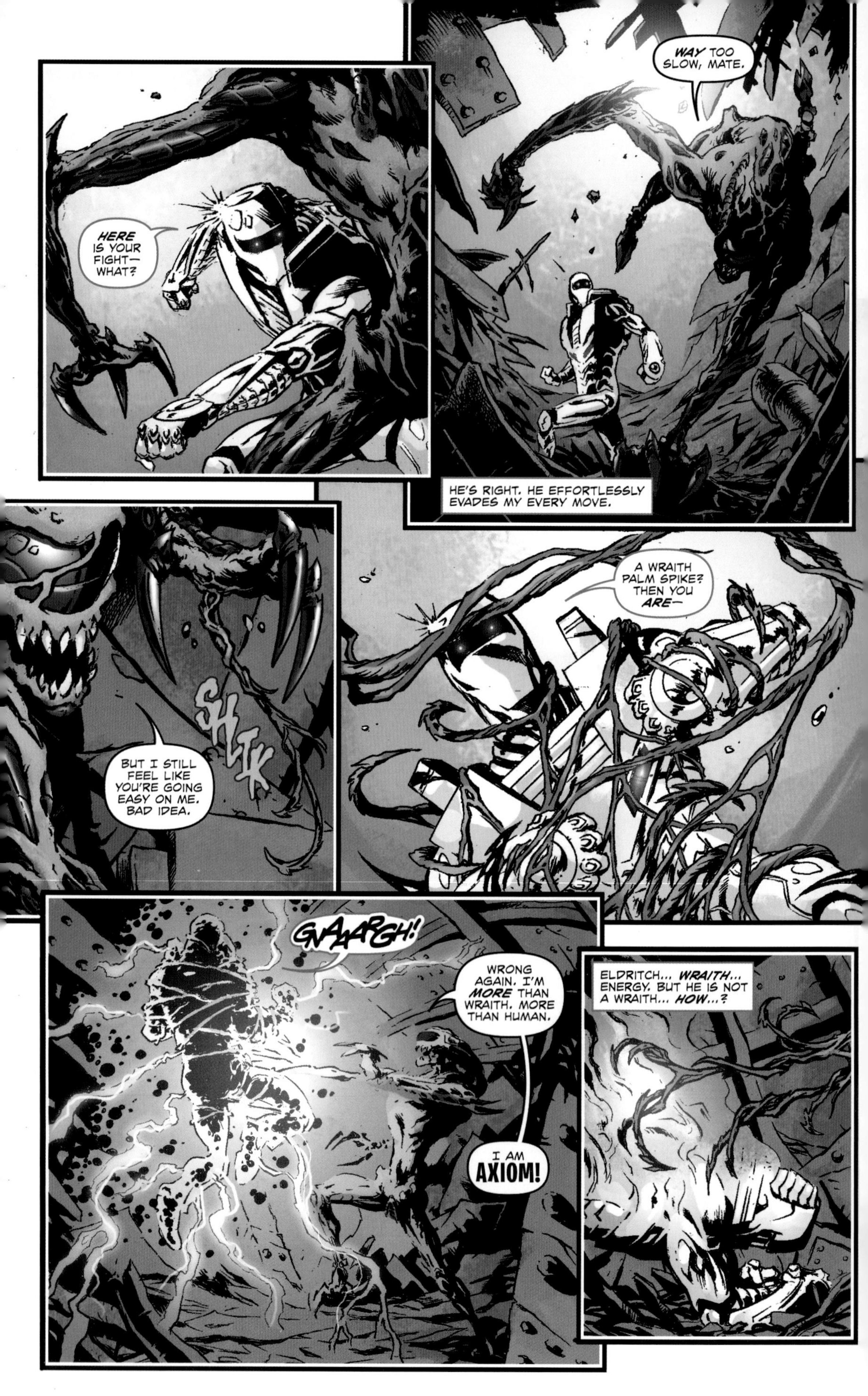
HERE IS YOUR FIGHT— WHAT?
WAY TOO SLOW, MATE.
HE'S RIGHT. HE EFFORTLESSLY EVADES MY EVERY MOVE.
SHIK
BUT I STILL FEEL LIKE YOU'RE GOING EASY ON ME. BAD IDEA.
A WRAITH PALM SPIKE? THEN YOU ARE—
GNAAARGH!
WRONG AGAIN. I'M MORE THAN WRAITH. MORE THAN HUMAN.
I AM AXIOM!
ELDRITCH... WRAITH... ENERGY. BUT HE IS NOT A WRAITH... HOW...?

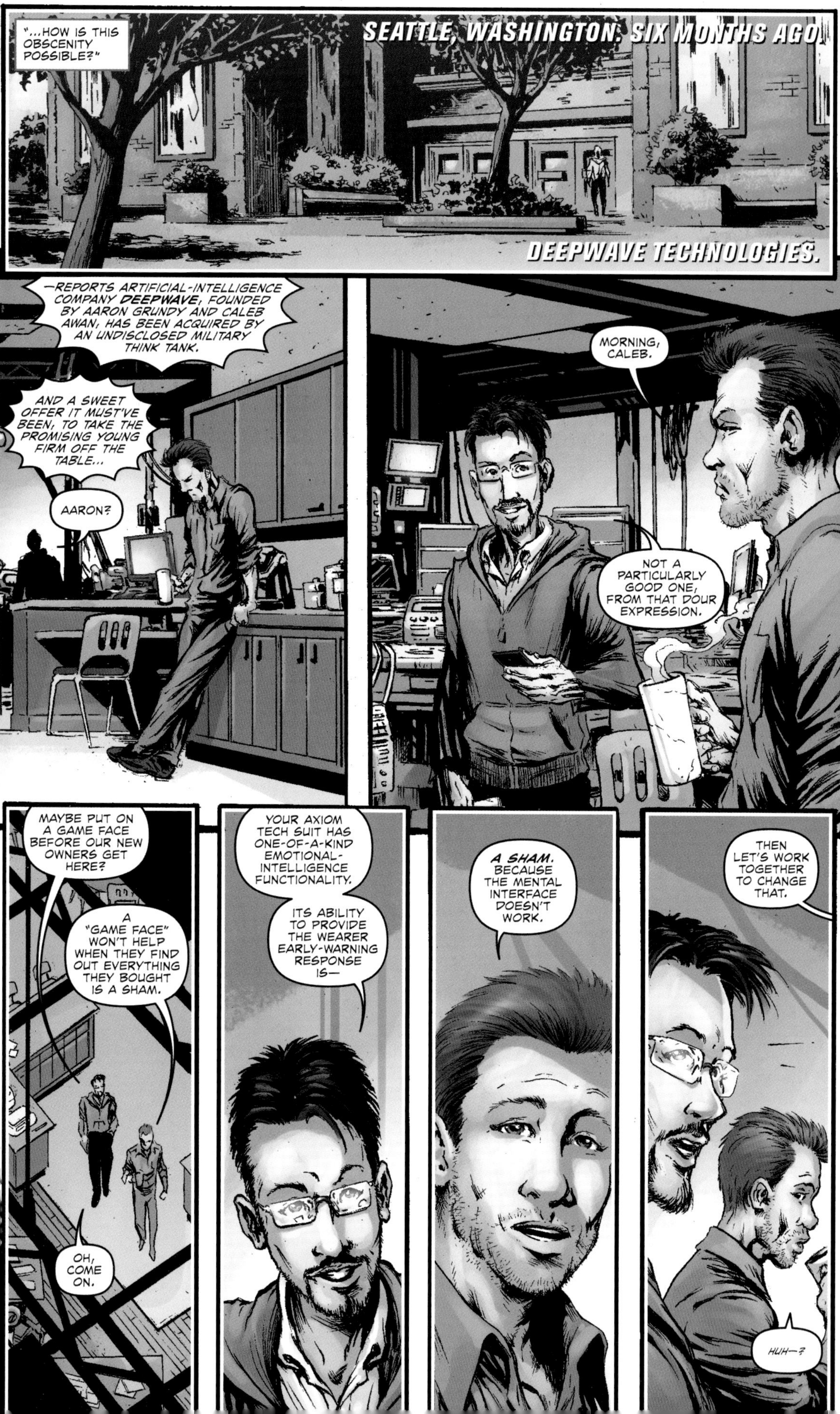

"...HOW IS THIS OBSCENITY POSSIBLE?"
SEATTLE, WASHINGTON. SIX MONTHS AGO.
DEEPWAVE TECHNOLOGIES.
—REPORTS ARTIFICIAL-INTELLIGENCE COMPANY DEEPWAVE, FOUNDED BY AARON GRUNDY AND CALEB AWAN, HAS BEEN ACQUIRED BY AN UNDISCLOSED MILITARY THINK TANK.
AND A SWEET OFFER IT MUST'VE BEEN, TO TAKE THE PROMISING YOUNG FIRM OFF THE TABLE...
AARON?
MORNING, CALEB.
NOT A PARTICULARLY GOOD ONE, FROM THAT DOUR EXPRESSION.
MAYBE PUT ON A GAME FACE BEFORE OUR NEW OWNERS GET HERE?
A "GAME FACE" WON'T HELP WHEN THEY FIND OUT EVERYTHING THEY BOUGHT IS A SHAM.
OH, COME ON.
YOUR AXIOM TECH SUIT HAS ONE-OF-A-KIND EMOTIONAL-INTELLIGENCE FUNCTIONALITY.
ITS ABILITY TO PROVIDE THE WEARER EARLY-WARNING RESPONSE IS—
A SHAM. BECAUSE THE MENTAL INTERFACE DOESN'T WORK.
THEN LET'S WORK TOGETHER TO CHANGE THAT.
HUH—?

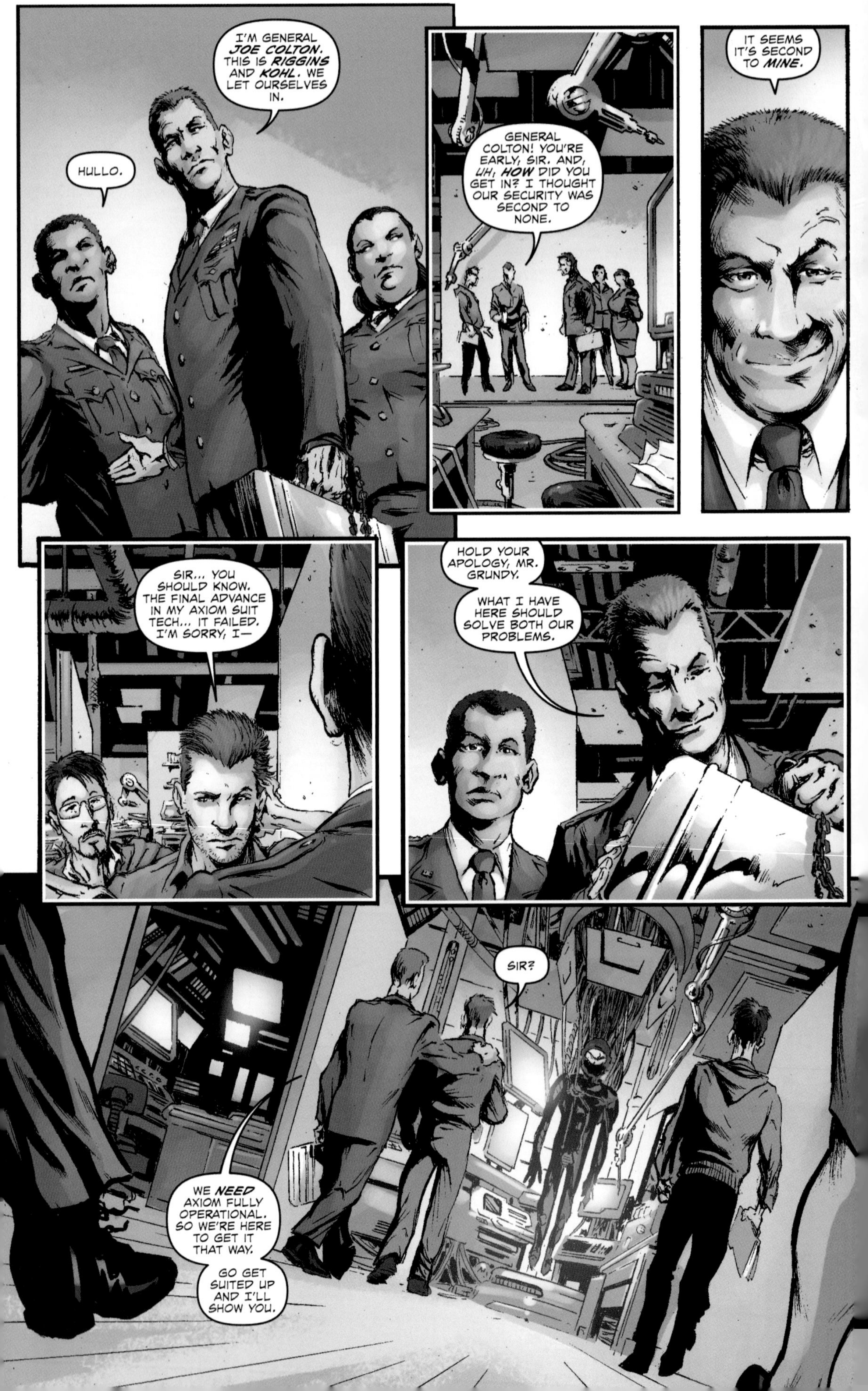
HULLO.
I'M GENERAL JOE COLTON. THIS IS RIGGINS AND KOHL. WE LET OURSELVES IN.
GENERAL COLTON! YOU'RE EARLY, SIR. AND, UH, HOW DID YOU GET IN? I THOUGHT OUR SECURITY WAS SECOND TO NONE.
IT SEEMS IT'S SECOND TO MINE.
SIR... YOU SHOULD KNOW. THE FINAL ADVANCE IN MY AXIOM SUIT TECH... IT FAILED. I'M SORRY, I—
HOLD YOUR APOLOGY, MR. GRUNDY.
WHAT I HAVE HERE SHOULD SOLVE BOTH OUR PROBLEMS.
SIR?
WE NEED AXIOM FULLY OPERATIONAL. SO WE'RE HERE TO GET IT THAT WAY.
GO GET SUITED UP AND I'LL SHOW YOU.

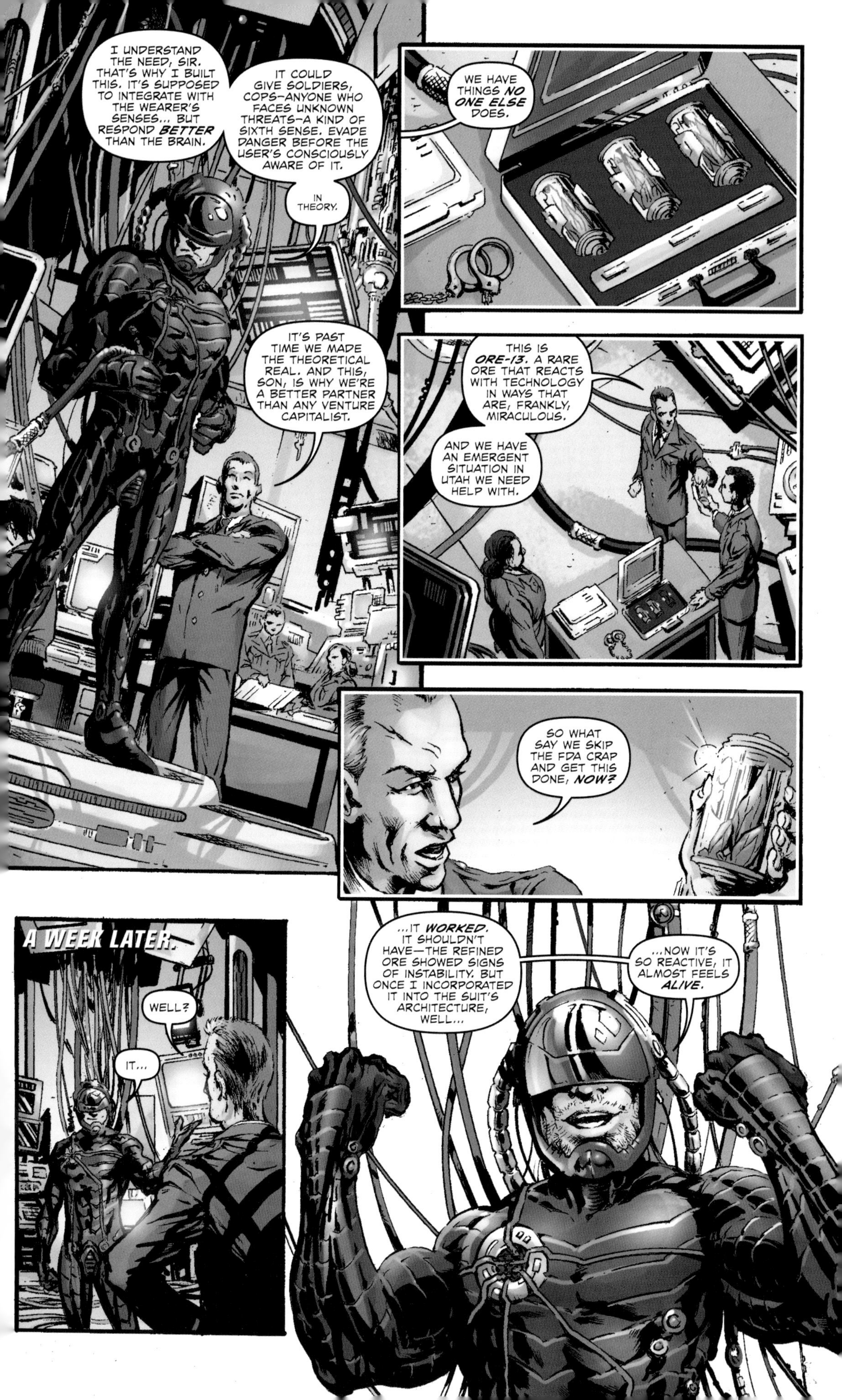
I UNDERSTAND THE NEED, SIR. THAT'S WHY I BUILT THIS. IT'S SUPPOSED TO INTEGRATE WITH THE WEARER'S SENSES... BUT RESPOND BETTER THAN THE BRAIN.
IT COULD GIVE SOLDIERS, COPS—ANYONE WHO FACES UNKNOWN THREATS—A KIND OF SIXTH SENSE. EVADE DANGER BEFORE THE USER'S CONSCIOUSLY AWARE OF IT.
IN THEORY.
IT'S PAST TIME WE MADE THE THEORETICAL REAL. AND THIS, SON, IS WHY WE'RE A BETTER PARTNER THAN ANY VENTURE CAPITALIST.
WE HAVE THINGS NO ONE ELSE DOES.
THIS IS ORE-13. A RARE ORE THAT REACTS WITH TECHNOLOGY IN WAYS THAT ARE, FRANKLY, MIRACULOUS.
AND WE HAVE AN EMERGENT SITUATION IN UTAH WE NEED HELP WITH.
SO WHAT SAY WE SKIP THE FDA CRAP AND GET THIS DONE, NOW?
A WEEK LATER.
WELL?
IT...
...IT WORKED. IT SHOULDN'T HAVE—THE REFINED ORE SHOWED SIGNS OF INSTABILITY. BUT ONCE I INCORPORATED IT INTO THE SUIT'S ARCHITECTURE, WELL...
...NOW IT'S SO REACTIVE, IT ALMOST FEELS ALIVE.

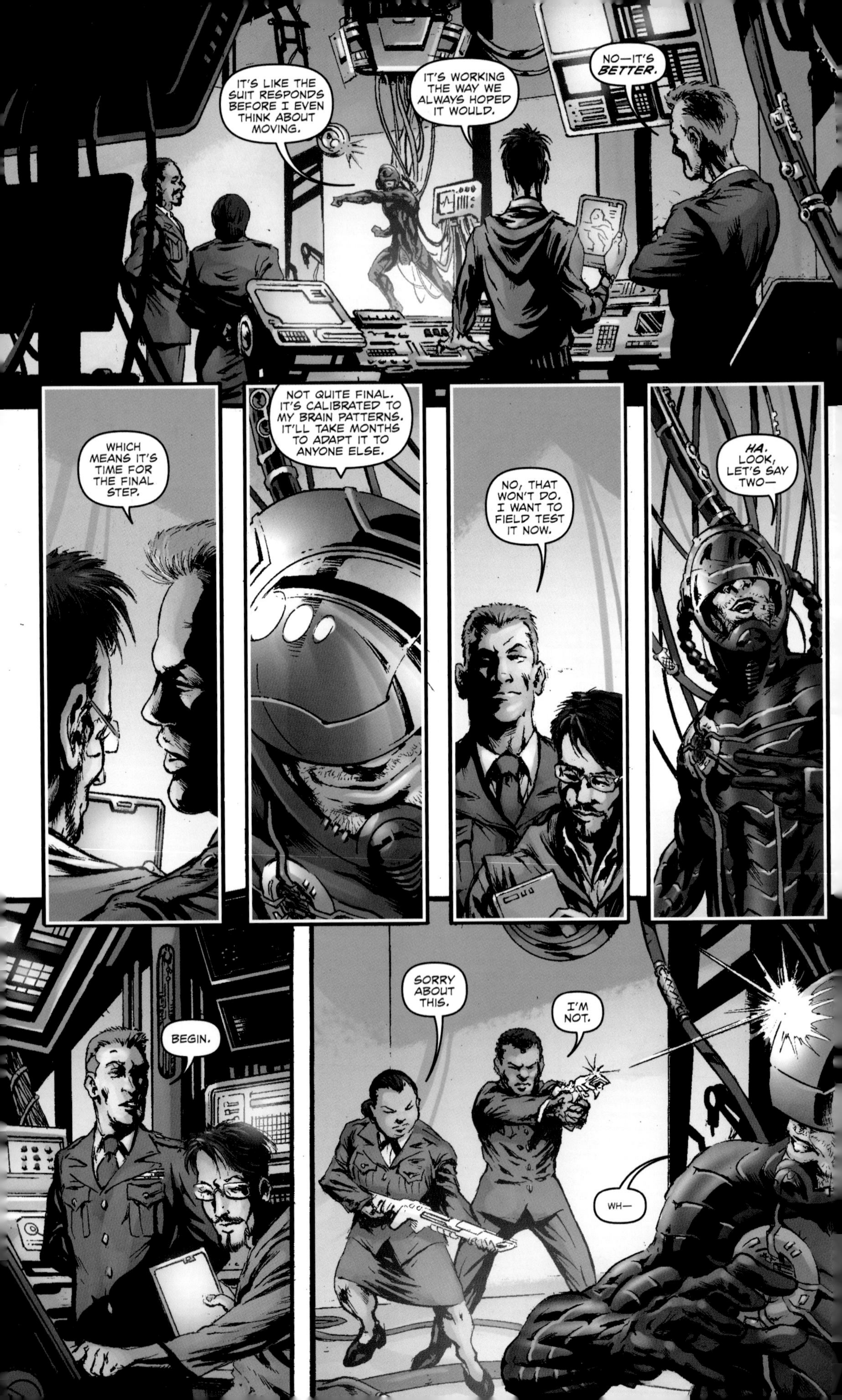
IT'S LIKE THE SUIT RESPONDS BEFORE I EVEN THINK ABOUT MOVING.
IT'S WORKING THE WAY WE ALWAYS HOPED IT WOULD.
NO—IT'S *BETTER*.
WHICH MEANS IT'S TIME FOR THE FINAL STEP.
NOT QUITE FINAL. IT'S CALIBRATED TO MY BRAIN PATTERNS. IT'LL TAKE MONTHS TO ADAPT IT TO ANYONE ELSE.
NO, THAT WON'T DO. I WANT TO FIELD TEST IT NOW.
HA. LOOK, LET'S SAY TWO—
BEGIN.
SORRY ABOUT THIS.
I'M NOT.
WH—

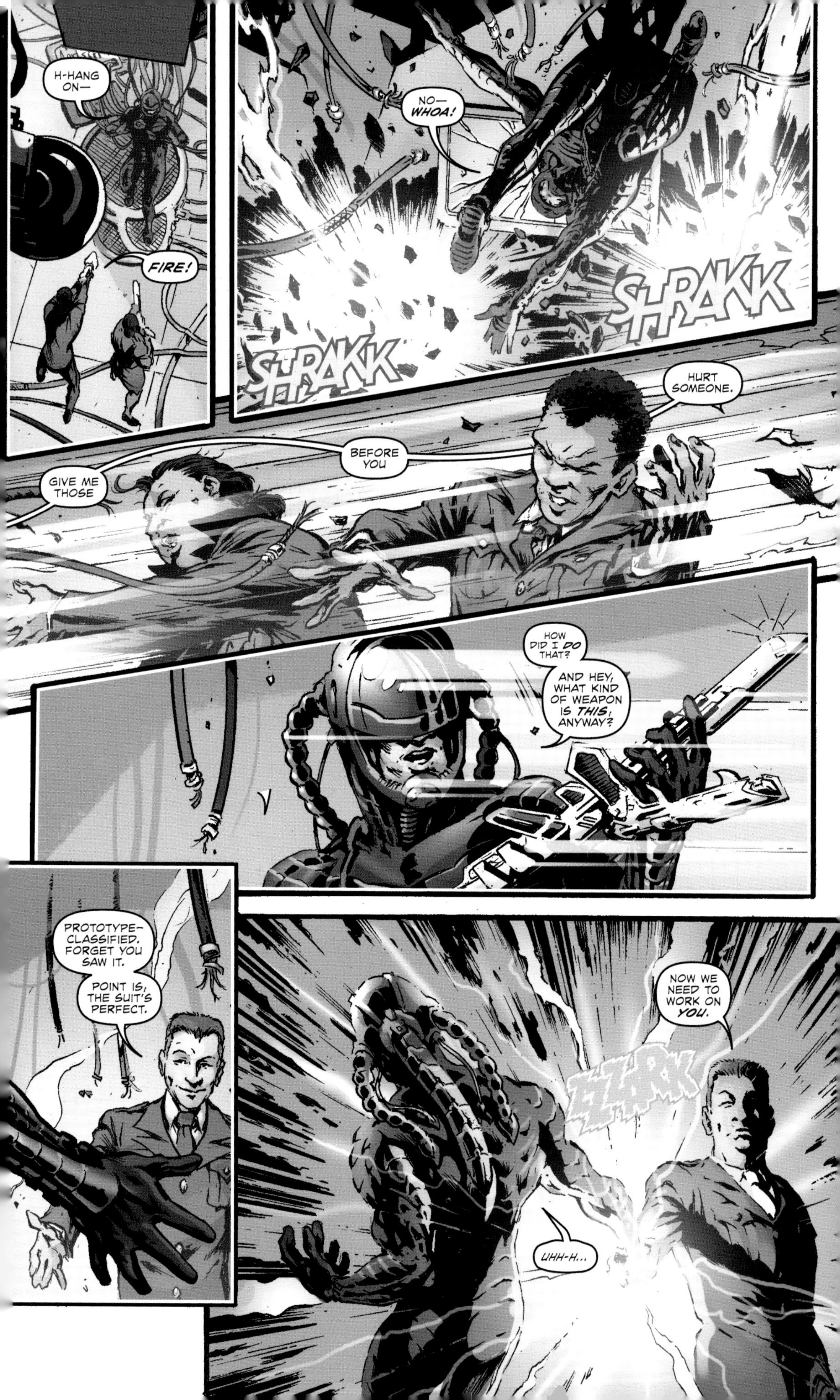
H-HANG ON—
FIRE!
NO— WHOA!
SHRAKK
SHRAKK
HURT SOMEONE.
BEFORE YOU
GIVE ME THOSE
HOW DID I DO THAT?
AND HEY, WHAT KIND OF WEAPON IS THIS, ANYWAY?
PROTOTYPE-CLASSIFIED. FORGET YOU SAW IT.
POINT IS, THE SUIT'S PERFECT.
NOW WE NEED TO WORK ON YOU.
ZZZARK
UHH-H...

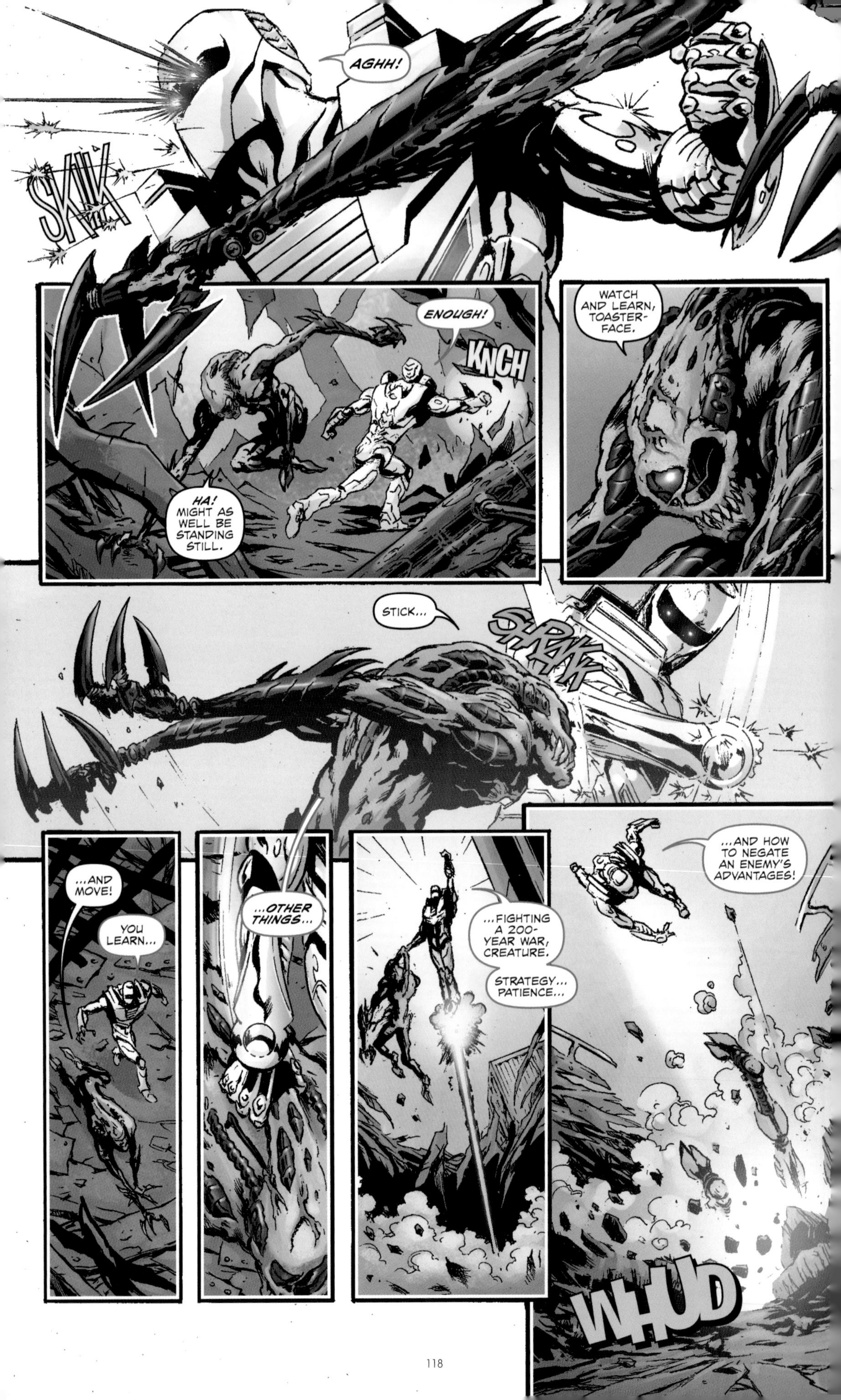
AGHH!
SKIK
ENOUGH!
KNCH
HA! MIGHT AS WELL BE STANDING STILL.
WATCH AND LEARN, TOASTER-FACE.
STICK...
SHRAKK
...AND MOVE!
YOU LEARN...
...OTHER THINGS...
...FIGHTING A 200-YEAR WAR, CREATURE.
STRATEGY... PATIENCE...
...AND HOW TO NEGATE AN ENEMY'S ADVANTAGES!
WHUD

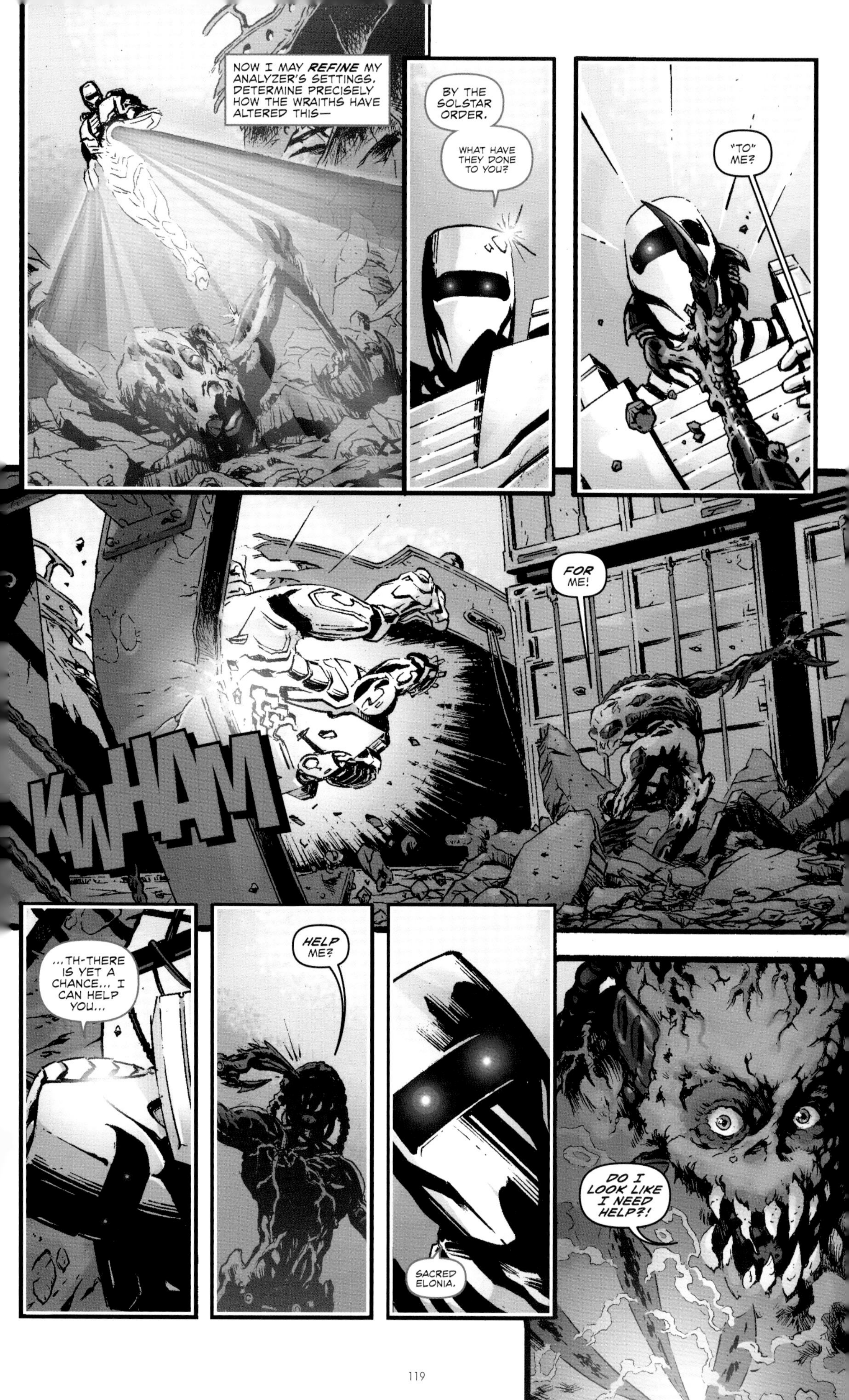
NOW I MAY REFINE MY ANALYZER'S SETTINGS. DETERMINE PRECISELY HOW THE WRAITHS HAVE ALTERED THIS—
BY THE SOLSTAR ORDER.
WHAT HAVE THEY DONE TO YOU?
"TO" ME?
FOR ME!
KWHAM
...TH-THERE IS YET A CHANCE... I CAN HELP YOU...
HELP ME?
SACRED ELONIA.
DO I LOOK LIKE I NEED HELP?!

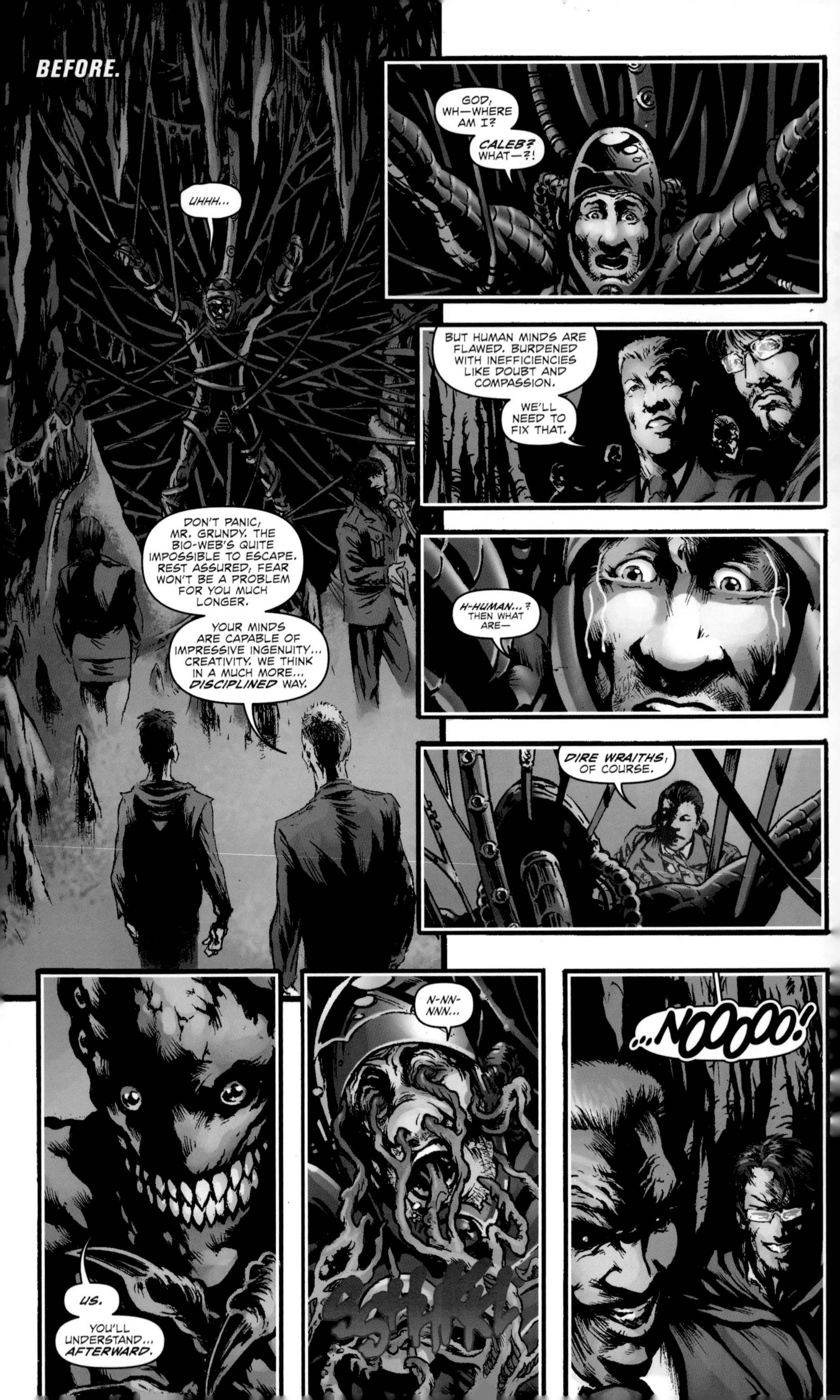
BEFORE.
UHHH...
GOD, WH—WHERE AM I?
CALEB? WHAT—?!
DON'T PANIC, MR. GRUNDY. THE BIO-WEB'S QUITE IMPOSSIBLE TO ESCAPE. REST ASSURED, FEAR WON'T BE A PROBLEM FOR YOU MUCH LONGER.
YOUR MINDS ARE CAPABLE OF IMPRESSIVE INGENUITY... CREATIVITY. WE THINK IN A MUCH MORE... DISCIPLINED WAY.
BUT HUMAN MINDS ARE FLAWED. BURDENED WITH INEFFICIENCIES LIKE DOUBT AND COMPASSION.
WE'LL NEED TO FIX THAT.
H-HUMAN...? THEN WHAT ARE—
DIRE WRAITHS, OF COURSE.
US.
YOU'LL UNDERSTAND... AFTERWARD.
N-NN-NNN...
...NOOOOO!

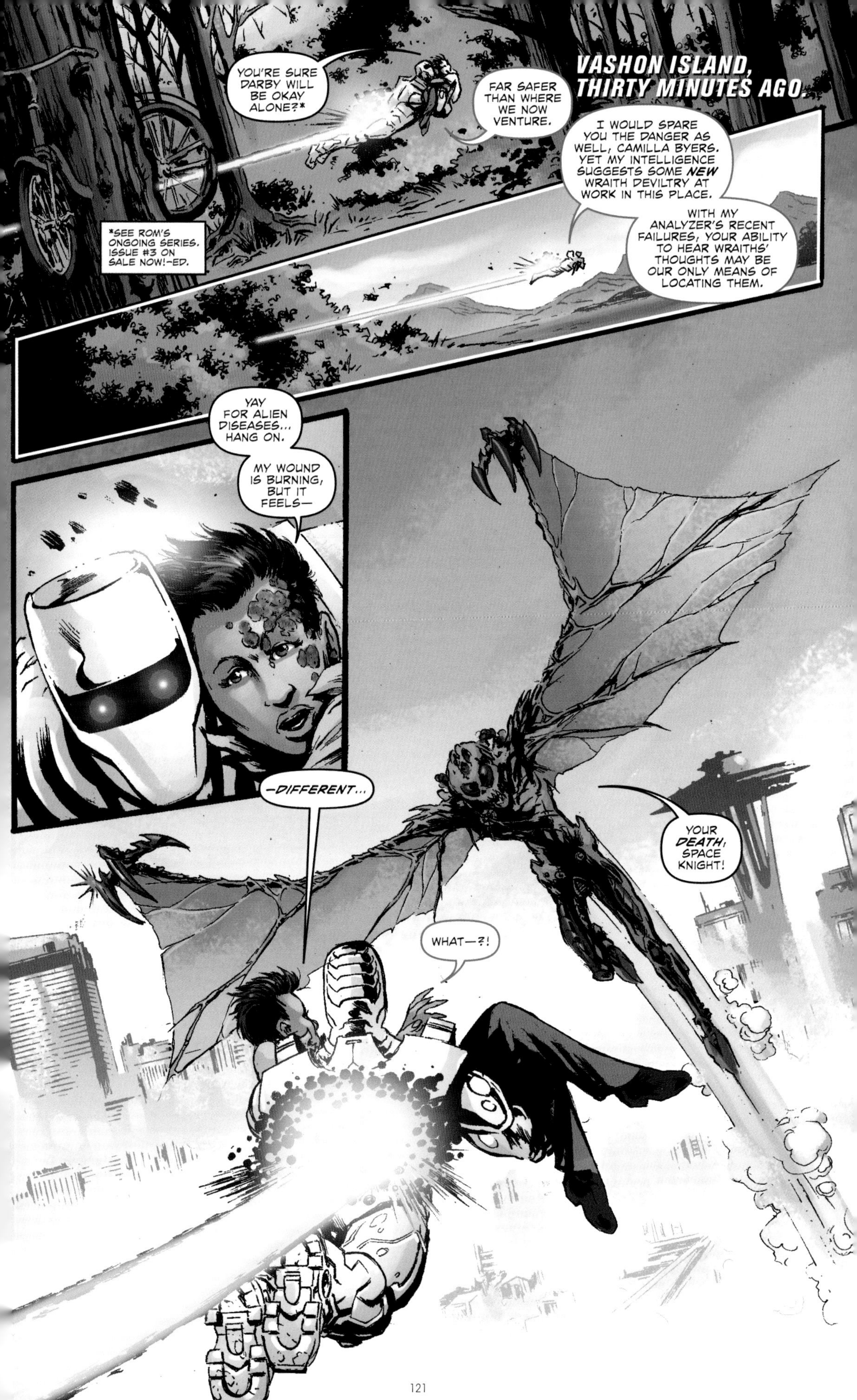

VASHON ISLAND, THIRTY MINUTES AGO.
YOU'RE SURE DARBY WILL BE OKAY ALONE?*
FAR SAFER THAN WHERE WE NOW VENTURE.
*SEE ROM'S ONGOING SERIES. ISSUE #3 ON SALE NOW!-ED.
I WOULD SPARE YOU THE DANGER AS WELL, CAMILLA BYERS. YET MY INTELLIGENCE SUGGESTS SOME NEW WRAITH DEVILTRY AT WORK IN THIS PLACE.
WITH MY ANALYZER'S RECENT FAILURES, YOUR ABILITY TO HEAR WRAITHS' THOUGHTS MAY BE OUR ONLY MEANS OF LOCATING THEM.
YAY FOR ALIEN DISEASES... HANG ON.
MY WOUND IS BURNING, BUT IT FEELS—
—DIFFERENT...
YOUR DEATH, SPACE KNIGHT!
WHAT—?!

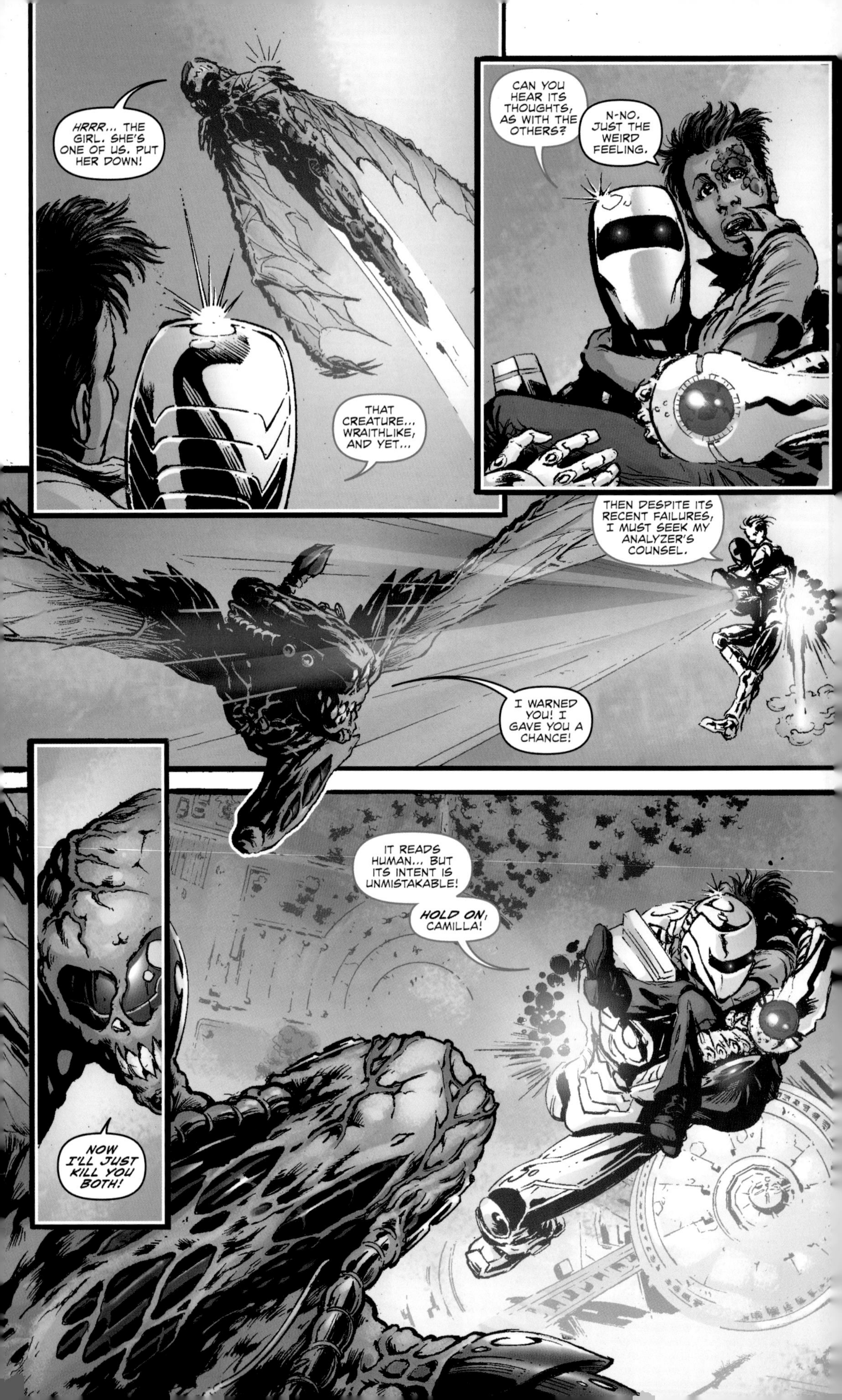
HRRR... THE GIRL. SHE'S ONE OF US. PUT HER DOWN!
THAT CREATURE... WRAITHLIKE, AND YET...
CAN YOU HEAR ITS THOUGHTS, AS WITH THE OTHERS?
N-NO. JUST THE WEIRD FEELING.
THEN DESPITE ITS RECENT FAILURES, I MUST SEEK MY ANALYZER'S COUNSEL.
I WARNED YOU! I GAVE YOU A CHANCE!
IT READS HUMAN... BUT ITS INTENT IS UNMISTAKABLE!
HOLD ON, CAMILLA!
NOW I'LL JUST KILL YOU BOTH!

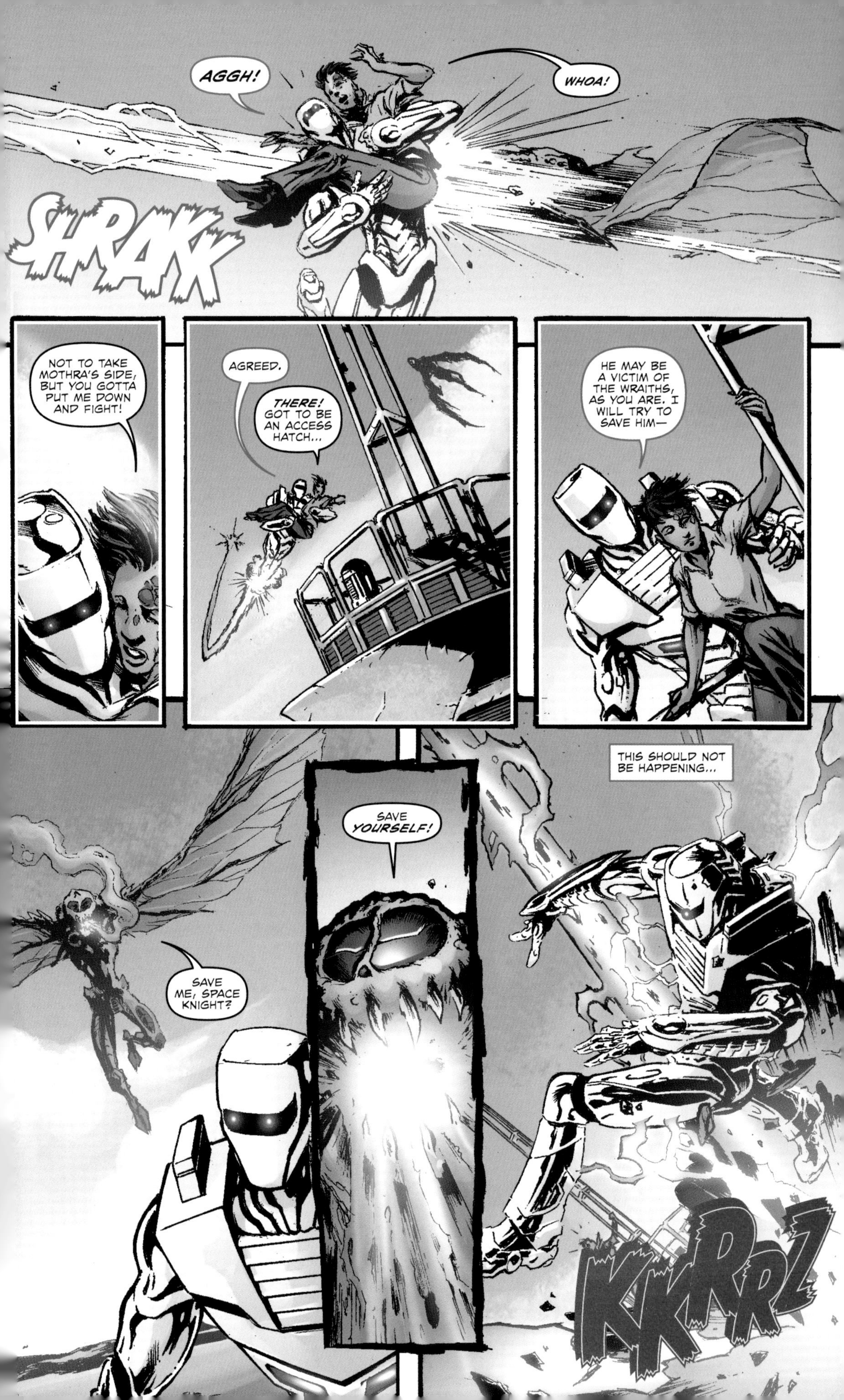
AGGH!
WHOA!
SHRAKK
NOT TO TAKE MOTHRA'S SIDE, BUT YOU GOTTA PUT ME DOWN AND FIGHT!
AGREED.
THERE! GOT TO BE AN ACCESS HATCH...
HE MAY BE A VICTIM OF THE WRAITHS, AS YOU ARE. I WILL TRY TO SAVE HIM—
THIS SHOULD NOT BE HAPPENING...
SAVE ME, SPACE KNIGHT?
SAVE YOURSELF!
KKRRZ

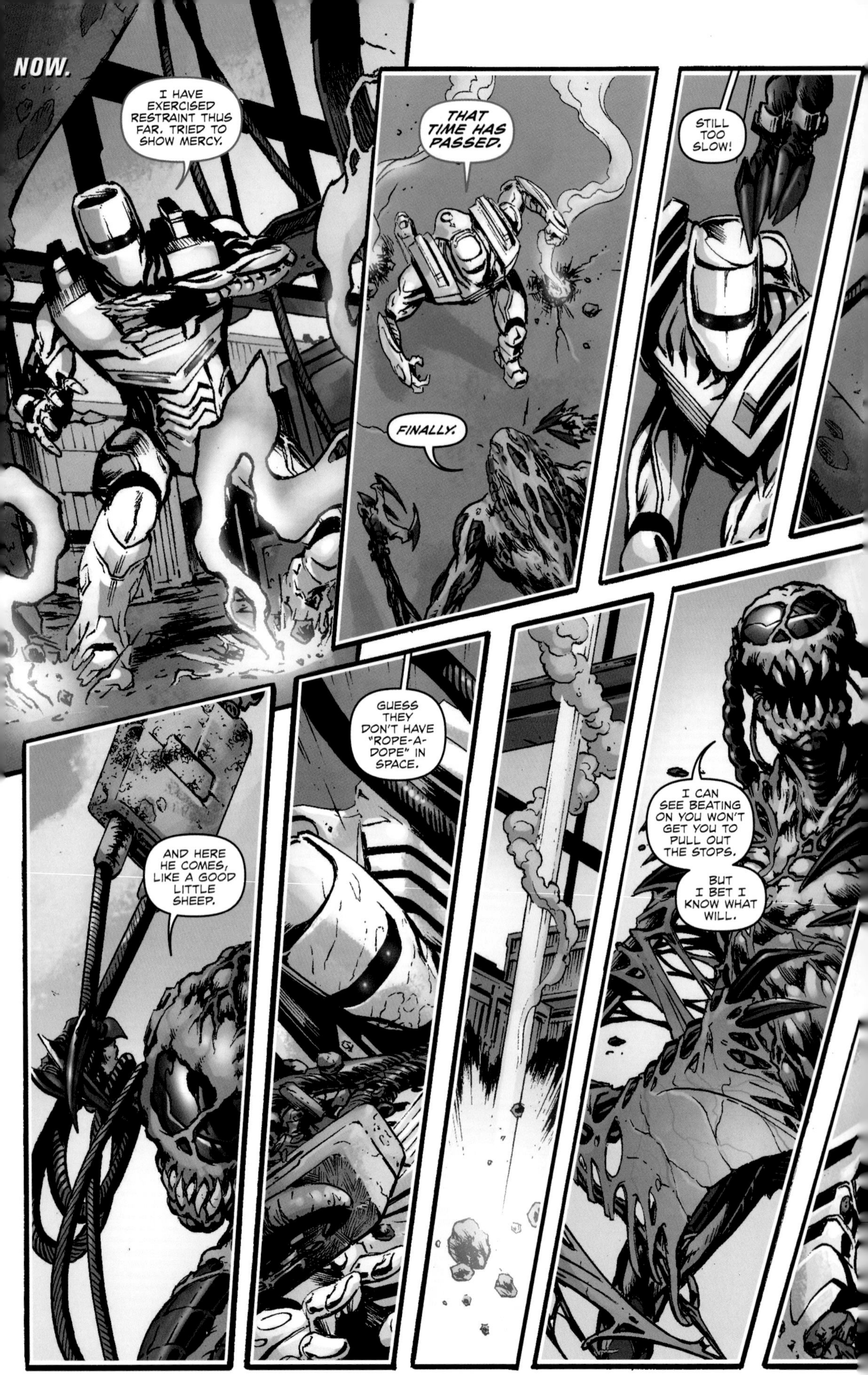

NOW.
I HAVE EXERCISED RESTRAINT THUS FAR. TRIED TO SHOW MERCY.
THAT TIME HAS PASSED.
FINALLY.
STILL TOO SLOW!
AND HERE HE COMES, LIKE A GOOD LITTLE SHEEP.
GUESS THEY DON'T HAVE "ROPE-A-DOPE" IN SPACE.
I CAN SEE BEATING ON YOU WON'T GET YOU TO PULL OUT THE STOPS.
BUT I BET I KNOW WHAT WILL.

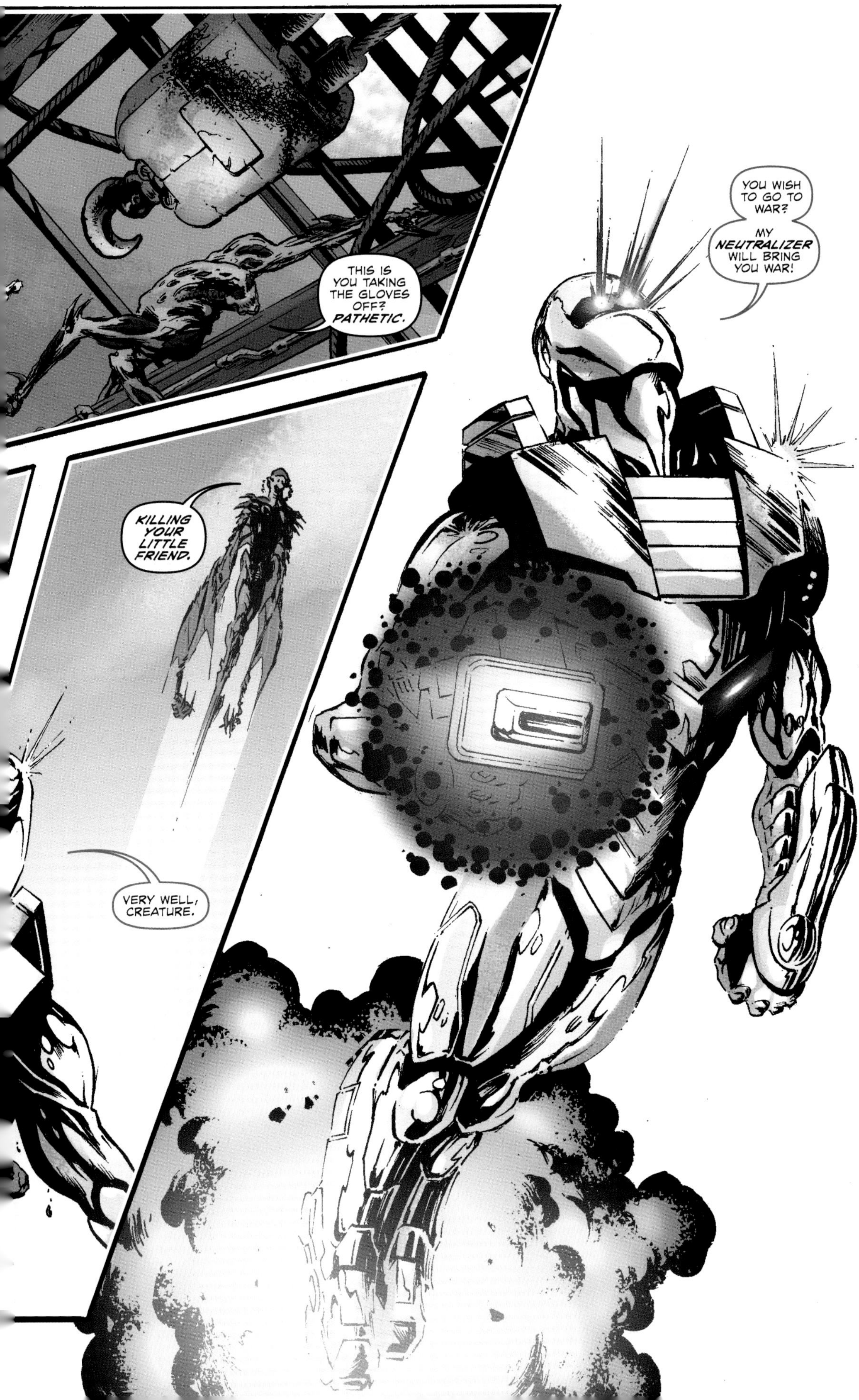
THIS IS YOU TAKING THE GLOVES OFF? PATHETIC.
YOU WISH TO GO TO WAR?
MY NEUTRALIZER WILL BRING YOU WAR!
KILLING YOUR LITTLE FRIEND.
VERY WELL, CREATURE.

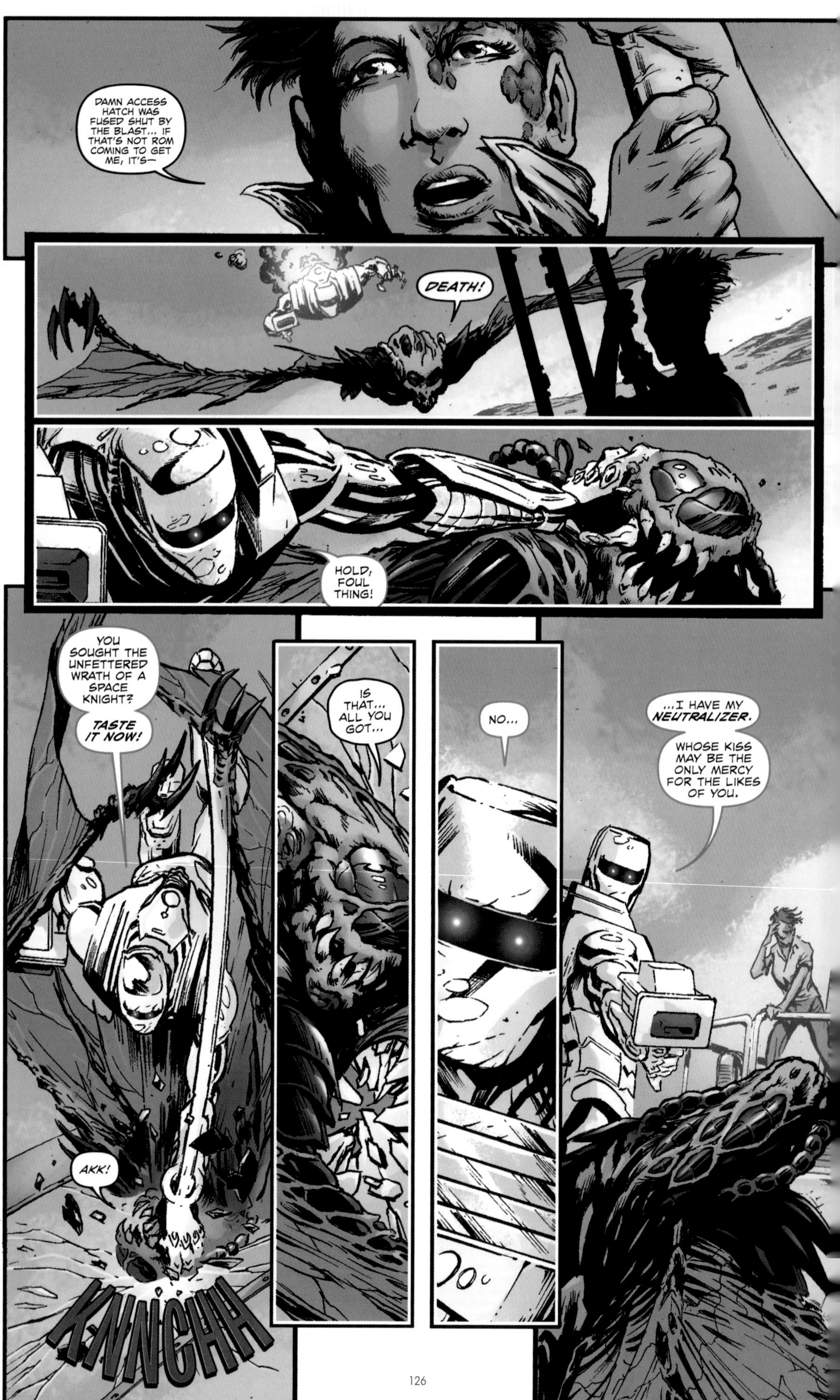
DAMN ACCESS HATCH WAS FUSED SHUT BY THE BLAST... IF THAT'S NOT ROM COMING TO GET ME, IT'S—
DEATH!
HOLD, FOUL THING!
YOU SOUGHT THE UNFETTERED WRATH OF A SPACE KNIGHT?
TASTE IT NOW!
AKK!
KNNCHH
IS THAT... ALL YOU GOT...
NO...
...I HAVE MY NEUTRALIZER.
WHOSE KISS MAY BE THE ONLY MERCY FOR THE LIKES OF YOU.

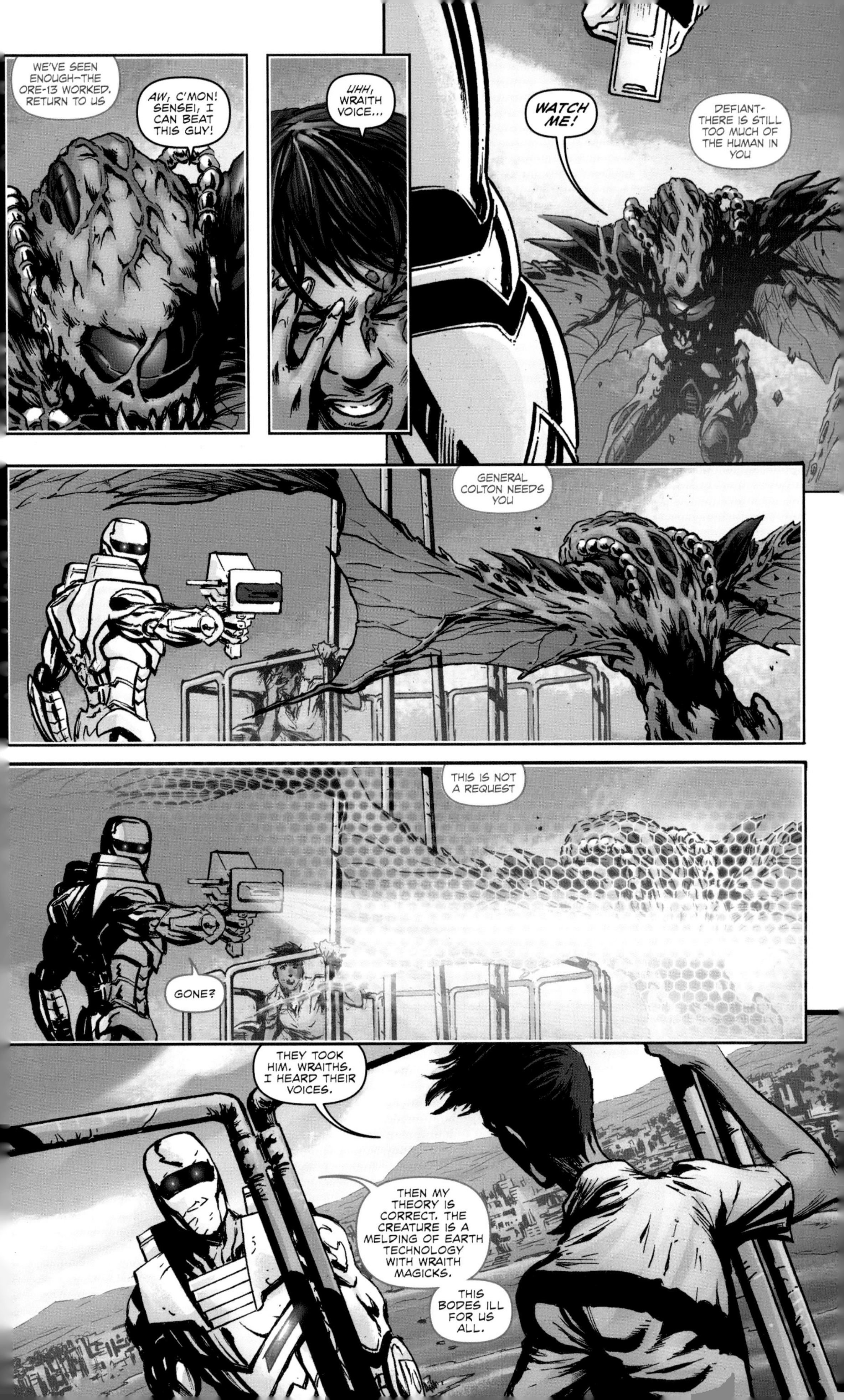
WE'VE SEEN ENOUGH—THE ORE-13 WORKED. RETURN TO US
AW, C'MON! SENSEI, I CAN BEAT THIS GUY!
UHH, WRAITH VOICE...
WATCH ME!
DEFIANT- THERE IS STILL TOO MUCH OF THE HUMAN IN YOU
GENERAL COLTON NEEDS YOU
THIS IS NOT A REQUEST
GONE?
THEY TOOK HIM. WRAITHS. I HEARD THEIR VOICES.
THEN MY THEORY IS CORRECT. THE CREATURE IS A MELDING OF EARTH TECHNOLOGY WITH WRAITH MAGICKS.
THIS BODES ILL FOR US ALL.

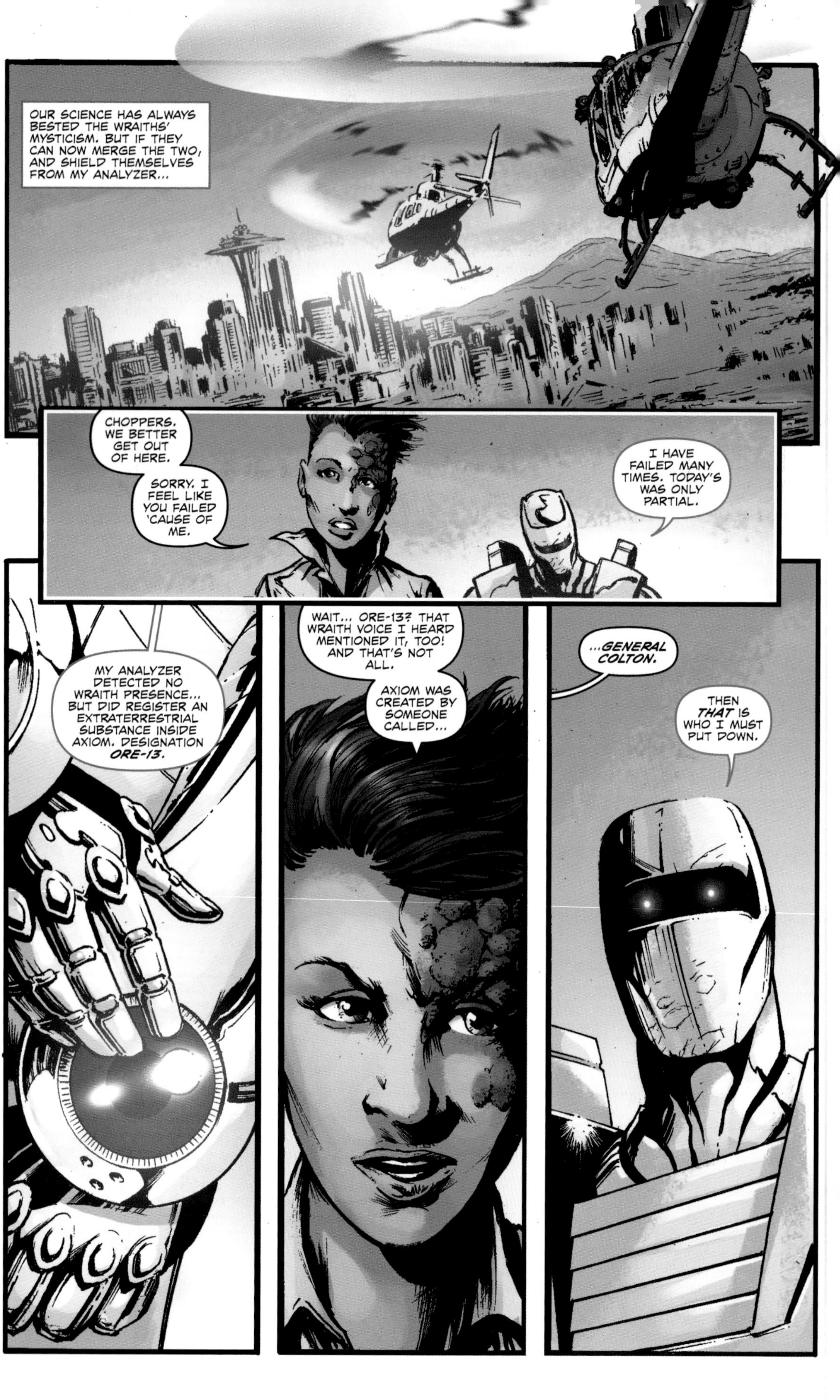

OUR SCIENCE HAS ALWAYS BESTED THE WRAITHS' MYSTICISM. BUT IF THEY CAN NOW MERGE THE TWO, AND SHIELD THEMSELVES FROM MY ANALYZER...
CHOPPERS. WE BETTER GET OUT OF HERE.
SORRY. I FEEL LIKE YOU FAILED 'CAUSE OF ME.
I HAVE FAILED MANY TIMES. TODAY'S WAS ONLY PARTIAL.
MY ANALYZER DETECTED NO WRAITH PRESENCE... BUT DID REGISTER AN EXTRATERRESTRIAL SUBSTANCE INSIDE AXIOM. DESIGNATION ORE-13.
WAIT... ORE-13? THAT WRAITH VOICE I HEARD MENTIONED IT, TOO! AND THAT'S NOT ALL.
AXIOM WAS CREATED BY SOMEONE CALLED...
...GENERAL COLTON.
THEN THAT IS WHO I MUST PUT DOWN.

ART BY **ROB LIEFELD**, COLORS BY **JESUS ABURTO**

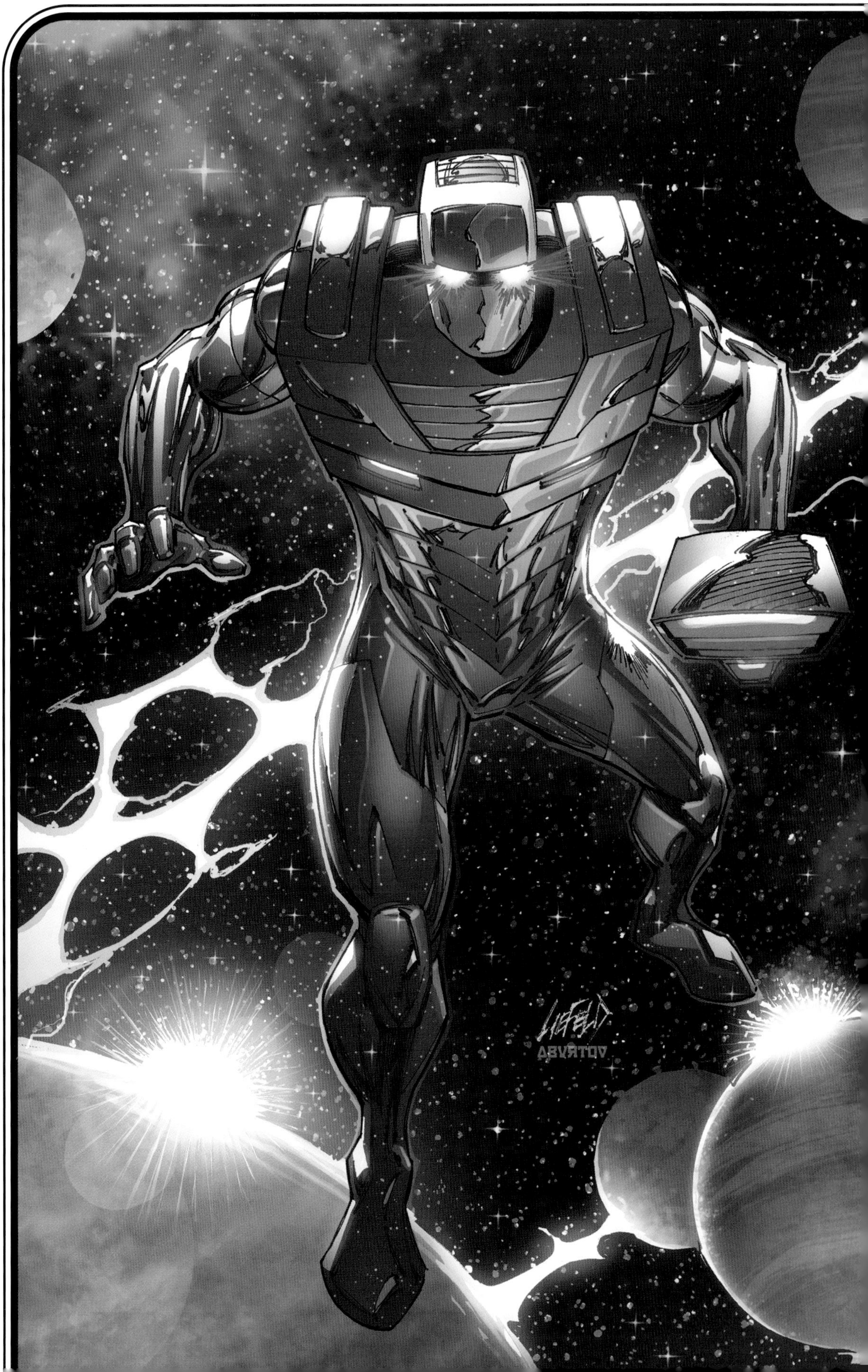
LIEFELD
ABURTO

ART BY **MICHAEL GOLDEN**

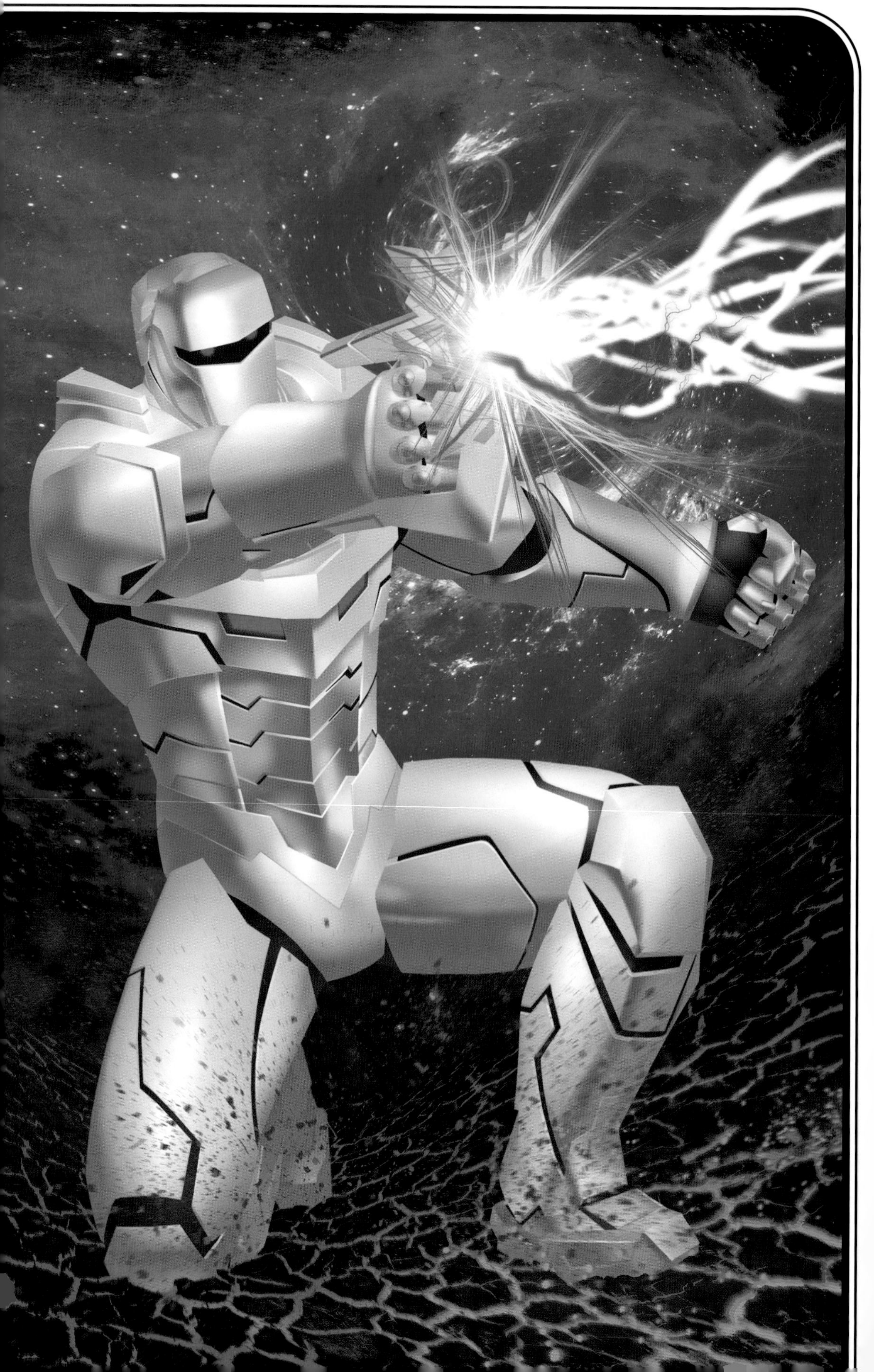

ART BY **P. CRAIG RUSSELL**, COLORS BY **LOVERN KINDZIERSKI**

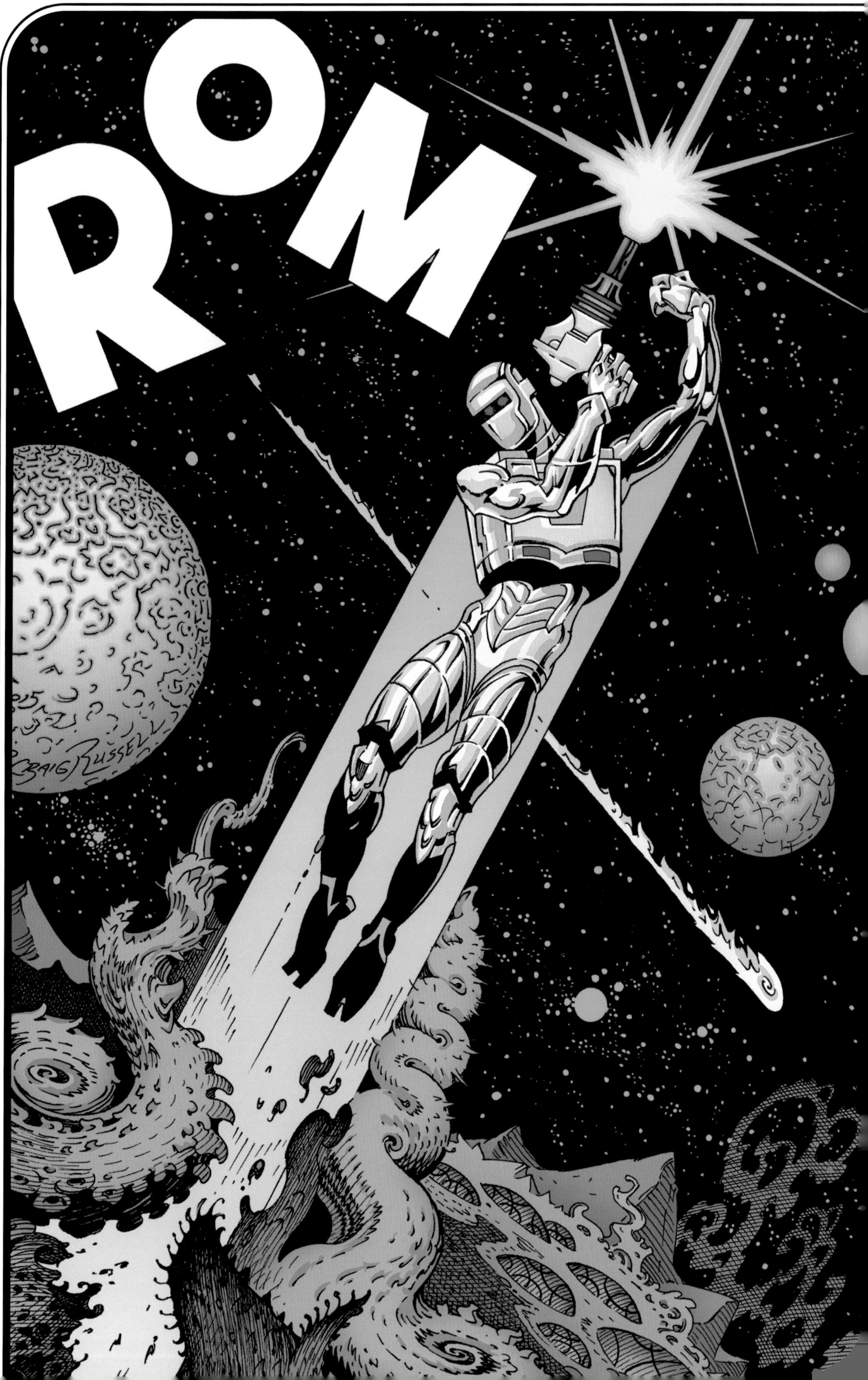
ROM
P. CRAIG RUSSELL

ART BY **ZACH HOWARD**, COLORS BY **NELSON DÁNIEL**

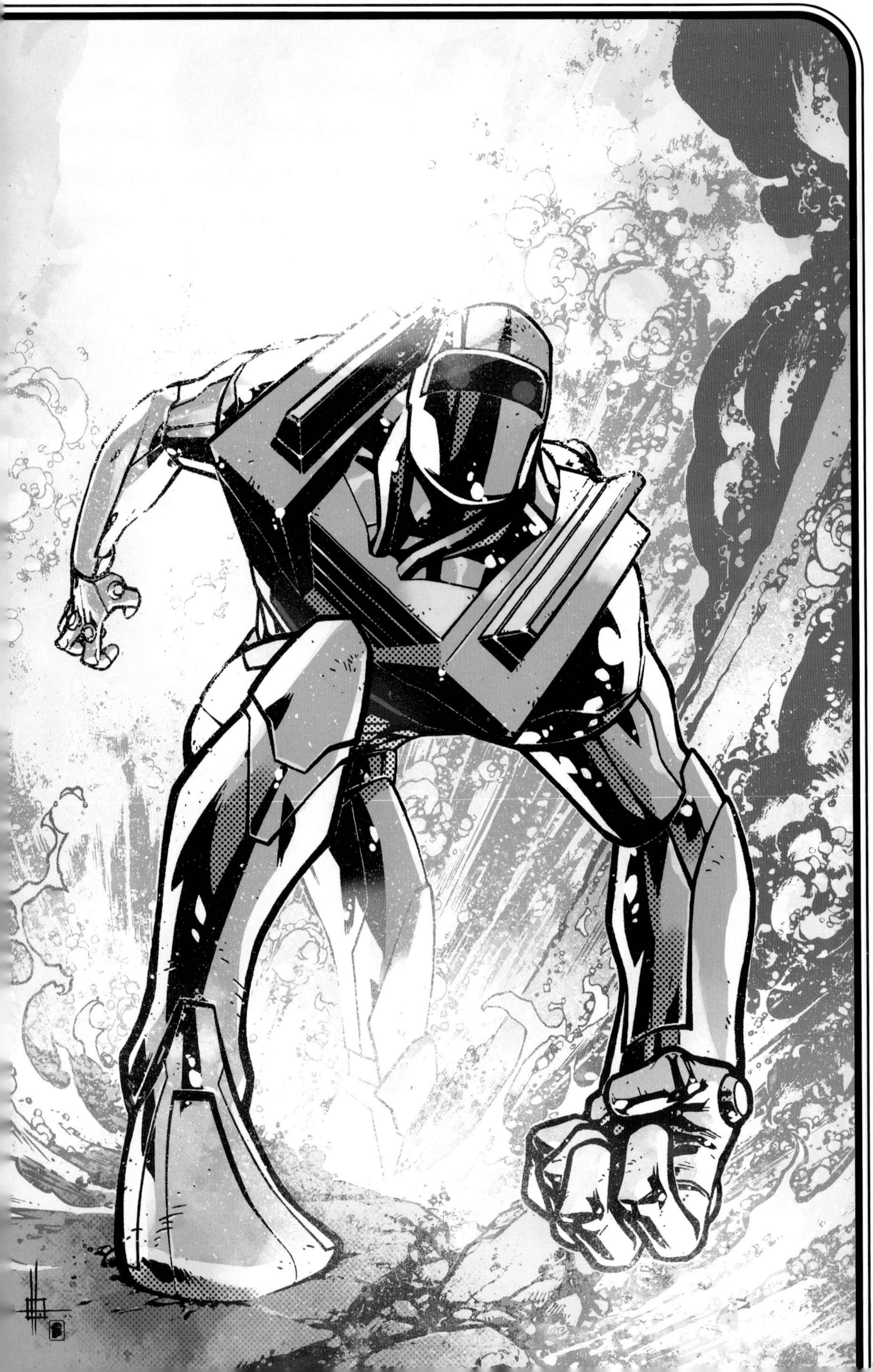

ART BY **TOM WHALEN**

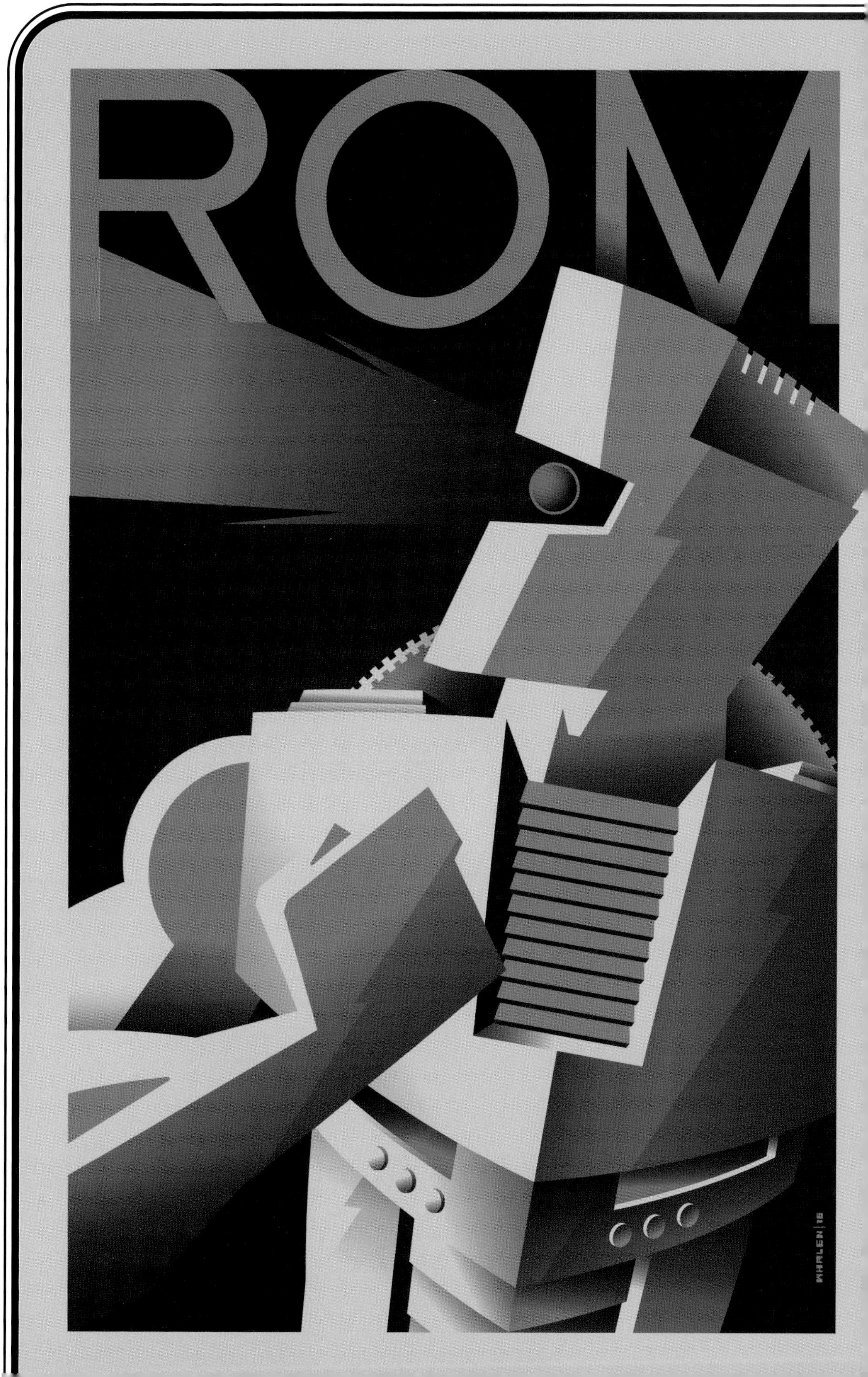
ROM
WHALEN | 16

ART BY **BOB LAYTON**, COLORS BY **MIKE CAVALLARO**

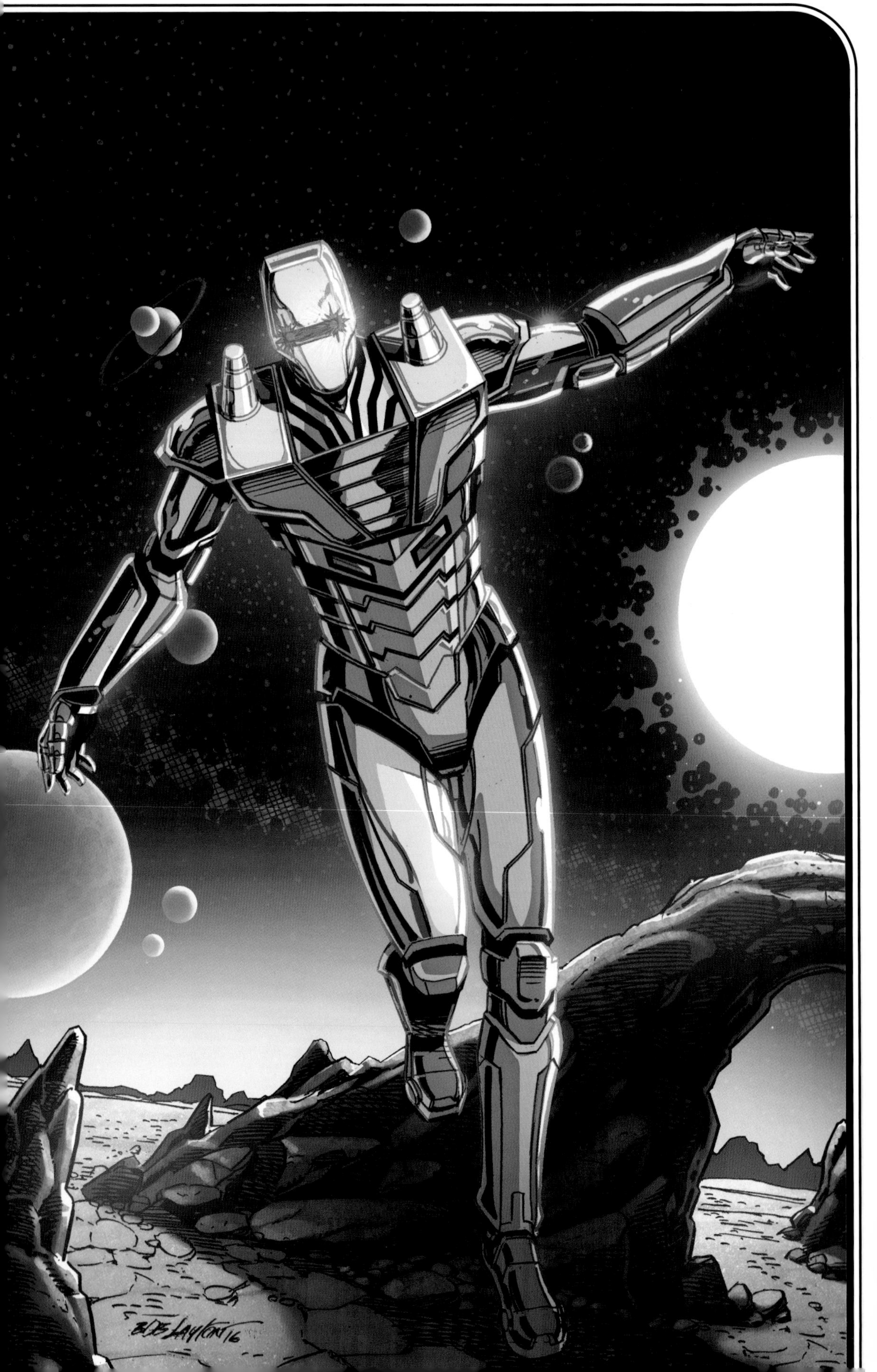

ART BY **ADAM RICHES**

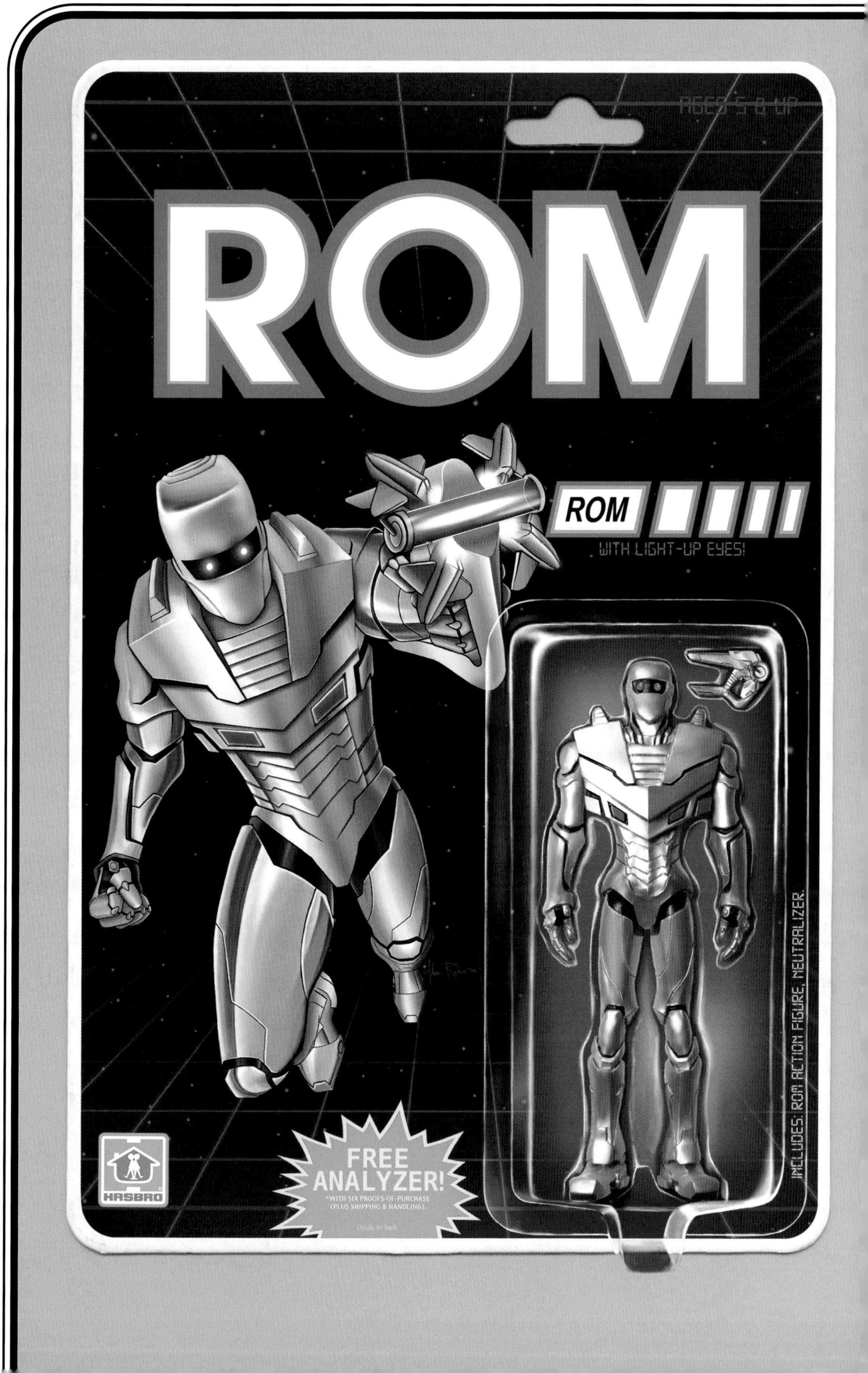

AGES 5 & UP
ROM
ROM
WITH LIGHT-UP EYES!
INCLUDES: ROM ACTION FIGURE, NEUTRALIZER.
HASBRO
FREE ANALYZER!
*WITH SIX PROOFS-OF-PURCHASE (PLUS SHIPPING & HANDLING).
Details on back.

ART BY **MARCELO MATERE**

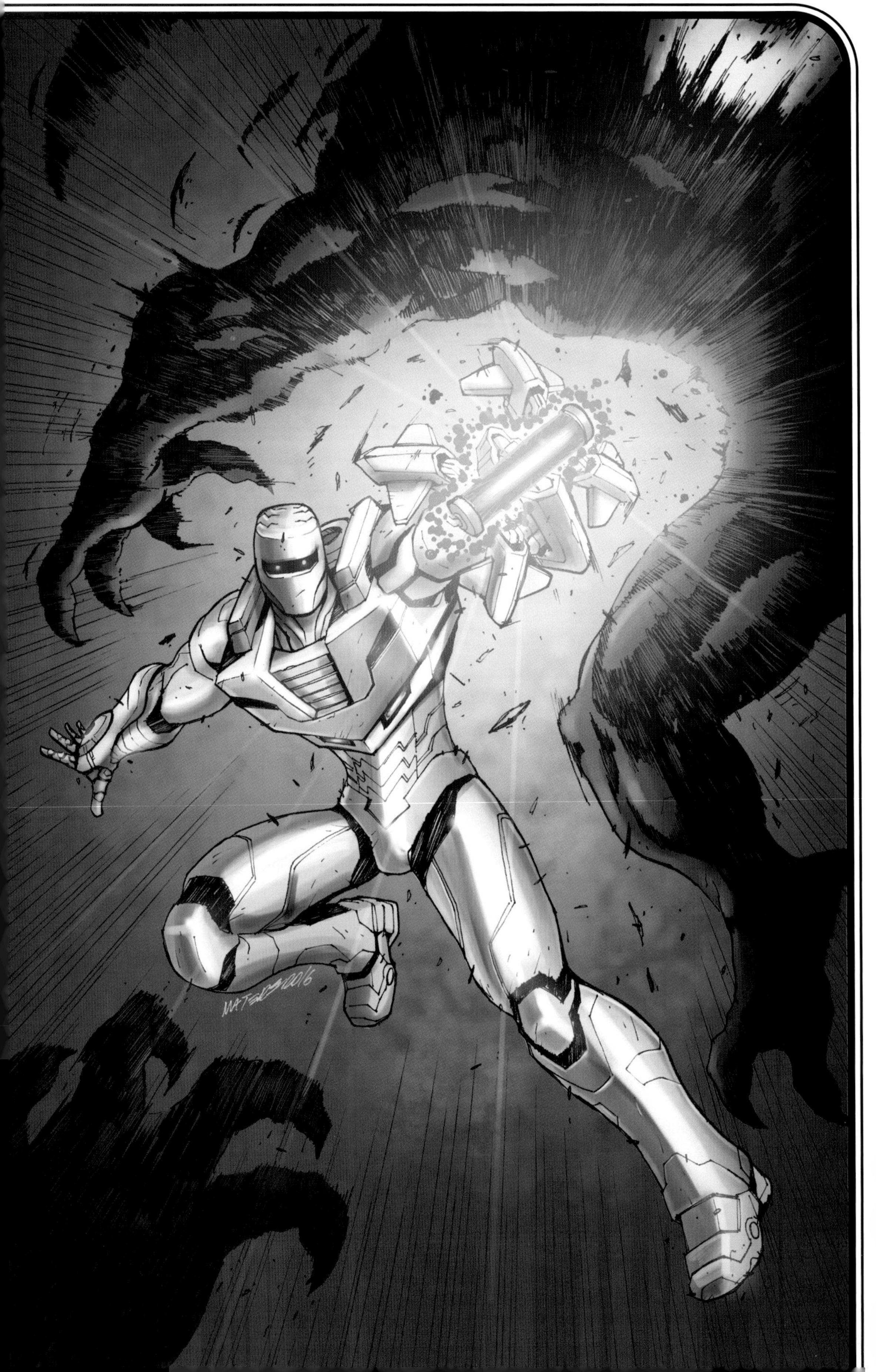

MATERE 2016

ART BY J.K. WOODWARD

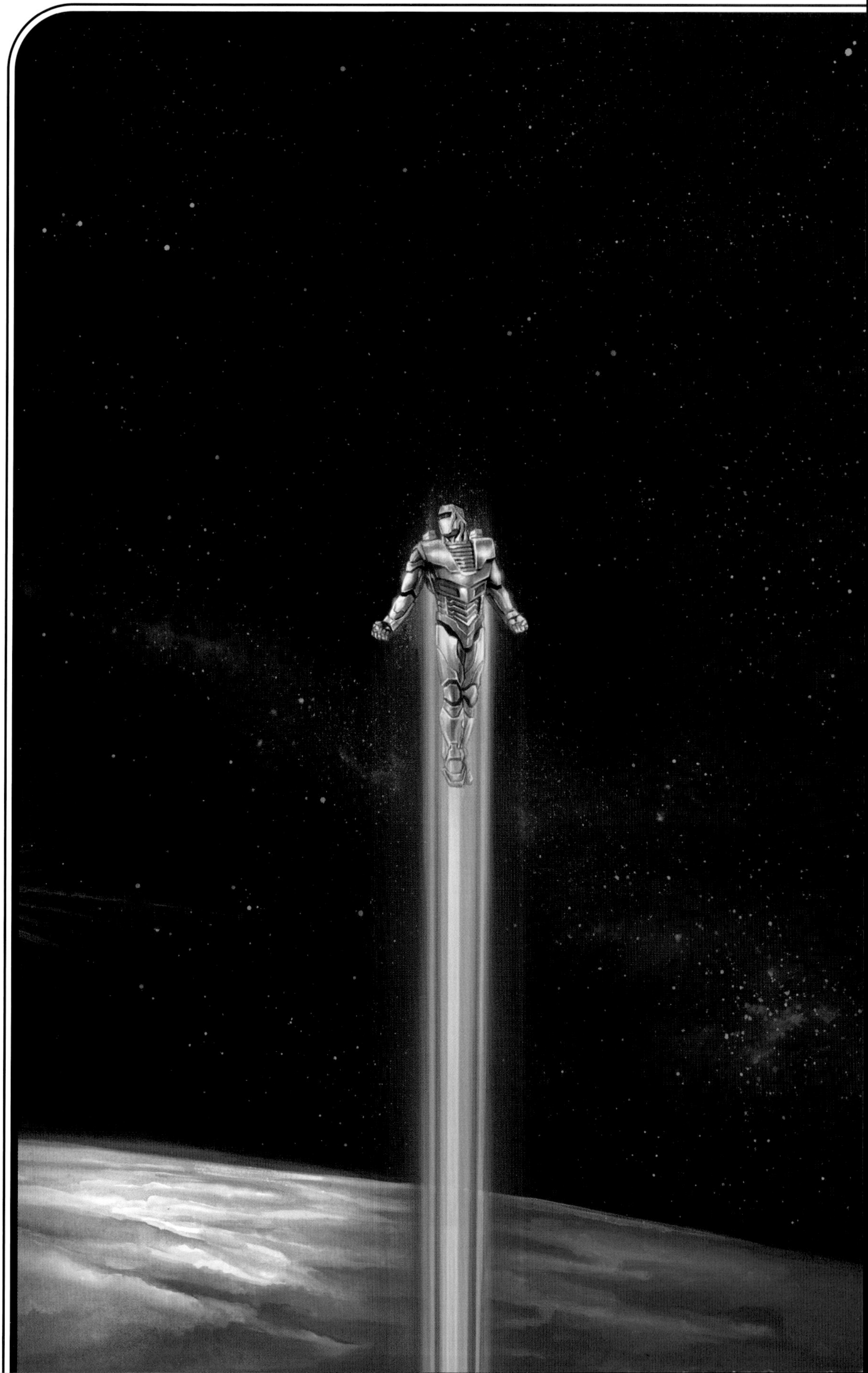

ART BY **DAVID MESSINA**

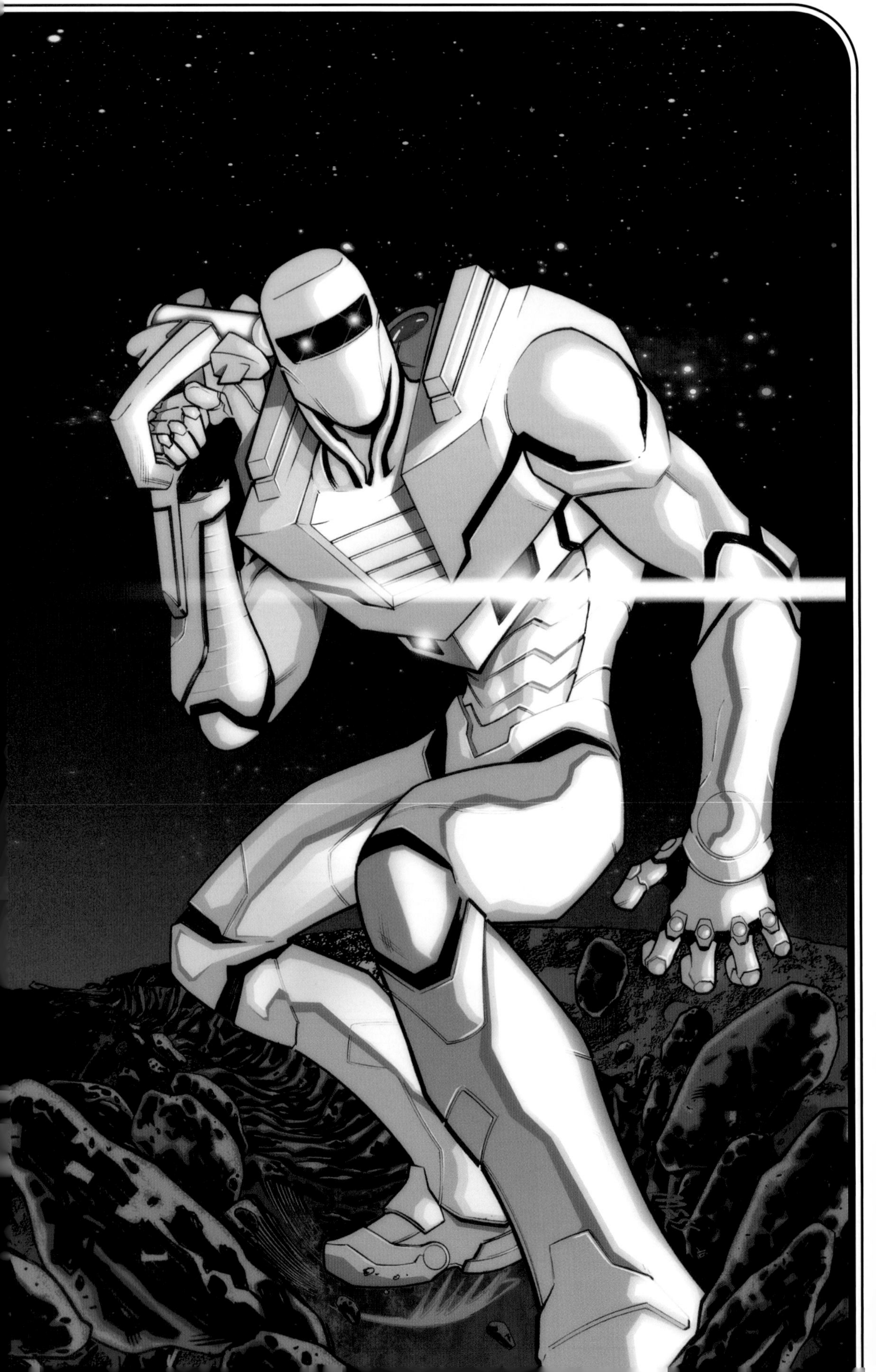

ART BY **POP MHAN**

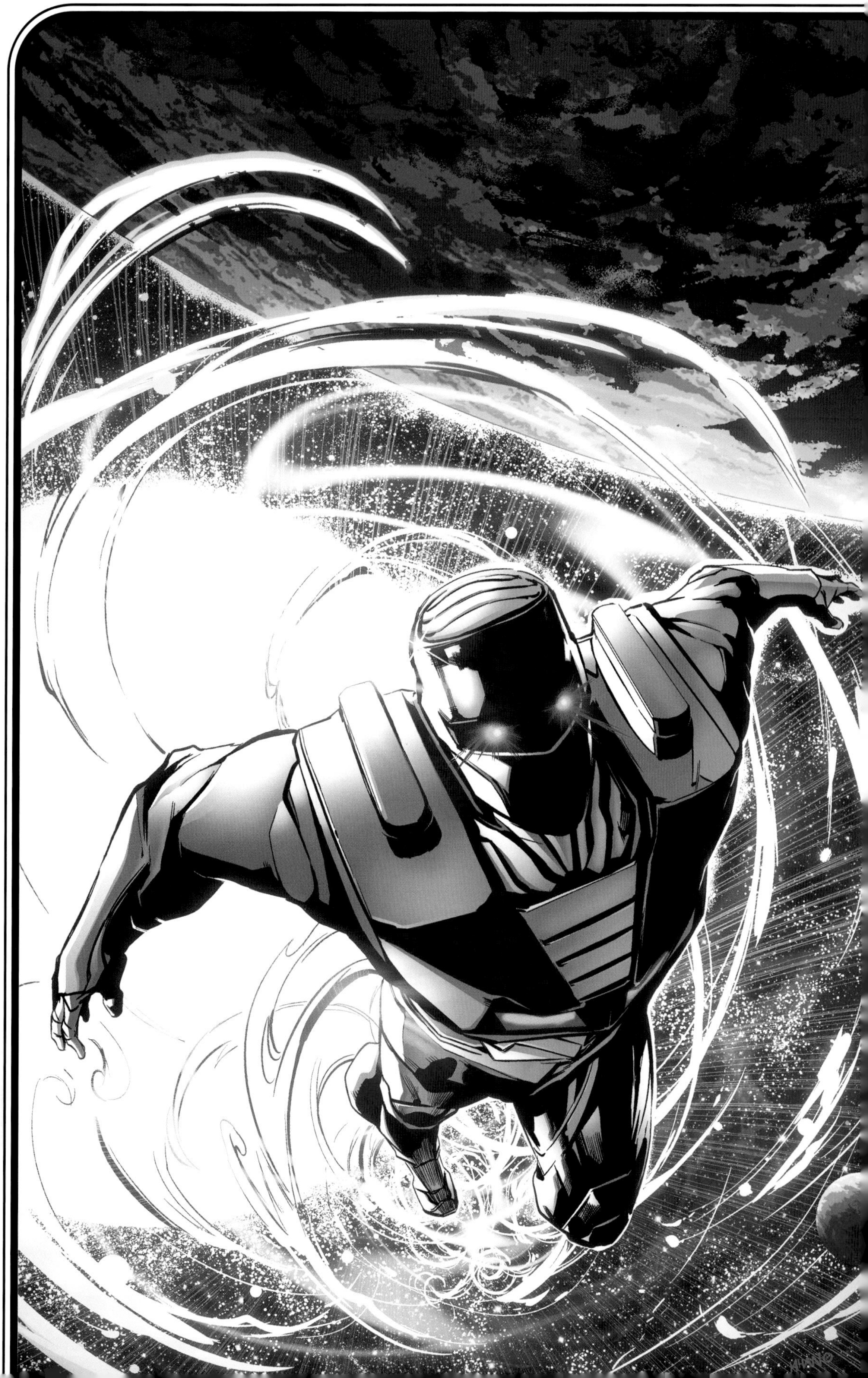

ART BY **LOSTON WALLACE**, COLORS BY **STEPHEN DOWNER**

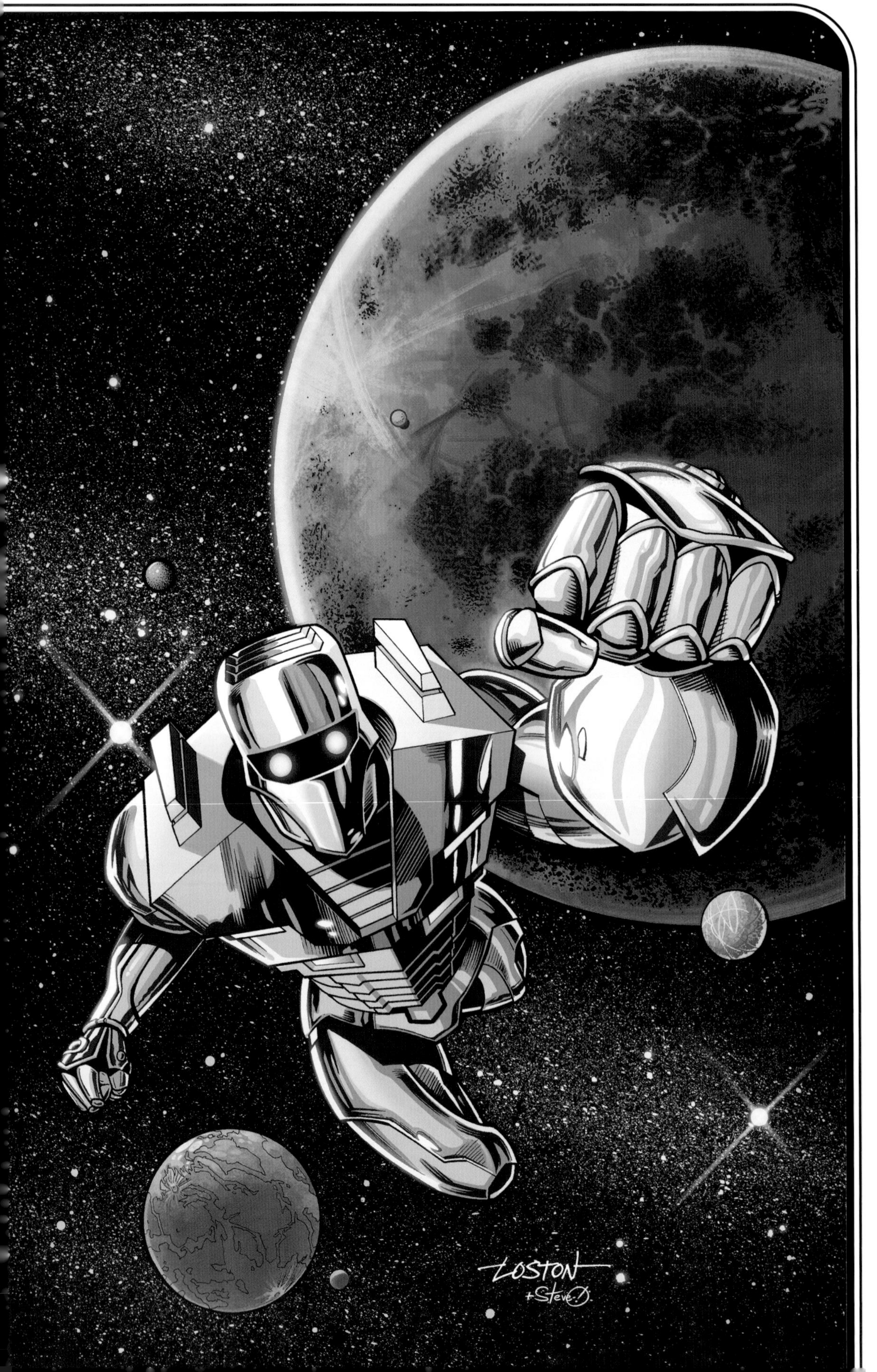
LOSTON
+Steve Ø.

ART BY **JEFFREY VEREGGE**

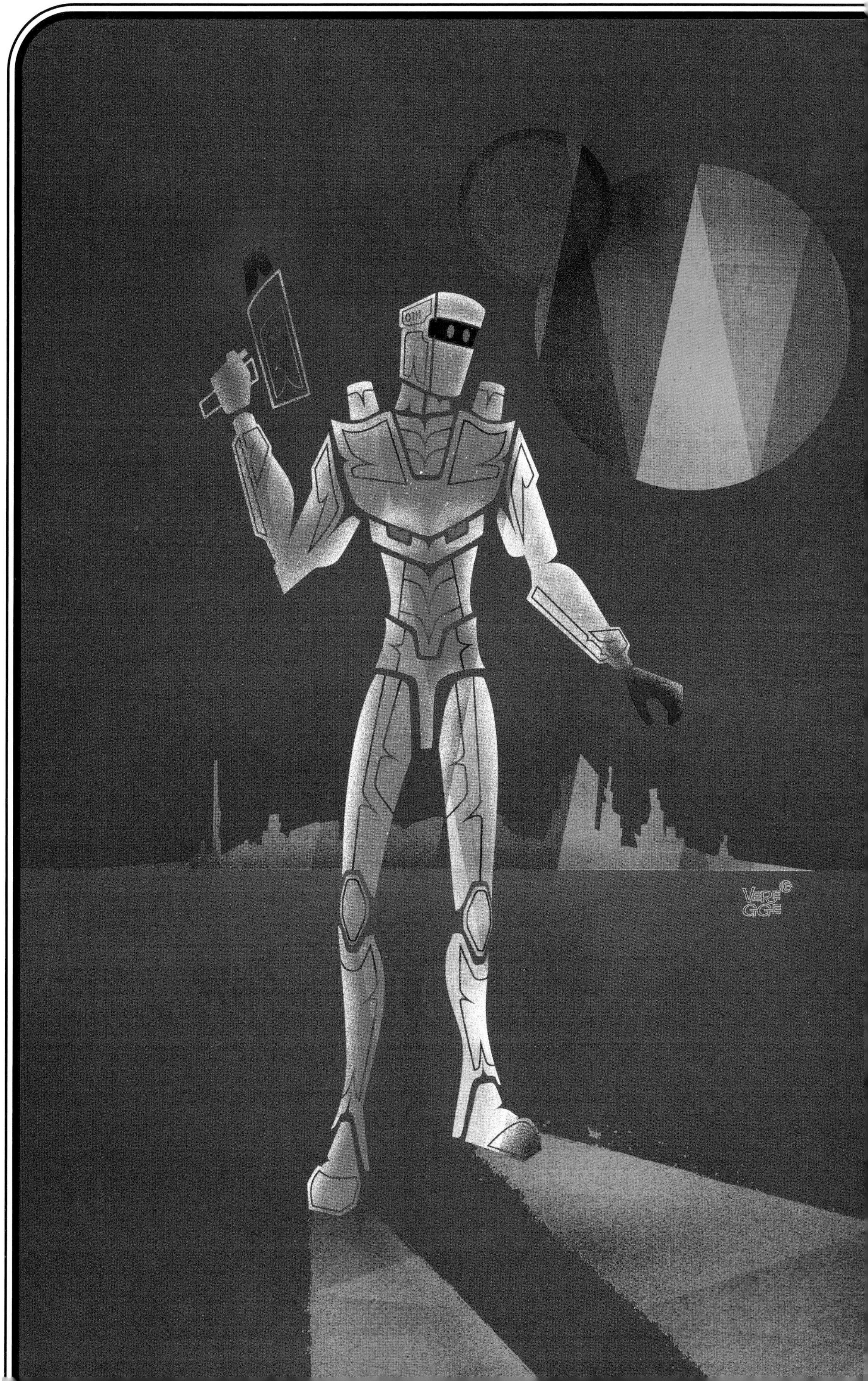
VEREGGE

ART BY **KEN CHRISTIANSEN**

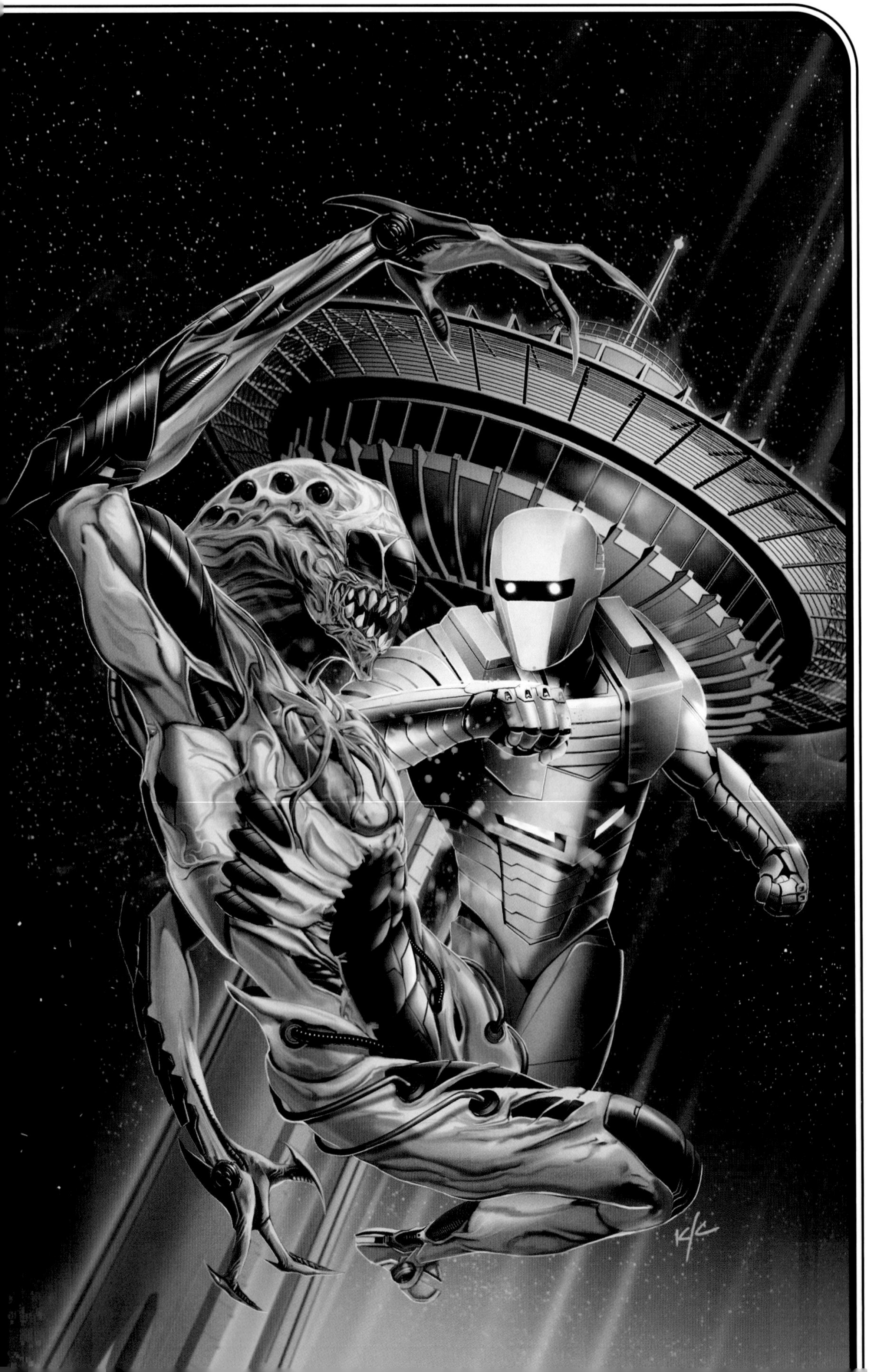

ART BY **ZACH HOWARD**, COLORS BY **NELSON DÁNIEL**

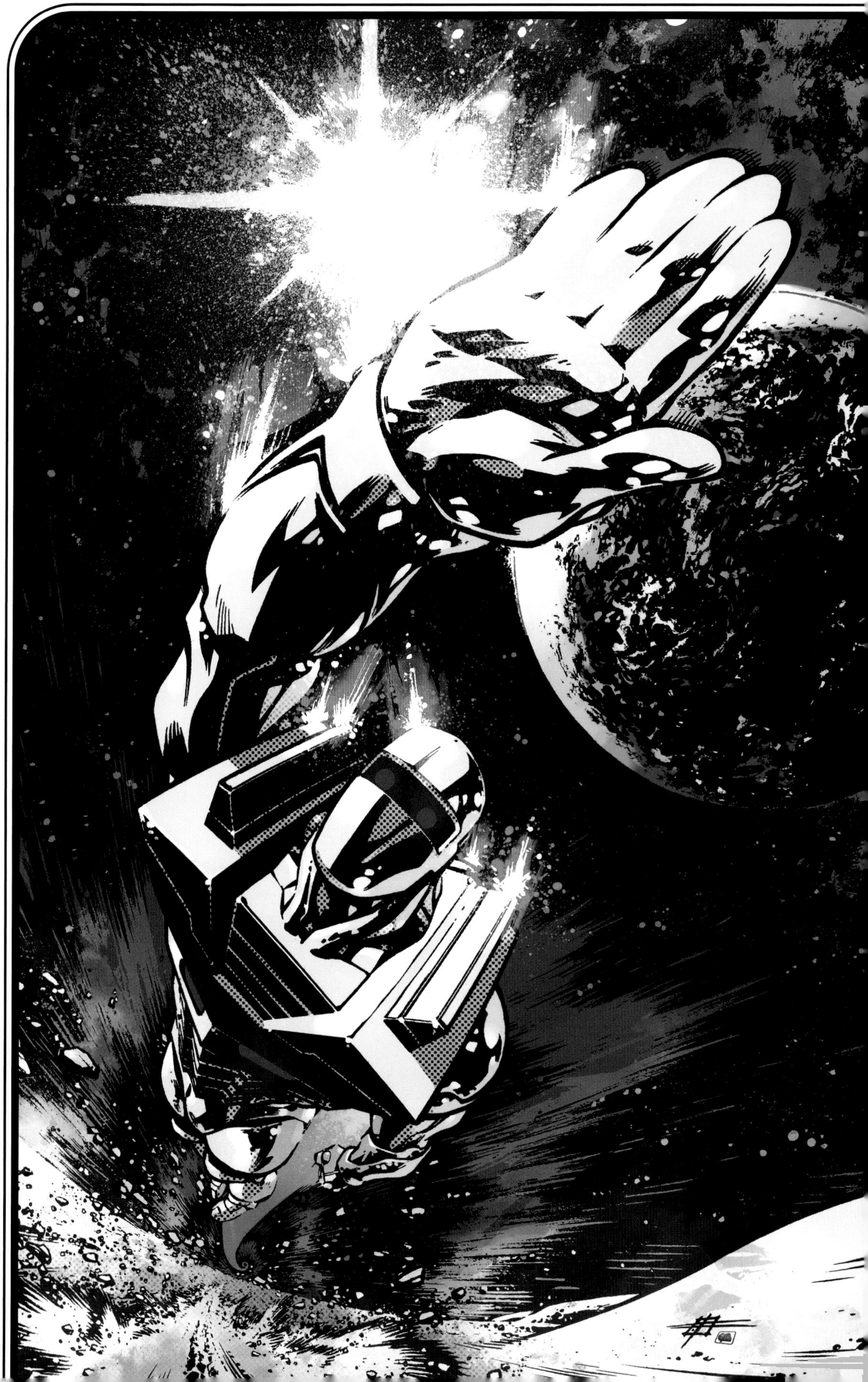

INITIAL DESIGNS BY **DAVID MESSINA** AND **PAOLO VILLANELLI**

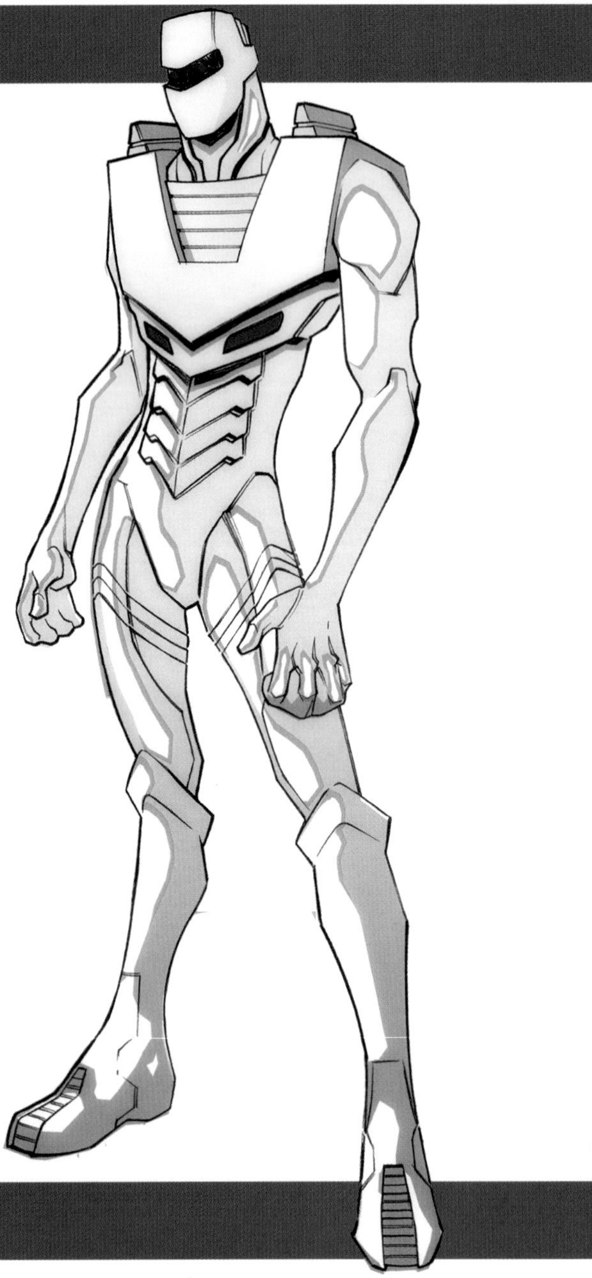

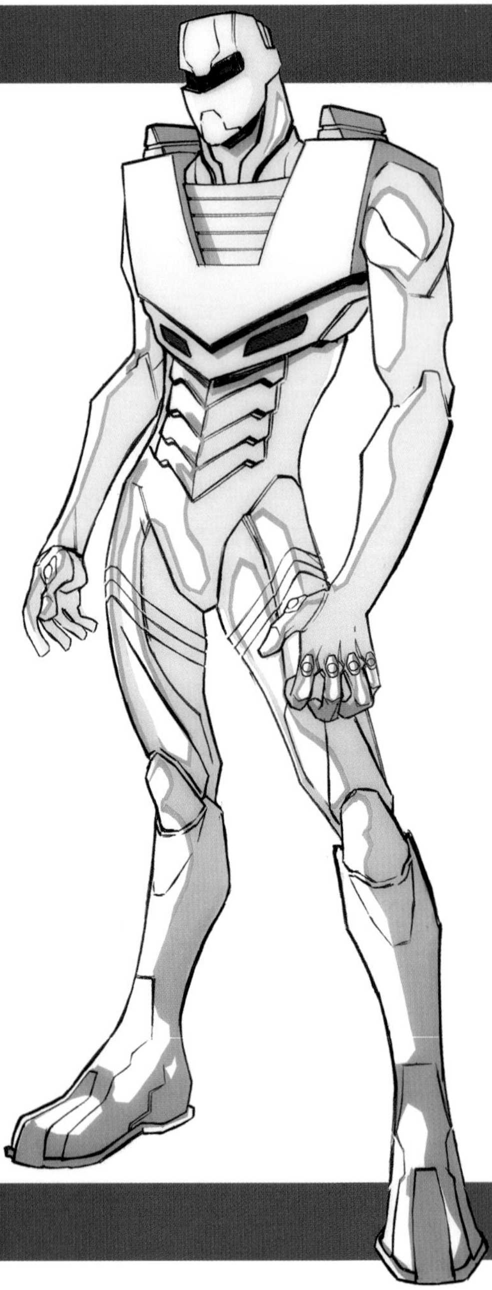

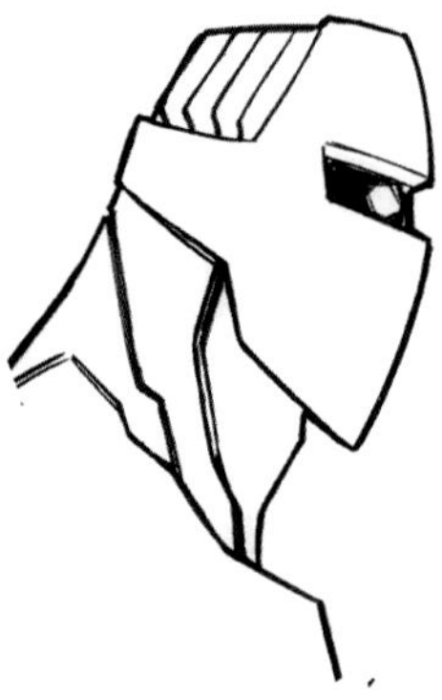

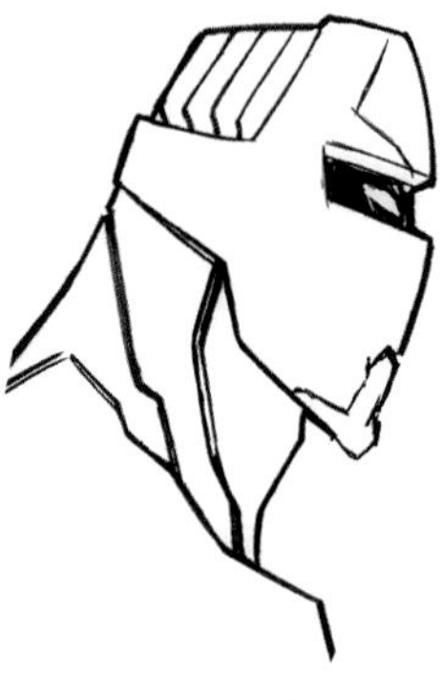

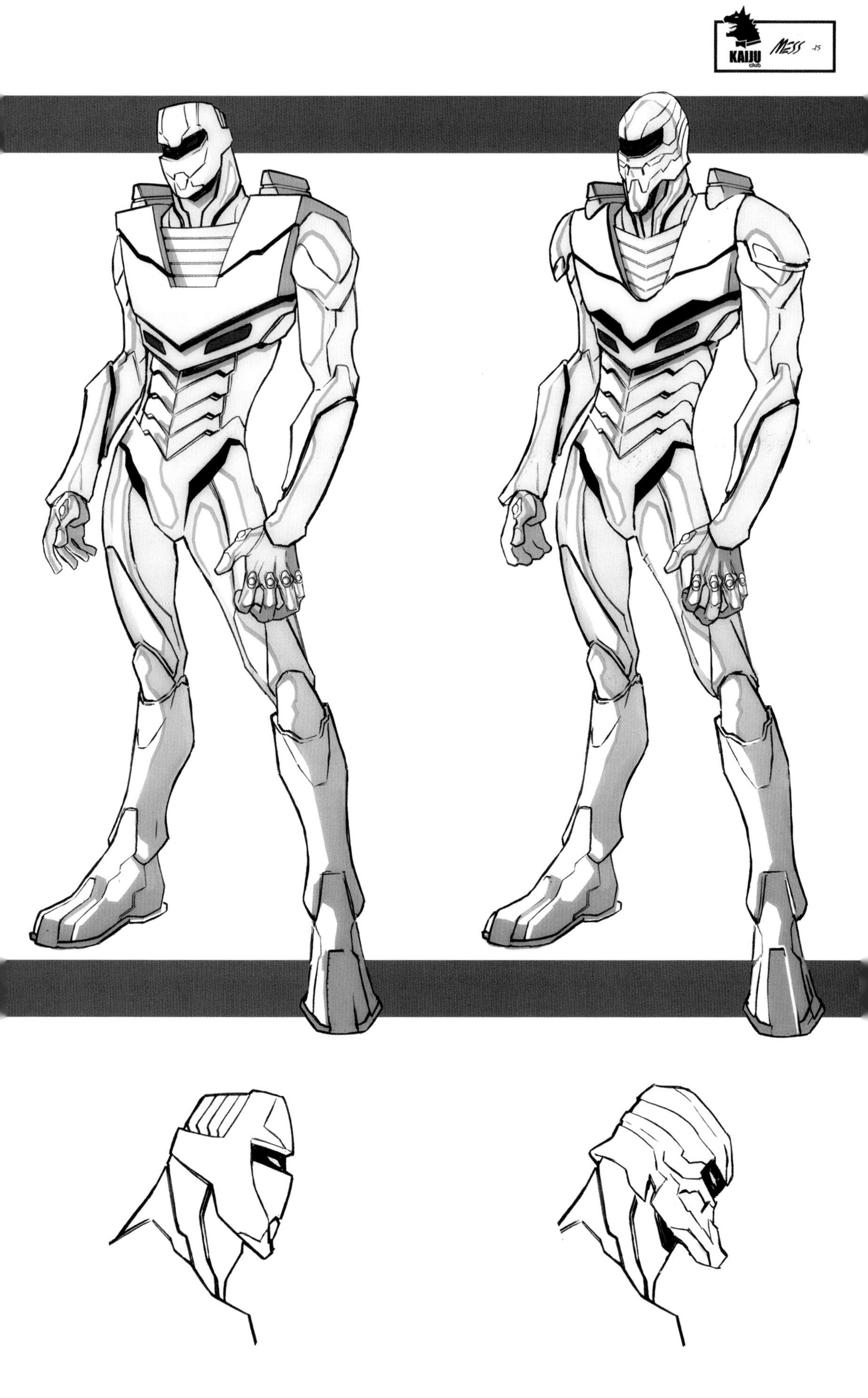
KAIJU club
MESS -15

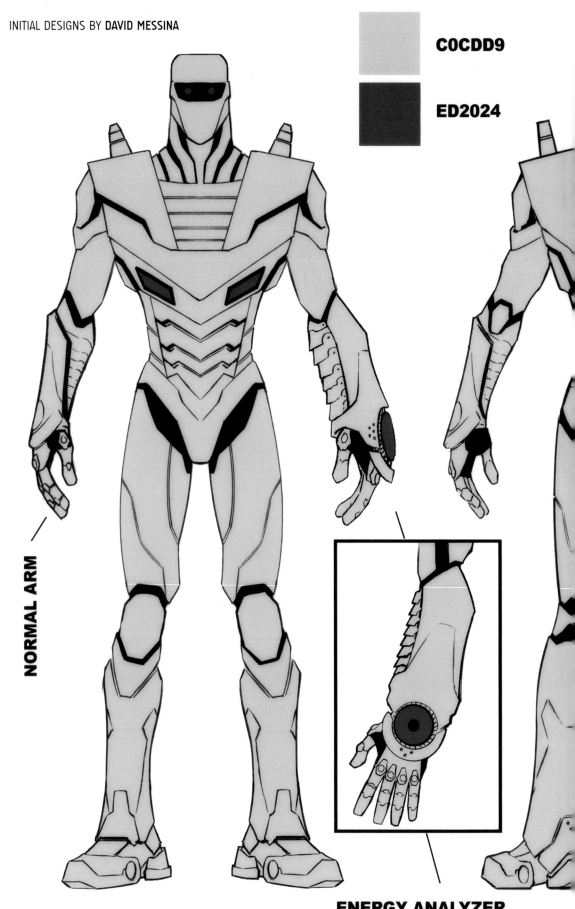

INITIAL DESIGNS BY **DAVID MESSINA**

C0CDD9

ED2024

NORMAL ARM

**ENERGY ANALYZER
MODE**

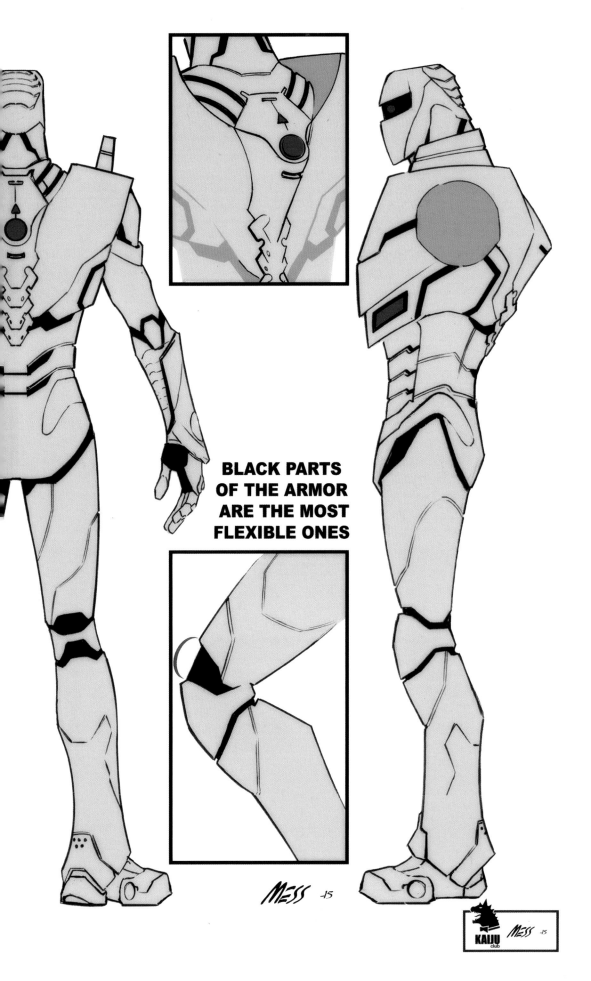

**BLACK PARTS
OF THE ARMOR
ARE THE MOST
FLEXIBLE ONES**

MESS -15

MESS -15

ROM

Real name: Rom (surname not yet known)
Occupation: Solstar Order Space Knight
Legal Status: Citizen of Elonia
Place of birth: Elonia
Marital status: Unknown
Known relatives: Unknown
Group affiliation: The Solstar Order
Current Base of operations: Northern California, USA, Earth
First appearance (historical): 1979 toy line
First appearance (this continuity): Rom Free Comic Book Day 2016 #0

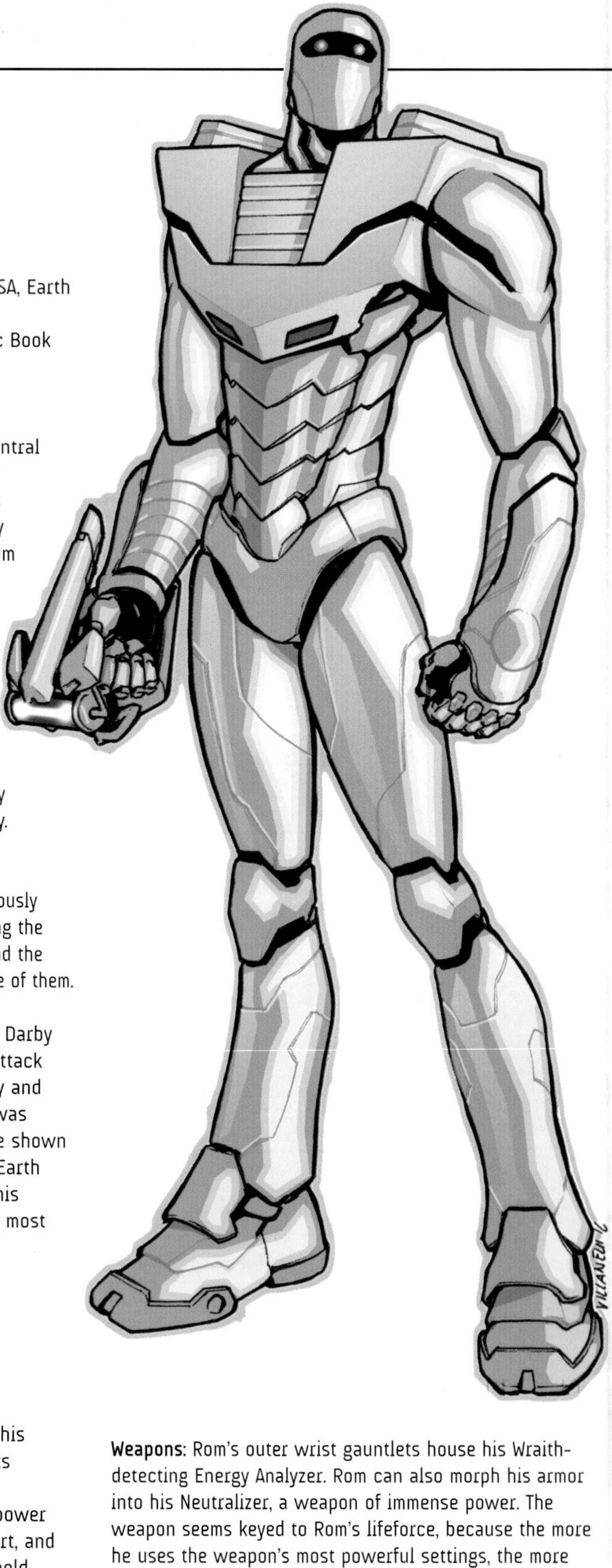

History: Not much is yet known of Rom before his fiery arrival in a forested area near California's central coast. The impact brought in soldiers from nearby Vandenberg Air Force Base and the local police as well. Some of whom Rom discovered were actually Dire Wraiths, the shape-shifting alien race that Rom has pursued across the galaxy.

Dire Wraiths use black-magic abilities to assume the forms of other lifeforms they possess and kill—flora and fauna alike. Two hundred years ago, Wraiths used their insidious magicks to devastate Rom's home planet of Elonia for purposes still unknown to Rom. For the past two centuries, he and other Space Knights have gallantly fought the Wraiths' growing threat across the galaxy.

Rom was victorious in his initial battle. Two humans caught in the crossfire were less lucky: a Wraith viciously slashed a human police officer, Camilla Byers, creating the Wraithmark, as Rom called it, which allows her to read the Wraiths' thoughts even as it slowly turns her into one of them.

Rom also came into contact with a woman named Darby Mason, the sole survivor of a subsequent Wraith attack on the nearby town of Cooper's Mill. At first, Darby and Camilla questioned what they saw, thinking Rom was killing other humans. But subsequent attacks have shown them the reality, that the Wraiths have infiltrated Earth at all levels, including the military. The fact that this killer "robot" from space is telling the truth is the most frightening thing of all.

Height: 7'2"
Weight: 900 lbs
Eyes (humanoid): Unknown
Eyes (in armor): Red
Hair: Unknown
Strength level: Rom's metal suit greatly enhances his life support, longevity, strength and stamina but its upper levels are thus-far unknown.
Unusual powers: Rom's metal suit possesses the power of interstellar travel, seemingly endless life support, and the ability to mentally morph the metal into handheld weapons and scanners that allow him to determine if any living thing is secretly a Wraith. Trained as a soldier in a war stretching out over centuries, Rom has great military acumen and battle-honed decision-making.

Weapons: Rom's outer wrist gauntlets house his Wraith-detecting Energy Analyzer. Rom can also morph his armor into his Neutralizer, a weapon of immense power. The weapon seems keyed to Rom's lifeforce, because the more he uses the weapon's most powerful settings, the more it weakens him overall. His armor is also equipped with a built-in Translator that converts his language to others'.

Text: Chris Ryall Art: Paolo Villanelli & David Messina